Teaching Culture in Introductory Foreign Language Textbooks

W0115225

Carol A. Chapelle

Teaching Culture in Introductory Foreign Language Textbooks

palgrave
macmillan

Carol A. Chapelle
Iowa State University
Ames, Iowa, USA

ISBN 978-1-137-49598-3 (hardcover)   ISBN 978-1-137-49599-0 (eBook)
ISBN 978-1-349-69767-0 (softcover)
DOI 10.1057/978-1-137-49599-0

Library of Congress Control Number: 2016946757

© The Editor(s) (if applicable) and The Author(s) 2016, First softcover printing 2018
The author(s) has/have asserted their right(s) to be identified as the author(s) of this work in accordance
with the Copyright, Designs and Patents Act 1988.
This work is subject to copyright. All rights are solely and exclusively licensed by the Publisher, whether
the whole or part of the material is concerned, specifically the rights of translation, reprinting, reuse of
illustrations, recitation, broadcasting, reproduction on microfilms or in any other physical way, and trans-
mission or information storage and retrieval, electronic adaptation, computer software, or by similar or
dissimilar methodology now known or hereafter developed.
The use of general descriptive names, registered names, trademarks, service marks, etc. in this publication
does not imply, even in the absence of a specific statement, that such names are exempt from the relevant
protective laws and regulations and therefore free for general use.
The publisher, the authors and the editors are safe to assume that the advice and information in this book
are believed to be true and accurate at the date of publication. Neither the publisher nor the authors or
the editors give a warranty, express or implied, with respect to the material contained herein or for any
errors or omissions that may have been made.

Cover illustration: © Ulrich Schade / Alamy Stock Photo

Printed on acid-free paper

This Palgrave Macmillan imprint is published by Springer Nature
The registered company is Macmillan Publishers Ltd. London

For Barbara Chapelle

Acknowledgments

A large project without a large funder is a long project. Fortunately, this large project found enough funding at each step of the way to get off the ground, gain momentum, and finally succeed. I am very grateful to each of the funders and people, who through their interest, dedicated work, advice, hospitality, and funding contributed the pieces to allow it all to come together. I will not be able to name all of the people who have contributed to this work in various ways, but I want to acknowledge some who have been so instrumental in making it happen.

Cultural studies is itself a long project. For me my study of Quebec began with an invitation to teach a course on language assessment at Université Laval in the 1990s, where the enthusiastic faculty in the *département de langues, linguistique et traduction* welcomed me warmly and were eager to establish an exchange program with Iowa State University. This program has created an ongoing point of contact between the two universities, which years later paved the way for the study abroad course, Language Policy and Practice, which I have taught there regularly, giving both Iowa State and Laval students the opportunity for cross-cultural discovery. This engagement with Laval and the opportunity to learn with the students about Quebec fueled my textbook research project when funding did not.

Thanks to multiple sources of support at Iowa State University, I was able to make continuous, incremental progress on the study. I have regularly received funding from College of Liberal Arts and Sciences small grants program established by Associate Dean David Oliver. I was also granted a study leave by the College to go to Quebec during the fall of 2010, where I was generously hosted by the *département de langues, linguistique et traduction* at Laval and received funding from the Québec Studies Program Grants for Professors and Researchers. The project got a substantial boost in the summer of 2012 with grants from Iowa State's Center for Excellence in Arts and Humanities and the Culture Corps Grant Program in the Office of International Students and Scholars. Most recently, at Iowa State University I was awarded a named professorship, so as the Angela B. Pavitt Professor of English, I have had the additional resources needed to finish the project.

Along this path, I have encountered many people who saw the importance of the project and its relevance even as it was being formulated. I have had the good fortune of working with many university students at Laval and at Iowa State, who were able to provide insight and information to help me understand how textbook content intersects with students' perceptions. In particular, I would like to acknowledge the diligent efforts of Haley Comisky and Carly Sommerlot who did substantial work as research assistants on the project. As I come to the end of the project, I am again bolstered by the precise and professional assistance of two research assistants, Hyewon Lee and Yundeok Choi.

For this research program, I am most grateful to Diane Huot, the source of the original invitation to Laval twenty-plus years ago, who shared her expertise in examining the French textbooks with me while I was on leave in 2010. I sincerely thank Kirsten Hummel for her initiation of the exchange with Iowa State University and continued care of and enthusiasm for my study abroad course. I appreciate the encouragement and support I have received for my Canadian Studies work from Stacey Weber-Feve and Jean-Pierre Taoutel, who teach French at Iowa State University. I am grateful to my colleagues in the Association for Canadian Studies in the United States for the welcoming collegiality that prompted me years ago to apply for a Canadian Studies grant, which funded my first textbook study. Among my Canadian Studies colleagues, I am most grateful to James McCormick, who has helped me navigate across the many facets of cross-disciplinarity that exist in area studies, from the concepts that make sense of political practice to analysis of current news from Canada as well as editorial comments on my writing about Canadian Studies.

December 6, 2015
Ames, Iowa, USA

Contents

List of Figures

List of Tables

1

The Significance of Culture in Language Teaching

Teachers of world languages today have an unprecedented range of materials to select from on the Internet to introduce their students to the people and places that are home to the languages they are studying. Before students embark on a study abroad program, they have access to all of the texts, media, reference materials, and even opportunities for interaction with the cultures that they will visit and study. The material capacity offered by the Internet for learning about people and their culture lays bare the limited knowledge of most teachers and materials developers about how to teach culture. Today's resources are an embarrassment of riches in the face of limited professional understanding of culture teaching in first year foreign language courses, but the question of how to teach culture in foreign language courses predates the Internet. Instead, the teaching of culture has been a topic of critical importance to the profession for over fifty years.

This chapter explains how my research investigating culture teaching in French language textbooks fits into this larger interest in the profession. It presents the background for my research by explaining the rationale for studying how culture is presented in foreign language textbooks, justifying my choice to focus on cultural narrative and politics and defining

© The Editor(s) (if applicable) and The Author(s) 2016
C.A. Chapelle, *Teaching Culture in Introductory Foreign Language Textbooks*, DOI 10.1057/978-1-137-49599-0_1

textbook analysis as an area of inquiry in applied linguistics. The first part examines the rationale for studying culture through textbook analysis and sketches the goals of culture teaching in foreign language pedagogy as they have been discussed in the USA, which is the context for my research. I show the continuous quest to improve culture teaching and suggest that textbook analysis is needed to connect teachers and materials developers to the academic discussion of culture teaching. The second part of the chapter introduces my particular area of interest, cultural narrative, and explains the basis for a politically informed cultural narrative as a central area of interest for beginning-level textbooks. The third part lays out the methodological implications for textbook analysis as an area of applied linguistics that intends to offer results of practical utility.

1   Why Study the Presentation of Culture in Textbooks?

What and how students should be taught about culture has been central to the discussion of foreign language teaching for decades. This discussion takes place at multiple levels from theoretical consideration of culture and meaning, the development of conceptual frameworks to inform curricula, and the practical decisions made in the creation of textbooks. Regardless of all efforts toward formulating culture theory and curriculum frameworks, the course textbook remains the cornerstone of the language course at the beginning level. It provides the basis for the syllabus, the springboard for other activities and discussion, guidance for new teachers, and socialization into the practice of language teaching and learning for students. Authors and editors of language textbooks select cultural content that provides an important starting point for students to construct images of the places where the language is spoken and to forecast key aspects of culture that they may study in greater depth in the future when their language abilities increase. Textbook cultural content also provides a starting point from which teachers add explanations in class and build additional materials into the curriculum. Because of the critical role of the textbook in foreign language teaching, it is deserving of careful analysis.

1.1   Culture Teaching Goals in Foreign Language Teaching

Foreign language textbooks reflect the goals of the profession to teach culture as part of the introductory courses. Despite the variation in how this goal is approached in specific textbooks, the commitment of authors to the teaching of language and culture has been evident since the 1960s at least. For example, in the 1968 textbook *Basic French: An Oral Approach*, this statement about the interconnection of language and culture appears in the introduction that lays out the goals and approach of the textbook:

> It is the intention of this book to provide a practicable introduction to contemporary French. As students deal most readily with situations familiar to them, the material is presented first in the form of Conversations situated generally in the university environment, and which have to do with the problems and interests of young people attending the university of Paris. Many of the Conversations will thus lead naturally to discussions on French science, art, education, and other aspects of French culture. The vocabulary tends to be that of the modern spoken language, sanctioned by good usage (Mainous, 1968, p. v).

In the 1960s, the culture aspect of the teaching goals in this French textbook was clear even though the idea of pluricentrism of cultural content had not yet affected French foreign language textbooks in the USA. By the 2000s, French textbooks still stated the intent to teach culture, but they did so from a pluricentric view. In *Vis-à-vis: Beginning French*, published in 2004, the authors included culture of the Francophone world in their statement of the main goal: 'To promote a balanced four-skills approach to learning French throughout a variety of listening, speaking, reading, and writing activities, while introducing students to the richness and diversity of the Francophone world' (Amon, Muyskens, & Omaggio Hadley, 2004, p. XVIII). The authors included a detailed explanation about how students were supposed to learn the cultural aspects that they had chosen to focus on:

> The cultures of the French-speaking world are an integral part of every page of *Vis-à-vis: Beginning French*. In particular, they are prominently displayed in the central Correspondance section of each chapter. Located between

Leçons 2 and 3, Correspondance brings to life the immense richness and variety of French and Francophone cultures in a single, easy-to-use section. (Amon et al., 2004, p. XVII)

The goal statements in the textbooks typically reflect contemporary professional perspectives as stated in the *Standards of the American Council on the Teaching of Foreign Languages* (ACTFL). A synopsis of the most recent version of the official standards document, the *World-Readiness Standards for Learning Languages*, summarizes the five goal areas:

> Communication: Communicate effectively in more than one language in order to function in a variety of situations and for multiple purposes.
> Cultures: Interact with cultural competence and understanding.
> Connections: Connect with other disciplines and acquire information and diverse perspectives in order to use the language to function in academic and career-related situations.
> Comparisons: Develop insight into the nature of language and culture in order to interact with cultural competence.
> Communities: Communicate and interact with cultural competence in order to participate in multilingual communities at home and around the world (ACTFL n.d.).

These *Standards* are open to interpretation as to the way that they encompass culture learning. Lange (1999) argued that 'culture permeates all of the standards, [and] that it appears in any of the topics related to Communication, in any of the disciplines suggested in Connections, and in any use of language in Communities' (p. 59). Three of the standards direct teachers to attend to developing students' cultural competence. Culture, comparisons, and communities all indicate that students should learn to 'interact with culture competence' (ACTFL, n.d.). Schulz (2006) sees culture additionally in the communication standard: 'Cultural knowledge and culture-appropriate communication skills play an important role in all three modes of communication: interpersonal (implying, of course, culturally appropriate interaction); interpretive (implying sufficient knowledge of the target culture to understand culture-specific meanings); and presentational (implying selection of culture-appropriate contents and use of style and register, that is, the conscious or subconscious understanding of what can be said to whom, how, and in what circumstances)' (Siskin, 1998, p. 10). What appears in the textbooks is in part the result of such interpretations of the *Standards*, but the *Standards* are only one source of input for textbook producers who are influenced by factors such as international intellectual trends, business calculations, teachers' judgments, and students' reactions.

Before the 1960s, professional inquiry into culture teaching in textbooks in the USA was extremely rare. For example, only one textbook analysis study appeared in *The Modern Language Journal* before the 1960s (Reinhardt, 1928). Risager (2007) attributes the growth of modern culture teaching in the USA in the 1960s to Lado's (1957) book about teaching language and culture. From that point researchers began to define and theorize culture in foreign language teaching in the USA, primarily from the perspective of cultural anthropology, which highlighted 'the need to make visible the cultural content of language teaching' (Risager, 2007, p. 36). The American anthropological perspective values the language as it is used by real people rather than the study of the classic literature, and accordingly, at least in theory, would be open to a polycentric presentation of the culture of the people who speak the target language. In the 1970s, many American foreign language teachers became aware of the distinction between what was called large 'C' and small 'c' culture. The former refers to the canon of the traditional art, literary, and intellectual history of a people. The latter refers to the everyday way of doing things and developing relationships among people in society. The small 'c' anthropological approach that sees culture as embedded in the everyday practices of people was preferred in the USA, where the emphasis was on teaching everyday cultural practices.

The shift toward polycentrism in French language teaching in the USA is evident in the professional discussion in the 1980s when Ogden (1981) criticized French textbooks because they presented French 'not just as the language of France, but sometimes, one feels, as the language of Paris alone' (p. 1). Almost two decades later, Siskin (1998) offered a similar analysis, suggesting that Spanish was taking the lead over French in popularity for foreign language study in the USA because of students' perception that the former is spoken widely throughout the world. He argued that French appeared to be perceived as less useful because it is 'predominantly associated with France, and perhaps Québec; however, its importance as a significant world language, which is spoken on five continents, is largely ignored' (Siskin, 1998, p. 260). These types of statements by professionals in French language teaching reveal shifting views, but with respect to what is actually taught in textbooks, empirically based studies of actual textbooks are few.

To bring the idea of pluricentrism closer to more tangible goals for teaching and materials development, the American Association of Teachers of French (AATF) and the National Commission on Cultural Competence developed a monograph entitled *Acquiring Cross-Cultural Competence: Four Stages for Students of French* (Singerman, 1996). As the title indicates, four levels of competence are delineated for conceptualizing the culture-related abilities that students are expected to develop through the study of foreign language and, therefore, what should be taught. These abilities are defined as consisting of two dimensions: understanding culture and knowledge of French-speaking societies, the latter of which includes France and major French-speaking regions where French was the language of the European conquerors and settlers: North America, Sub-Saharan Africa, The Caribbean, and North Africa. The AATF document recommended that students should know specific aspects about France in addition to one other French-speaking area. Students should also know what other areas belong to the French-speaking world. Further, the document contained categories of cultural knowledge including communication in cultural context, the value system, social patterns and conventions, social institutions, geography and the environment, history, literature, and the arts.

The clearest message to emanate from these standards and their interpretations is that the need for improvement in culture teaching is continuous. There is a constant quest to better understand and define the goals of culture learning in order to improve the teaching of culture in foreign language in the USA.

1.2   The Need to Improve Culture Teaching

The continuous quest for improvement within the profession was amplified in the first decade of the new century with the public attention attracted by the intercultural and linguistic dimensions of 9/11. Reflections on the events of 9/11 in the USA resulted in connections being drawn between foreign language teaching and national politics, perhaps most prominently through Bush's National Security Language Initiative. In this context of heightened national attention for foreign language teaching, a report was conceived by the Modern Language Association (MLA). It recommended curricular reform to 'situate language study in cultural, historical, geographic, and cross-cultural frames' (MLA, 2007, p. 4). The MLA (2007) report defines the goal of foreign language study as developing students who are 'educated speakers who have deep translingual and transcultural competence' (p. 3). It asserted that 'This kind of foreign language education systematically teaches differences in meaning, mentality, and worldview as expressed in American English and in the target language.' (p. 4)

In order to better understand and improve the cultural dimensions of foreign language teaching, the MLA report strongly recommended that the profession rethink the way languages are taught at universities:

> The kind of curricular reform we suggest will situate language study in cultural, historical, geographic, and cross-cultural frames within the context of humanistic learning. We expect that more students will continue language study if courses incorporate cultural inquiry at all levels and if advanced courses address more subject areas. This means faculty members will have the opportunity to bring into the classroom the full breadth of their knowledge of the society about which they teach, including that society's languages and language variants, literatures, and cultures. Many colleges and universities have made a successful transition toward this broad understanding of language study, and we urge others to follow (2007, p. 4).

The MLA report's recommendations were seen as a fundamental change in the organization of the foreign language curriculum at universities because of its recognition of the importance of culture teaching at the introductory levels. The *ACTFL Standards* are written in a way that highlights the more advanced capacities of interpreting texts, making comparisons across cultures, and engaging in cross-cultural conversations. Accordingly, the discussion of culture teaching goals has implicitly focused on culture teaching at the intermediate and advanced levels, leaving aside questions about the prerequisites for students to get into these levels.

This problem with the report is nowhere better articulated than in the first chapter of *The Modern Language Journal Special Issue, Volume 94, Realizing Advanced Foreign Language Writing: Development in Collegiate Education: Curricular Design, Pedagogy, Assessment* (Byrnes, Maxim, & Norris, 2010). The authors point out the insufficiency of the suggestion that curricular revision should focus on 'cultural narratives' (MLA, 2007, p. 4). Part of the limitation of cultural narrative, which encompasses considerable scope requiring a high level of foreign language competence, is that it naturally directs attention to advanced-level program curricula. 'To be credible, the MLA report's stated goals would have to be accompanied by a well-considered proposal for how such high levels of ability might be attained' (Byrnes et al., 2010, p. 20). Fortunately, the purpose of their monograph is to put forth such a proposal. At its core is the explanation of a more robust intellectual foundation for revising a curriculum for all four years of collegiate foreign language study. Based on the social-semiotic linguistic theory systemic functional linguistics, the authors demonstrate how curriculum can be developed that takes into account the progression of students' abilities to use language resources to create meaning. Key to this proposal is the fact that the theory links language (e.g., words and phrases) and meaning (e.g., cultural narratives), thereby providing a means of considering both in the development of language curriculum and materials. My research also necessarily draws upon systemic functional linguistics in order to offer insights relevant to language education.

1.3   The Role of Language Textbook Analysis

Improvements in the treatment of culture in foreign language textbooks and in other aspects of language courses are difficult to invent and even more difficult to implement without a clear idea of existing practices. Current practices need to be investigated in part through research on textbooks, or textbook analysis. Weninger and Kiss (2015) help to define textbook analysis by distinguishing it from textbook evaluation. The former is intended to imply a more theoretical and principled approach to the examination of language teaching materials. Textbook analysis in our interpretation points further than judging the appropriateness of a particular book in a given educational context for use with specific students in mind. Analysis is concerned with identifying general trends using different theories as frameworks of investigation, while evaluation is situated in the practice and context of the language teacher to offer practical and immediately applicable answers. (Weninger and Kiss, 2015, pp. 51–52)

Several papers reporting such research have appeared in *The Modern Language Journal*, one of which analyzed the cultural topics in German textbooks (Dechert & Kastner, 1989). Ramirez and Hall (1990) published a study of high school Spanish textbooks that examined the Hispanic cultures represented, the cultural topics and communicative situations taught, as well as the linguistic functions included in the textbooks. Their study raised the issue of polycentrism in language teaching in concrete terms. But the next textbook studies did not appear in *The Modern Language Journal* for almost twenty years, when French textbooks were analyzed to assess the representation of Canada (Chapelle, 2009). Russian textbooks were examined to reveal the representation of ethnic minorities in Russia (Azimova & Johnson, 2012), and a study of Swahili textbooks analyzed the representation of Swahili users and their cultures (Thompson, 2013). Despite these individual studies investigating foreign language textbooks in the USA, the majority of research and broader methodological issues have been raised primarily in the study of textbooks for English as a second/foreign language. A recent edited volume containing analyses primarily of English textbooks, *Critical Perspectives on Language Teaching Materials* (Gray, 2013), outlines the assumptions underlying textbook analysis as consisting of (1) their commercial situatedness, (2) emphasis on meaning, and (3) interdisciplinarity.

1.3.1   Textbooks Are Commercially Situated

Gray (2013) points out that commercially produced materials are core commodities in textbook publishing and that this commercial aspect cannot be ignored in seeking to understand their contents. Kramsch (1988) described the central dilemma of foreign language textbook culture as follows: 'a text whose purpose is to teach a foreign language is caught in an interesting dilemma that arises from the discrepancy between its monocultural educational parameters and its multicultural educational goals' (p. 66). The dilemma leaves textbook producers with no clear answers to at least three questions that Kramsch (1988) identified. First, what kind of rules should be taught? Second, what are the cultural topics that should be covered? Third, which cultures should be taught?

Kramsch's (1988) insight came from her view of textbooks as both curriculum artifacts and cultural artifacts which make languages mean in particular ways. The commercial and cultural situatedness of textbooks makes them particularly rich as objects of investigation. Kramsch (1988) observed, 'Like any work of art, [the textbook] is a construct, one that represents the way the author and publisher conceive of language, culture, and learning, and the way they construe an integrated world of foreign reality for instructional purposes. ... [A] text is not the authentic experience, but a culturally coded educational construct' (p. 65). With the goal of identifying the factors affecting textbook content, Kramsch (1988) expanded the view of the social and political situation, in which textbooks are produced, that is, 'the textbook culture' (p. 67). She examined the national educational culture, the interests and resources of publishers, state departments of education, and teachers—all types of mediation on what is an author's work of art.

The assumption about the context-situatedness of the French textbooks that I am investigating is critical to my study. I have defined the population of textbooks of interest by delineating their geographical context (the USA), historical point in time (1960–2010), and level (beginning). Moreover, as background to the study, I have studied and described (in Chap. 2) the politics of language in Québec that provides potential cultural material for each of the five decades that I have studied. I have also outlined the efforts made by the Québec government to promote French language teaching through its foreign policy during this period (Chapelle, 2014). These contextual factors are likely to exert an influence on knowledge and attitudes of teachers, students, and the public. Because these factors within Québec changed dramatically between the period of 1960 and 2010, the historical perspective taken in this study offers a new vantage point from which the cultural context of foreign language textbooks can be seen.

1.3.2 Textbook Analysis Encompasses Analysis of Meanings in the Textbooks

The meanings in textbooks are many, but the papers in Gray's (2013) edited collection emphasize the ways in which the textbooks used language to convey representation and identity of the people portrayed in text and image. He identified two broad categories of representation. One is the way that the geographical spaces are represented graphically in maps showing which land masses are politically connected or separated from various countries and showing where a particular language is spoken. Representations are also conveyed in texts where geography is made reference to in a manner that represents a certain view of political alliances and language policy. In my study, I examine the evolution of the amount and manner of representation of Québec in the textbooks' display of the French-speaking world. Maps are included in my analysis of the political aspects of cultural narrative in Chap. 5.

The second broad category is the representation of certain people, which conveys some aspects of their identity. The most salient example of identity representation in textbooks, Gray (2013) points out, is the presence of women and the roles that they are depicted as holding. Gray's (2013) analysis of identity representation includes the idea that 'The struggle to be represented, or to be represented in particular ways, arises out of a response to the related politics of erasure and misrecognition' (p. 6). Erasure refers to the omission of certain identities from textbooks. He cites the absence of the working class from English as a foreign language (EFL) textbooks in the UK, but the absence of certain national or ethnic groups has been the topic of study in foreign language textbooks (Azimova & Johnson, 2012; Chapelle, 2009; Ramirez & Hall, 1990). He refers to 'misrecognition' as a 'demeaning or stereotypical representation' (Gray, 2013, p. 6) of certain identities, noting that the inclusion of tokens from various identities to counter erasure frequently results in misrepresentation. In my study, the chronological analysis of Canadian and Québec content in both text and image across multiple textbooks provides a strong indication of the degree of erasure or at least invisibility as it changes over the five decades. A quantitative analysis with a defensible sample is needed to make statements about erasure that pertain to a context larger than the books in the study because the represented minority tends to appear infrequently. Determining with some credibility the degree to which an infrequent occurrence of a topic or image is actually absent requires examination of a large sample. My research uses a large sample to report quantitative data about the absence of text and images.

1.3.3   Textbook Analysis is Interdisciplinary

In view of the multifaceted contents of language textbooks and their role in the course, the research perspective underlying foreign language textbook analysis is necessarily interdisciplinary. Gray (2013) points out that the authors in the edited collection draw upon a wide range of disciplines in their analysis of foreign language textbooks 'including sociology, philosophy, cultural studies and political economy' (p. 1). If research is to yield results that can raise professional consciousness about materials development and selection, theoretical lenses need to guide examination of all aspects of content. In Gray's collection, each of the researchers interprets the materials in view of larger historical, societal, and cultural perspectives to draw connections between language textbook content and the world of events and ideas beyond the language classroom. The interdisciplinarity of my research is its use of social-semiotic theory of meaning and Canadian/Québec Studies. The former provides the basis for my analysis of the language and images in the textbooks by offering the concepts needed to examine the connection between the content and resources for making meaning, the accessibility of the language for beginning-level students, as well as the meanings conveyed in images. More specifically, I have relied on the application of social-semiotic theory to the development of foreign language curriculum and materials (Byrnes et al. 2010) and analysis of images (Kress & VanLeuveen, 2006). Canadian Studies and Québec Studies are themselves highly cross-disciplinary fields; I have drawn primarily on research on history and language politics for my analysis, but other areas of Canadian and Québec Studies such as Canadian politics and geography have proven to be relevant as well.

1.3.4 There Is a Need for More Textbook Analysis

Textbooks retain their 'enduring centrality in classrooms around the world' (Gray, 2013, p. 2). They provide a window on how the profession operationalizes its theoretical principles of language teaching and learning. At the same time, they have a real impact on hundreds of thousands of language learners every day. Despite the key place of textbooks, Risager's (2007) survey concludes that there is a 'lack of awareness of the choices of content and thus the choices of areas of insight and interest for all participants' in language teaching and learning' (p. 238). The few studies of foreign language textbook content begin to offer food for thought. But interpreting results of such research necessarily returns researchers to the vexing questions about normative goals for the teaching of culture. Schulz (2006) points out that theory and standards have proven to be insufficient for making decisions for teaching practice because they fail to 'offer a realistic delineation of contents for culture teaching in the context of foreign language education' (p. 13). This pessimistically accurate observation is complemented by Byrnes, Maxim, and Norris' (2010) view that the preoccupation with culture in foreign language teaching inappropriately sidelines language. Their proposal for a better balance, which has been carried out in curriculum development, uses an analytic approach to connect the language and cultural content in the courses. I will describe that and use it as the basis for analysis of my Québec content in Chap. 3. Their approach offers a relevant, language-based means of analysis but does not attempt a systematic response to the question of what aspects of culture to teach.

Moving forward on questions of culture teaching in foreign language textbooks will require that the specific goals of culture teaching be included as part of textbook analysis, and that textbook analysis include the study of integrated language and culture. My research on French textbooks therefore outlines the cultural narrative that should be central to the cultural content and then examines how the narrative has been presented. This approach to textbook analysis assumes that the goal of foreign language teaching includes introducing the students to the political aspects of the cultural narrative of French speakers in Canada with the aim of allowing them to eventually be able to make sense of the daily life in Québec.

2   Cultural Narrative and Politics

The MLA (2007) report's positioning of the learning of cultural narratives as central to foreign language teaching connects politics to language teaching in an unprecedented way. The report does not define cultural narrative, but it introduces it as the key to gaining a full understanding of written, oral, and visual cultural artifacts of a culture.

> One possible model defines transcultural understanding [the goal of foreign language study] as the ability to comprehend and analyze the cultural narratives that appear in every kind of expressive form—from essays, fiction, poetry, drama, journalism, humor, advertising, political rhetoric, and legal documents to performance, visual forms, and music (MLA, 2007, p. 4).

Cultural narrative in the MLA report probably refers to the collective understanding of a people about their history, which explains who they are and how they came to be. Stories of coming to be as a group inevitably include the political and sometimes violent pushing of others and pulling toward assimilation. In applied linguistics, the idea of cultural narrative is seldom stated in exactly those terms. Instead, narrative research in applied linguistics (e.g., Barkhuizen, 2013) can focus on stories told on one or more levels of abstraction including the language of the actual recounting or forecasting of an event or experience and the larger social metanarratives that capture understandings of the past. The assumption in critical discourse analysis is that particularly the ideological dimensions of metanarratives affect the narratives that people tell and their interpretation. The idea alluded to in the MLA (2007) report is that if foreign language learners can learn the cultural narrative of the people whose language they are studying, they will be in the position to interpret the texts and images that they encounter. Because the language spoken by a group of people is typically central to their collective identity, their cultural narrative at least to some extent will include the role their language played in their history. Such narratives of identity and language involve highly political dimensions of struggle for recognition within existing states as well as the creation of nation-states. Thus, an understanding of any cultural narrative requires engagement with political concepts such as nations, states, and sovereignty in addition to ideological concepts such as identity and group rights.

The irony of the MLA (2007) report's suggestion to teach a political and ideological understanding of culture is striking in view of the cardinal rule for materials developers in foreign language education in the USA: avoid controversy. Despite this practice in materials development, the argument for a politically informed approach to foreign language pedagogy has clearly made its way into applied linguistics. It is not difficult to find the rationale for bringing political dimensions to culture teaching in three lines of argument: the definition of the competence that students are to achieve, the needs of students as they develop their language, and the societal needs that are the focus of the MLA (2007) report.

2.1   Defining the Target Competence

The political dimensions of the competence that learners are expected to achieve have gradually increased through various reconceptualizations of the apolitical communicative competence of the 1980s. Political dimensions of competence and culture teaching are included in discussions in the USA, but probably the most influential approach internationally was introduced by Byram (1997) in his book, *Teaching and Assessing Intercultural Communicative Competence*, which named the target competence for learners as 'intercultural communicative competence' (ICC). His book defined ICC as consisting of the following capacities:

Attitudes: curiosity and openness, readiness to suspend disbelief about other cultures and belief about one's own.

Knowledge: of social groups and their products and practices in one's own and in one's interlocutor's country, and the general processes of societal and individual interaction.

Skills of interpreting and relating: ability to interpret a document or event from another culture, to explain it and relate it to documents of events from one's own.

Skills of discovery and interaction: ability to acquire new knowledge of a culture and cultural practices and the ability to operate knowledge, attitudes and skills under the constraints of real-time communication and interaction.

Critical cultural awareness/political education: an ability to evaluate, critically and on the basis of explicit criteria, perspectives, practices, and products in one's own and other cultures and countries. (pp. 57–63)

Pedagogy intended to help students increase their ICC has been developed even though specific emphasis on political education is rare. Furstenberg (2010) developed a third-semester French course to allow students 'to access and understand core but essentially invisible aspects of a foreign culture—namely, the attitudes, beliefs, and values that underlie it' (p. 330) through structured communication over the Internet with a peer who is a member of the target culture. Students begin by responding to questionnaires that highlight each student's perspectives and then they discuss their responses with their partners and progress to analysis of various texts with their partner. Through this process, students of French, for example,

explore how and why such notions as *individualism/individualisme, success/ réussite, democracy/démocratie,* or *freedom/liberté* are viewed differently. They discuss their various attitudes toward privacy, hierarchy, government, or religion; they debate what kind of behaviors are 'expected' within a variety of contexts and interactions; they reflect about notions such as formality versus informality, implicit versus explicit, and about the importance of context in understanding people's attitudes and behaviors; and they share their views about current topics such as the environment, unemployment, or terrorism. In the process, they discover the underlying values inherent in their own culture as well as in the other. (Furstenberg, 2010, pp. 330–331).

This course, which has been conducted in a variety of languages, offers a concrete model aimed at fostering cultural knowledge, skills of interpreting and relating, and skills of discovery in students who are capable of using their French to do so. Work on ICC in foreign language teaching in the USA tends to focus on students beyond the beginning level when they would have at least minimum linguistic skills to converse with native speakers of the languages they are studying.

A second approach for addressing the development of ICC is presented in a book, *Language Learners as Ethnographers* (Roberts, Bryan, Barro, Jordan, & Street, 2001), which reported on a project that taught language learners preparing for study abroad to act as ethnographers seeking data and local understanding of cultural artifacts. The approach is 'multi-disciplinary' drawing upon 'social and linguistic anthropology, and aspects of sociolinguistics' (Roberts et al., 2001, p. 3). Students are educated in the use of frameworks for observation and interpretation of actions they observe in the daily lives of the speakers of the language they are studying. Students are also taught to write up their ethnographic reports in a manner that reflects their ethnographic stance as an interpreter of another culture. Such an ethnographic approach illustrates one dimension of what Byram (1997) sees as the complementary roles of the classroom, fieldwork, and independent learning. Byram (1997) questions the assumption that the classroom is solely preparation for experience to be gained later out in the real world, suggesting instead that 'engagement with otherness in the contemporary world is simultaneous—through media on a daily basis, through occasional visiting and receiving visitors, or working and learning together with people of another culture. This means that the dichotomy of "classroom" and "real world"' (1997, p. 65) is not productive for planning culture learning, as most foreign language teachers would agree.

These approaches to teaching that take culture learning outside of traditional school frameworks inevitably step into the realm of politics. Students' prior learning about the historical, political, and national narratives that shape every day understandings of events will be critical to their ability to understand and interpret what they observe. Risager's (2007) definition of the targeted competence takes a step beyond Byram's. She defines transnational cultural competence as including the knowledge of how languages are connected to nations and states in addition to how these language-nation-state relationships can evolve. She sees the goal of global citizenship as integral to the learner's ability to use language to act as an independent agent, not tied to nations and states. In order for learners to attain such a degree of effective agency, Risager argues, they need to have an understanding of the political and ideological meanings of nation, state, and identity, as well as how popular conceptions of the world uncritically link these entities to language.

2.2   Research on Students' Developmental Needs

A second argument for inclusion of politics in culture teaching comes from research that has attempted to document how and how well students perform in their target language use beyond the first year. The two domains of research come from the conversations that learners engage in over the Internet while working on structured learning collaborations and in study abroad programs. Findings from research in both of these areas suggest that whatever the benefits of undertaking the projects, intermediate language learners are unprepared to fully engage in productive conversation in the target language.

In research on collaborations over the Internet, Kramsch and Thorne (2002) investigated the conversation that took place when students studying French in the USA worked with students studying English in France. The researchers identified points of conflict in the conversation that likely arose because of the students' differences in their approach to the communication tasks as well as their lack of cultural understanding, inability to analyze the cultural aspects of the communication, and absence of strategies for maintaining cultural topics without offending each other. One of the American students who participated in this process later reflected that he felt the American students were doing the task that had been set in class but 'it seemed like, [the students in France] didn't know what they were doing. [laughs]' (Kramsch & Thorne 2002, p. 97).

The researchers' reflection on the American students' planning conversations about what to ask their French interlocutors added another level of analysis. One of the researchers commented:

but how is this idealistic communicative agenda ever to be realized without a knowledge of basic facts and understanding of the different social and cultural conventions under which each party is operating? This idealism, I am afraid is not based on knowledge and information about the Other, but on some vague attempts at establishing trust based on a supposedly shared youth culture. (Kramsch & Thorne, 2002, p. 90)

In other words, when students are not taught about any of the basic facts and understanding needed to interpret their interlocutors' words, they are left to their own conversational devices.

Another study investigated miscommunication between an American learning German and a German learning English in an Internet collaboration. Ware and Kramsch (2005) concluded that the causes of the miscommunication, which ultimately led to a communication breakdown, were complex, but partly a result of the students' lack of understanding of each other's histories and communication styles as well as a failure to see the activity as an occasion where presentation of one's self needs to be managed in a manner that respects the fact that they are engaging in cross-cultural communication. In reflecting on the miscommunication, Ware and Kramsch (2005) pointed out that typically students learn about culture 'as the national social institutions and dominant ways of life in a given country' (p. 199), but that such Internet collaborations actually require more of students because they need to have a 'willingness to imagine another person as different from oneself, to recognize oneself, to recognize the other in his or her historicity and subjectivity, and to see ourselves through the eyes of others' (p. 202).

Research has also revealed similar communication problems encountered by students in cross-cultural conversations while on study abroad because of their lack of basic cultural knowledge. Investigating students on study abroad in France during spring semester of 2003, Kinginger (2008) gathered data through interviews, biweekly journals, observations, and language assessments. The interview and journal data contained students' narrative accounts of their successes and failures in engaging with their peers, host families, and the community. The data revealed that students were unprepared to gain insight from the potentially rich opportunities that study abroad was intended to offer, and it showed specific areas of frustration and limitations for the students as a result of their lack of knowledge about France, the USA, politics, and how to discuss any of these areas. One consequence of the lack of knowledge Kinginger (2008) noted was that when students were called upon to talk about their political and ideological perspectives, they were challenged because 'they had given little thought or effort to the achievement of informed personal views on current political events. As a result, when asked to articulate their view, they reported feeling doubly challenged: to develop such a view in the first place and then to give expression to their views in French' (p. 64). She concluded that because students 'do not necessarily understand the local meanings of events and interactions' (pp. 11–12), it was difficult for them to engage with prospective interlocutors.

American students studying in Latin America recognized the limitations imposed by their lack of critical cultural awareness and political education. Students studying Spanish were interviewed in a multiple case study investigating the motivations of study abroad students in Latin America (Shedivy, 2004). All five of the students, who had studied Spanish in the USA for at least two years, mentioned their lack of historical and political knowledge about the countries that they visited. Upon their arrival in Latin America, students recognized that America is a controversial and, in some cases, unpopular force in this part of the world. It was through conversations while they were away that they discovered their lack of knowledge about their own country and its foreign policy. On the basis of these reports from students, Shedivy (2004) recommended 'aspects of political controversy, including those that might position the US in an unfavorable light should be part of the foreign language curriculum' (p. 118). One of the participants pointed out, 'I think it's unfortunate that the Spanish major in college is a literature major, so the professors don't really go into a lot of political issues. It's really only at the discretion of the professor if any political issues are discussed at all' (p. 114).

Kinginger's (2009) interpretation of the study abroad research depicts the learner as an agent whose motivation, decision-making, and strategic behavior are critical to the quality of the learning experience. The agent-learner intersects dynamically within the context of a host family, their beliefs, and attitudes toward foreign students and toward Americans. These factors can seem to conspire against students to put them into a position of incompetence, taking on the role of a young student, who is the recipient of regular corrective linguistic guidance, a family pet who is loved but not communicated with linguistically, a foreigner who is not expected to communicate accurately, or even the object of harassing behavior. Her interpretation portrays study abroad students as regularly engaging in a 'socialization process toward strategic cultivation of communicative *incompetence*' (p. 181) because of the roles they construct for themselves jointly with others in the study abroad context.

When students take on the reduced social roles in the target language community afforded by their communicative incompetence, they can communicate in English with their American peers in the study abroad program or in their own circle of friends and family, who are readily available through the Internet. Thus, students on study abroad who have developed neither the knowledge and strategies for engaging in cross-cultural conversations nor the impetus for doing so have alternatives to remaining in a role as a communicatively incompetent. These alternatives of retreating to the English-speaking world are unlikely to allow students to benefit from the type of conversations conducive to understanding others' perspectives and increasing intercultural competence. In view of the opportunities that students need to be prepared to choose beyond their first year, the type of political education that is part and parcel of cultural narrative appears to be an imperative.

2.3   Social Impact

A third argument for a politically rich presentation of a foreign language asserts the need for foreign languages to play a positive role in society by developing the international perspectives of students in higher education. In the USA, this argument is presented as the impetus for curricular change in foreign language teaching. The MLA (2007) report uses the political and social conditions of the USA after 9/11 to argue for the important role of foreign languages in a national response to current events. The document does not cite researchers in second language acquisition. Instead, the document quotes from Senator Daniel Akaka of Hawaii, who stated, 'Americans need to be more open to the world; we need to be able to see the world through the eyes of others if we are going to understand how to resolve the complex problems we face.' (as cited in MLA, p. 2) This grounding of the report's recommendations in global politics positions foreign language learning as a social and political good for the nation.

A decade earlier, a similar perspective was introduced in Europe, even if without the same sense of crisis. Working with a Council of Europe document, Starkey (1999) pointed out, 'In a European context, language education contributes to the political project of creating a more integrated market and transnational political entity' (as cited in Starkey, p. 156). Starkey quotes from a document stating the goals of foreign language education from the Council of Europe. It includes among the goals that foreign language teaching and learning aims 'to promote the personal development of the individual with growing self-awareness, self-confidence and independence of thought and action combined with social responsibility as an active agent in a participatory, pluralist democratic society and a well-informed, positive attitude toward other peoples and their cultures, free from prejudice, intolerance and xenophobia' (Trim 1997, p. 5).

Starkey's (1999) description of a language course with political content offers a step in this direction. The MLA (2007) report continues the argument by challenging the profession to meet society's social and political demand by teaching politically informed language courses in higher education. It criticizes the current typical organization of the curriculum in which the beginning-level courses fail to offer content that might engage students with a range of interests. Instead, it is argued that courses need to be organized to allow students to 'acquire a basic knowledge of the history, geography, culture, and literature of society or societies whose language they are learning; the ability to understand and interpret its radio, television, and print media; and the capacity to do research in the language using parameters specific to the target culture' (MLA, p. 4). In other words, the nonlinguistic content of foreign language courses is important at all levels.

Nothing better expresses the social significance of content in elementary courses than the numbers. The MLA report hints at the inappropriateness of a curriculum with its sole focus on literature for French majors by presenting the statistic that only 6.1 % of foreign language majors continue to attain a Ph.D., which is presumably in literature. This means that 93.9 % of French majors may go out to work in the world where their knowledge of cultural narratives is needed to interpret what is going on. However, the MLA's preoccupation with majors fails to serve a more powerful argument about social impact: the large majority of students in foreign language classes are not foreign language majors. In fact, the statistics showing recent enrollments in French classes in higher education in USA indicate that in 2013, 80 % of the enrollments in French classes were in the introductory courses, consisting of first and second year French. Figure 1.1 shows these relatively stable trends over a seven-year period, during which a slight decline in enrollments in both introductory and advanced courses is evident in the most recent period reported. Advanced courses are defined as third and fourth year courses. In 2013, with introductory course enrollments at 159,603 and advanced enrollments at 35,017, the ratio of students in the introductory course to those in the advanced course was 5:1. Introductory course students account for 82 % of all students in the USA studying French in higher education.

If French courses are to have social impact through their education of students to 'be open to the world' (as cited in MLA, 2007, p. 2), this education cannot wait until advanced-level courses. The MLA report, in its plea for faculty to rethink and make relevant university foreign language curricula, appropriately cites the need for a coherent vision for beginning-level foreign language courses. The authors argued that such a vision must be informed by cross-disciplinary collaboration, a position that has been echoed in the *The Modern Language Journal* 'Perspectives' columns. In particular, Bousquet (2008) pointed out that achieving successful collaboration requires a critical alliance with area studies and international studies programs. 'Area studies have embraced the goal of "transcultural competence" since their inception. Their curricula have an implicit collaborative agenda, built on interdisciplinarity, and offer students a vast array of courses aimed at developing an in-depth understanding of a particular area of the world or a thematic issue that crosses regions' (p. 304).

These three arguments for more politically oriented content at the beginning level are persuasive, but they are missing a critical element: data providing evidence of how and what political content is actually included in current introductory courses. Such data could come from classrooms, teachers, and students to provide a close-up view of a few

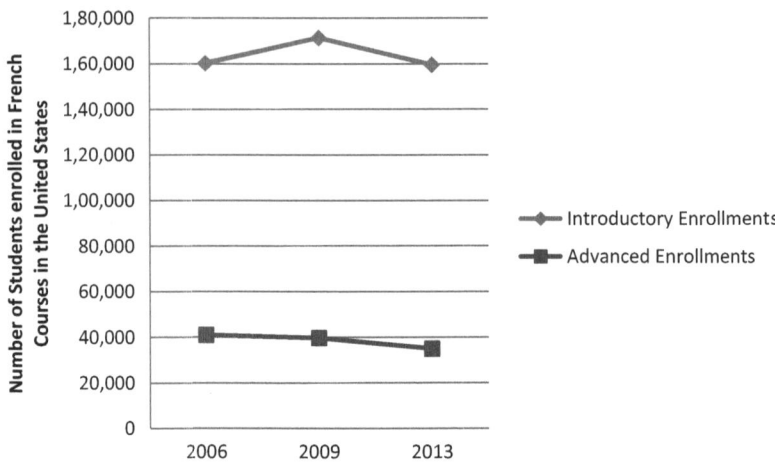

Fig. 1.1 Fall semester enrollments in introductory and advanced French courses in 2006, 2009, and 2013. Based on data from *Enrollments in Languages Other Than English in United States Institutions of Higher Education, Fall 2013* (pp. 40–42), by D. Goldberg, D., Looney, & N. Lustin, 2015, New York: Modern Language Association. Retrieved October 05, 2015, from http://www.mla.org/pdf/2013_enrollment_survey.pdf. Copyright 2015 by Modern Language Association of America

classes. They can also come from surveys to attempt to get a bigger picture perspective from 30,000 feet. My research investigates textbooks for beginning-level classes as the ground-level window on what textbooks bring to the classroom. I examine political content that is presented to help develop students understanding of Québec's cultural narrative in which the French language is the enduring pillar. If curricular change is to be undertaken seriously at the national or local level, such analyses of current practices are needed.

3   Textbook Analysis as Inquiry

The emergence of textbook analysis as an area of inquiry in applied linguistics is potentially important for the process of curricular change. But since textbooks are so central to curricular change, methodology for textbook analysis elevates in importance. Gray's (2013) statement of the assumptions underlying textbook analysis outlined above has implications for research in this area. Weninger and Kiss' (2015) methodological review of research investigating studies of textbooks for teaching English as an international language takes a first step toward building methodologies. Both the assumptions and the methodological review are useful in charting a way to define language textbook analysis as an area of inquiry in applied linguistics. They both suggest to me that textbook analysis should meet certain criteria for relevance and rigor, which I have defined as (1) cultural and historical grounding, (2) theoretical and practical relevance, and (3) methodological credibility.

3.1   Cultural and Historical Grounding

The assumption that textbook analysis encompasses the analysis of meanings in textbooks suggests that textbook analysis should be informed by the specific facts, values, and narratives of the relevant cultures. Risager (2007) pointed out that selection of cultural content does not follow deterministically from the language taught, but rather that materials developers need to be 'open to the diversity of contexts that might be relevant and interesting for their learners. Focusing on conditions in Spain in the teaching of Spanish, for example, is not a "natural" choice; it is a decision that has to be specifically motivated and justified' (pp. 236–237). This perspective is useful for prompting the study of representation of Mexico, for example, in Spanish textbooks in the USA, but it does not guide the analysis of how Mexico is presented to students.

The cultural content appearing in textbooks needs to be viewed through the lens of the potential content and ways of making meaning that are available to textbook producers for representing culture to students. Discussion of culture in applied linguistics tends to lack the necessary specificity. Instead, cultural topics tend to be referred to in the abstract (e.g., family relations and politics) and researchers tend to study universal concerns of reproduction of dominant power relations, exclusion of certain elements of society, and presentation of history in a Eurocentric fashion. These general themes are important aspects of critical awareness for teachers and learners at one level, but for materials writers, they are too abstract relative to the need to select specific materials and create effective means of presentation. In contrast, the acts of developing textbooks and selecting teaching materials require engagement with the particulars of specific cultures, understanding the important aspects of national cultural narratives, and examining not only what and how cultural aspects are presented but also what and how certain aspects are missing. Engagement with area studies is needed because the particulars to be analyzed in any textbook require knowledge on the part of the analyst that extends beyond the general observations that come from applied linguistics.

The assumption that textbook analysis is interdisciplinary provides a good foundation going forward for historically grounded analysis that takes into account the teaching of cultural narrative. In the past, the historical basis of culture teaching in foreign languages has received little attention in applied linguistics. A notable exception is a special issue of *L2 Journal* entitled *History and Memory in Foreign Language Study*, which published papers exploring the issues at the intersection of teaching history and teaching culture in foreign language classes. In the introduction to the special issue, Kramsch (2012) situates the topic in the historical and political context of the USA after 9/11, which she links to the goal set out in the MLA report for foreign language teaching to develop students' 'political consciousness' (as cited in Kramsch, p. 2) and to see themselves as Americans whose world view may be different from that of people from other parts of the world. Culture is itself historically constructed in the narrative of people and their interactions with other groups of people. Kramsch (2012) explains differences in world views that exist cross-culturally in part through their 'different interpretations of historical events, memories and aspirations,' all of which are 'linked to a sense of national identity' (p. 2). From this perspective, there is virtually nothing that one can learn about culture without also studying the historical cultural narratives that give rise to existing perspectives and practices. Textbook analysis needs to begin with knowledge of the important national narratives of the people and the multiple perspectives of those narratives among the people. Key questions for analysis are how the narrative is selectively retold through the texts, how language plays a role in the retelling, and how the students are engaged and positioned in the retelling.

3.2   Practical and Theoretical Relevance

The assumption that textbooks are commercially situated creates an impetus for conducting textbook analysis studies that are relevant for practice. The textbook industry creates products of value using complex methods of production, review, and trialing. In my experience, the competition is intense to develop products that will sell because of their perceived value for foreign language teaching and learning. In this environment, actionable research results from textbook analysis can have implications for practice. Currently, opportunities for the production process to connect the theoretical discussion with specific instances and issues in materials development are not abundant. However, the study of textbooks, if undertaken with the intent to inform practice, holds potential for making connections between practice and theory.

Such connections are needed because applied linguists raise important questions about culture teaching that pertain directly to issues faced by materials developers. For example, how useful is it to present a particular cultural topic in a neutral fashion? Byram's (1997) definition of ICC includes a critical, cultural dimension in addition to an understanding of one's own cultural perspective. Kinginger's review of study abroad research suggests the need for students to develop such self-awareness to benefit from conversation with interlocutors from other cultures. Accordingly, pedagogies aimed at developing ICC entail exploration and discovery of the learner's own positioning relative to culturally based meanings. Contrary to this goal, 'One of the characteristic features of foreign language textbooks is the great anonymity of the author(s). Though their names are known, they traditionally act as mere mediators with regard to sociocultural issues, at least at the elementary level' (Risager, 1991, p. 192). The neutral presentation of cultural material by a third-person narrator may not lend itself well to the type of critical positioning that students are expected to be able to adopt.

Applied linguists have regularly raised questions about representation and positioning of learners by textbook authors in the study of textbooks in English language teaching. Auerbach (1995) argued that such textbook and curriculum choices the author makes can have implications for the language and repertoire of social roles that learners learn to occupy. She observed that English as a second language (ESL) books for refugees teach the job-related functional language of requesting clarification of job instructions, calling in sick, and making small talk, but the students are 'rarely taught how to complain, file a grievance, challenge poor safety conditions, organize a union' (pp. 17–18). Similarly, with respect to cultural issues, one might argue that students who are exposed to the neutral, anonymous presentation of the textbook author are being subtly socialized into the use of the foreign language to take on a similar stance through the language they are exposed to. Such observations and insights emanate from theoretical perspectives of functional and critical discourse analysis and they raise questions of practical importance for materials developers and teachers.

3.3   Methodological Credibility

The assumption that more textbook analysis is needed demands that current practices be perceived as contributing to a credible area of inquiry in applied linguistics. Credibility is not linked to a single characteristic of a study, but a minimal requirement is the credibility of the research methodology. A variety of methods have been used for textbook analysis depending on the research goals. Weninger and Kiss (2015) reviewed textbook analysis research to identify 'what lines of argument are used, or what schools of thought are present in the analysis of cultural content of foreign/second language teaching textbooks' (Weninger & Kiss, p. 52). They found that some form of content analysis was the most prevalent approach to textbook analysis in their sample of studies. Researchers typically identified and counted particular instances of textbook content in order to summarize the content of interest. But they also found that some studies used critical discourse analysis, which begins with an assumption that certain social groups are marginalized and disadvantaged, and that the language used to represent them plays a role in perpetuating such injustice. In addition, they identified a trend toward using semiotic and multimodal approaches in the analysis of textbooks. Despite the fact that they identified a variety of methodological approaches, they noted that the authors of the studies themselves in most cases failed to make explicit the methodological perspectives guiding their analyses.

The methodological grounding for textbook analysis typically needs to be developed through a combination of quantitative and qualitative research methods. Such mixed-methods designs are complex because they are set up in a manner that is tailored to address particular research questions. The assumption that textbook analysis encompasses analysis of meaning in textbooks suggests a contribution from qualitative methods (e.g., Corbin & Strauss, 2015) whereas the reliance on quantitative approaches to content analysis in many studies suggests the utility of quantitative methodologies as developed by Krippendorff (2013). Social scientists have developed useful frameworks for combining qualitative and quantitative approaches, but these need to be justified for a particular study and applied in a way that makes sense for that study. Research methodology needs to be justified on the basis of the research questions and goals; it needs to be explained on the basis of accepted practices within the relevant research traditions.

For example, one fundamental research methodological issue that straddles the qualitative-quantitative research divide is how the sample of textbooks is chosen. Both research traditions as well as their combination recognize the sampling rationale and process as fundamental to interpretation of results. The issue is probably stated most clearly by quantitative researchers: 'When researchers analyze a sample of texts in place of a larger population of texts … they need a sampling plan to ensure that the textual units do not bias the answers to the research questions' (Krippendorff, 2013, p. 114). Limitations of time, money, and access result in the need to make explicit the relationship between the sample analyzed and the population of interest so as to identify potential bias due to selection or underrepresentation. Nevertheless, qualitative researchers include the sampling design in their evaluation of qualitative research as well: 'What was the target sample population? How was the original sample selected? How did sampling proceed?' (Corbin & Strauss, 2015, p. 350). In textbook analysis, the selection of the sample has direct implications for the population to which results can be generalized. For example, in the study of Spanish textbooks undertaken by Ramirez and Hall (1990), five textbook series used in public schools in the state of New York were included in the analysis, and therefore, results pertain to those textbook series. Chapelle (2009) investigated nine first-year French textbooks used at large universities in the northern USA, and results are interpreted in view of the geography and level of the textbooks in the study. If the results of textbook analysis are to be informative to the commercial industry of textbook producers, research questions and methodological choices need to be set up in a manner that allows for relevant and defensible interpretations about a population of interest to textbook producers.

3.4   The Current Study

The current study was designed in view of the four assumptions outlined by Gray (2013) and therefore reflects the methodological implications described above, as summarized in Table 1.1. The need for practical and theoretical relevance that can inform production practices of foreign language textbooks is addressed through the connections of this work with the recognized need in the profession to improve the introduction of culture at the beginning level of French instruction in the USA. In this context, I have taken into account the existing work that attempts to move forward on such an agenda. The description of curriculum development by Byrnes, Maxim, and Norris (2010) provides the necessary links between the profession's understanding of the problem, on the one hand, and a theoretically motivated way of beginning to conceptualize a solution, on the other hand. Their social-semiotic theoretical basis was also well suited to address the assumption that textbook analysis should encompass analysis of the meanings in textbooks. In addition, the study of meaning called for a qualitative approach, which was done in this study by identifying cultural themes through a grounded process of using expert judgment to identify themes, coding texts and images, and reexamining content for its relevance to cultural narrative.

The assumption about inclusion of meaning analysis went hand in hand with the assumption that the research must necessarily be interdisciplinary.

The study of cultural meaning requires more substantial engagement with area studies than what we as applied linguists and language teachers normally do. I have studied Canadian and Québec studies over the past ten years in order to be able to base the analysis of meaning conveyed in the textbooks on a cultural narrative compiled from the study of Québec's history and culture. The fourth assumption is that more textbook analysis is needed to ground the abundant professional discussion of culture teaching at the beginning level of foreign language study. This study was conceived on the assumption that actual data about the coverage of Québec's cultural narrative would be

Table 1.1 Assumptions underlying textbook analysis, their methodological implications with their instantiations in the current study

Assumptions	Methodological implications	This research
Textbooks are commercially situated	The need for practical and theoretical relevance	Addresses a recognized need in the profession to improve the introduction of culture at the beginning level of French instruction in the USA Draws upon social-semiotic theoretical perspectives as they have been used in foreign language curriculum development on language and visuals
Textbook analysis encompasses analysis of meanings in the textbooks	The need for qualitative approaches to research	Identified cultural themes through a grounded process of using expert judgment to identify themes and reexamine content
Textbook analysis is interdisciplinary	The need for cultural and historical grounding	Based analysis on a cultural narrative compiled from the study of Québec's history and culture
There is a need for more textbook analysis	The need for methodological credibility	Identified the population of interest, created a plan to sample from it, and explained the sampling logic Described the theoretical and methodological bases for all analyses

useful for future materials selection and development. To move such an analysis from the idea stage to actually affect practice requires a credible methodology for carrying out the study. To attain sufficient rigor, I drew upon the basic notion from mixed-methods research that the pragmatic aims of the research goals should guide the design of the research, which can draw upon both qualitative and quantitative approaches. Based on a combination of approaches, throughout the chapters I have described the rationale for each step in the analysis, all of which were built upon a sample of textbooks that had been identified on the basis of the intended interpretation.

4   Conclusion

The large majority of foreign language students in the USA begin their foreign language study by taking a course with a textbook. Despite the resources available on the Internet, textbooks serve as the starting point for their exposure to cultural content, which they may build on later in many ways, most immediately in their Internet collaborations and study abroad. The need for change in the ways that culture is integrated into the foreign language curriculum in the USA has been recognized for some time, and some pedagogical approaches have been suggested and investigated at the intermediate levels. However, culture teaching at the beginning level remains a problem, and it is clear that approaching solutions will require a better understanding of the issue. With a focus on the political dimensions of cultural narrative, the following chapters work toward building an understanding of how culture can be taught at the beginning level by examining how the cultural narrative of Québec has been taught in French textbooks in the USA over a fifty-year period. This chapter has provided the background motivation and assumptions as well as the general methodological parameters. The following chapter builds the cultural narrative and describes the sample of textbooks that was used for the analysis in the three following chapters. The final chapter summarizes the ways that this study offers a better understanding of culture teaching in foreign language textbooks.

References

ACTFL (n.d.) *World-Readiness Standards for Learning Languages*. Retrieved from http://www.actfl.org/sites/default/files/pdfs/World-ReadinessStandardsforLearningLanguages.pdf.

Amon, E., Muyskens, J. A., & Omaggio Hadley, A. C. (2004). *Vis-à-vis: Beginning French*. Boston: McGraw Hill.

Auerbach, E. R. (1995). The politics of the ESL classroom. In J. W. Tollefson (Ed.), *Power and inequality in language education* (pp. 9–33). Cambridge, UK: Cambridge University Press.

Azimova, N., & Johnston, B. (2012). Invisibility and ownership of language: Problems of representation in Russian language textbooks. *The Modern Language Journal, 96*(3), 337–349.

Barkhuizen, G. (Ed.) (2013). *Narrative research in applied linguistics*. Cambridge, UK: Cambridge University Press.

Bousquet, G. (2008). A model for cross-disciplinary collaboration. *The Modern Language Journal, 92*, 304–306.

Byram, M. (1997). *Teaching and assessing intercultural communicative competence*. Clevedon, UK: Multilingual Matters.

Byrnes, H., Maxim, H. H., & Norris, J. M. (2010). Realizing advanced foreign language writing: Development in collegiate education: Curricular design, pedagogy, assessment. *The Modern Language Journal, 94*(Supplement), 1–221.

Chapelle, C. A. (2009). A hidden curriculum in language textbooks: Are beginning learners of French at U.S. universities taught about Canada? *The Modern Language Journal, 93*(2), 139–152.

Chapelle, C. A. (2014). Five decades of Canadian and Québec content in French textbooks in the United States. *American Review of Canadian Studies, 44*(4), 415–432.

Corbin, J., & Strauss, A. (2015). *Basics of qualitative research: Techniques and procedures for developing grounded theory* (5th ed.). Thousand Oaks, CA: Sage Publications.

Dechert, C., & Kastner, P. (1989). Undergraduate student interests and the cultural content of textbooks for German. *The Modern Language Journal, 73*(2), 178–191.

Furstenberg, G. (2010). Making culture the core of the language class: Can it be done? *The Modern Language Journal, 94*(2), 329–332.

Goldberg, D., Looney, D., & Lusin, N. (2015). *Enrollments in Languages Other Than English in United States Institutions of Higher Education, Fall 2013.* Retrieved from http://www.mla.org/pdf/2013_enrollment_survey.pdf.

Gray, J. (Ed.). (2013). *Critical perspectives on language teaching materials.* Basingstoke, UK: Palgrave Macmillan.

Kinginger, C. (2008). Language learning in study abroad: Case studies of Americans in France. *The Modern Language Journal, 92*(s1), 1–124.

Kinginger, C. (2009). *Language learning and study abroad: A critical reading of research.* Basingstoke, UK: Palgrave Macmillian.

Kramsch, C. J. (1988). The cultural discourse of foreign language textbooks. In A. J. Singerman (Ed.), *Toward an integration of language and culture,* (pp. 63–88). Middlebury, VT: The Northeast Conference on the Teaching of Foreign Languages.

Kramsch, C. (2012). History and memory in foreign language study. *L2 Journal, 4*(1), 1–8.

Kramsch, C., & Thorne, S. (2002). Foreign language learning as global communicative practice. In D. Block & D. Cameron (Eds.), *Globalization and language teaching* (pp. 83–100). London: Routledge.

Kress, G. R., & Van Leeuwen, T. (2006). *Reading images: The grammar of visual design* (2nd ed.). London: Routledge.

Krippendorff, K. (2013). *Content analysis: An introduction to its methodology* (3rd ed.). Thousand Oaks, CA: Sage Publications.

Lado, R. (1957). *Linguistics across cultures: Applied linguistics for language teachers.* Ann Arbor, MI: University of Michigan Press.

Lange, D. L. (1999). Planning for and using the new national culture standards. In J. K. Phillips & R. M. Terry (Eds.), *Foreign language standards: Linking research, theories, and practice* (pp. 57–135). Lincolnwood, IL: National Textbook Company.

Mainous, B. H. (1968). *Basic French: An oral approach* (2nd ed.). New York: Charles Scribner's Sons.

Modern Language Association of America. (2007). *Foreign languages and higher education: New structures for a changed world: MLA Ad Hoc Committee on Foreign Languages.* New York: Modern Language Association of America.

Ogden, J. D. (1981). *Teaching French as a multicultural language.* Washington, DC: Center for Applied Linguistics.

Ramirez, A., & Hall, K. (1990). Language and culture in secondary level Spanish textbooks. *The Modern Language Journal, 74*(1), 48–65.

Reinhardt, E. (1928). French textbooks used in secondary schools. *The Modern Language Journal, 12*(6), 446–450.

Risager, K. (1991). Cultural references in European textbooks: An evaluation of recent trends. In D. Buttjes & M. Byram (Eds.), *Mediating languages and cultures: Towards an intercultural theory of foreign language education* (pp. 181–227). Clevedon, UK: Multilingual Matters.

Risager, K. (2007). *Language and culture pedagogy: From a national to a transnational paradigm.* Clevedon, UK: Multilingual Matters.

Roberts, C. Byram, M., Barro, A., Jordan, S., & Street, B. V. (2001). *Language learners as ethnographers.* Clevedon: Multilingual Matters.

Schultz, J. M. (2004). Towards a pedagogy of the francophone text in intermediate language courses. *French Review, 78,* 260–275.

Schulz, R. A. (2006). The challenge of assessing cultural understanding in the context of foreign language instruction. *Foreign Language Annals, 40*(1), 9–26.

Shedivy, S. L. (2004). Factors that lead some students to continue the study of foreign language past the usual 2 years of high school. *System, 32*(1), 103–119.

Singerman, A. J. (Ed.). (1996). *Acquiring cross-cultural competence: Four stages for students of French.* Lincolnwood, IL: National Textbook Company.

Siskin, C. (1998). *The work of writing: Literature and social change in Britain, 1700–1830.* Baltimore/London: Johns Hopkins University Press.

Starkey, H. (1999). Foreign language teaching to adults: Implicit and explicit political education. *Oxford Review of Education, 25*(1&2), 155–169.

Thompson, K. D. (2013). Representing language, culture, and language users in textbooks: A critical approach to Swahili multiculturalism. *The Modern Language Journal, 97*(4), 947–964.

Trim, J. L. M. (1997). *Modern languages: Learning, teaching, assessment: A common European framework of reference: A general guide for users: Draft 1.* Strasbourg, France: Council for Cultural Co-operation, Education Committee.

Ware, P. D., & Kramsch, C. (2005). Toward an intercultural stance: Teaching German and English through telecollaboration. *The Modern Language Journal, 89,* 190–205.

Weninger, C., & Kiss, T. (2015). Analyzing culture in foreign/second language textbooks. In X. Curdt-Christiansen, & C. Weninger, (Eds.), *Language, ideology and education: The politics of textbooks in language education* (pp. 50–66). London: Routledge.

2

Québec's Cultural Narrative and French Textbooks

This chapter lays the foundation for investigating aspects of Québec's cultural narrative in beginning-level French textbooks in the USA. It reports the amount of Canadian and Québec content appearing in text and images as well as the degree of variation among textbooks. The amount and variation of content are addressed for each of the five decades included in the study to show the chronological change in the amount of Canadian and Québec content from 1960 to 2010. The chapter begins by introducing Québec's language politics as potentially valuable content for language textbooks to explain why such content is worthy of investigation in foreign language textbook analysis. To provide the essential cultural and historical grounding, I outline the key events and actors in Québec's cultural narrative, which links the French language with Québec's history, politics, and identity. The second part of the chapter presents the methodology for choosing a sample of French textbooks for investigating the presentation of Québec cultural content from the five-decade period beginning in 1960 and ending in 2010. It describes how the Québec content was identified and coded. The third part of the chapter reports the quantity of Québec content appearing in the textbooks representing each decade. Based on the quantitative indicators, it is evident that the Canadian and

© The Editor(s) (if applicable) and The Author(s) 2016
C.A. Chapelle, *Teaching Culture in Introductory Foreign Language Textbooks*, DOI 10.1057/978-1-137-49599-0_2

Québec content has increased and was at an all-time high in the decade from 2000 to 2010. This finding about the upward trajectory of Québec content offers a valuable perspective on previous findings. In contrast to previous research and commentary suggesting underrepresentation and disinterest in Québec in French language teaching, the chronological perspective shows a clear trend of increasing Canadian and Québec content in the textbooks across the five decades studied.

1   Québec's Language Politics as Content

Visitors in Québec see artifacts of Québec's language politics on every street. The streets of Québec figure in Bernard Spolsky's (2004) *Language Policy*, which begins with a world tour of language in the news. The first stop is Hanover, Germany, where doctors had made a decision about treatment of a patient based on her inability to speak German. Next is Jerusalem, where the public signs are trilingual due to the linguistic history and politics of the city. The third stop is New Zealand, where it was reported that Transit New Zealand had agreed to include Mānori on the English road signs. The next two stops are also for observation of road signs: Wales and Québec. In Wales, a disagreement existed between people who supported the use of Welsh alone and those who supported the use of both Welsh and English. In Québec, no dispute was reported. Instead, the observation was, 'Québec law requires that all public signs be in French, permitting the addition, in smaller letters, of a translation into another language' (Spolsky, 2004, p. 1). Such laws are the result of a political process in which the interests of some prevailed to create conditions for all.

The content of Spolsky's (2004) book is language policy: It surveys the actions people have taken throughout history to manage the way that language is chosen and used for a variety of purposes, including its public display in signs. Québec's language laws appear in the first paragraph with the other important examples of language in the news. Spolsky's use of Québec as an example of interesting language policy is not an anomaly. This region of North America regularly appears amidst the international examples of language policy. To an American audience, the law seems curiously preemptive of individual liberty, unwelcoming to the large majority of the world, and simply strange. Six pages into Spolsky's text, he provides a brief story to explain Québec's sign laws: 'In Québec, the language problem in the 1950s … was that a French-speaking majority was required to learn English in order to communicate with the largely monolingual English-speaking minority, who effectively controlled the business life of the province. Taking advantage of their political power, the French speakers set out to change this policy' (Spolsky, 2004, p. 6). To begin to make sense of the French sign policy, the history is needed. But how did a French-speaking majority come to occupy such a disadvantaged position? More history is needed. Spolsky (2004) refers readers to later in his book, where religion, schools, the military defeat of the French by the English, and the 1867 Canadian constitution all come into the picture. Moreover, he points out the North American story of French has analogues in Europe with Catalan and Basque.

This content about the French language is politically intriguing, historically rich, and internationally significant. Spolsky's (2004) text only reveals the skeleton of the story as it is interwoven with the study of language policy at the global level, but a French language textbook should be able to dig deeper. What is the whole story of French language in Québec? What is the cultural narrative that forms the basis of a national identity in Québec? Is it even possible to maintain a national identity without having the geopolitical status of nation-state? What became of North American French speakers outside Québec? For students studying French in North America, these are questions of local interest. What could make better content for students who are beginning to learn French in the USA?

Beginning-level foreign language textbooks use cultural content intended to provide examples of the foreign language and convey content about the culture of its speakers. However, decisions about how to present cultures in language textbooks are made during the textbook development process, which remains undocumented except for a few recent case studies (Gray, 2013), revealing snapshots of the culture of textbook production (Kramsch, 1988). Singerman (1996) characterized culture presentation in French language textbooks as 'incidental fragments' (p. 1), but data-based research on foreign language textbooks remains rare, at best. The idea of fragments, which comports with my experience as a student, teacher, and materials developer, is at odds with the type of cultural narrative that is advocated in the MLA report, which is also critical of way that culture is presented in foreign language textbooks. Is the story of Québec's language politics really missing from beginning-level textbooks, leaving students of French without an introduction to this world-class cultural narrative?

2   Québec's National Cultural Narrative

A national or cultural narrative is a big story that helps to make sense of the people and places in their society. In Québec, the French signs figure prominently in Québec's cultural narrative, which forms the basis for the collective identity in Québec. The signs can be explained in part by the language law, which is in place as part of a Francophone movement to retake control of Québec from the Anglophones that Spolsky (2004) mentioned in his brief explanation. But what are the details of the actual story behind the French signs that textbook producers could select from? Who are the actors in this story? What are their positions, who do they interact with, and how do they get things done with language? How does such a historical cultural narrative help to shape the local interactions that residents of Québec have with each other? How do they interact with English Canadians today? How might all of these issues affect the experience that an American student might have in Québec?

Having investigated the sixty-five textbooks in my sample, I can attest that parts of the story of Québec, its history, identity, and politics have appeared in various forms in some French textbooks in the USA. These fragments can be identified, counted, and averaged over multiple textbooks as I have reported in the second part of this chapter. But ultimately if fragments of culture in textbooks are to be evaluated for the extent to which they represent a cultural narrative, the analysis needs to begin with an outline of what the cultural narrative includes. Spolsky's (2004) sketch gives a glimpse of the history, but it needs to be outlined in terms of the type of content that textbook developers can draw from to create textbooks.

In this section, I outline Québec's cultural narrative in terms of the people and events that form the basis of Québec's collective national identity. Such a cultural narrative might be construed in different ways depending on who is telling the story. I have developed my basic outline from a Québec government publication, *La langue française au Québec* (Gouvernement du Québec, 2008), which was published as a thirty-two-page, six-by-eight-inch glossy booklet for the 400th year anniversary celebration of the founding of Québec by Samuel de Champlain in 1608. Pages 5 through 30 contain important milestones in the story along with a brief description and images. The design is attractive, curated as one would expect in a museum or website. It is clearly a document for public consumption. In the process of its development, decisions were obviously made to omit the recent contentious political issues—most notably the two sovereignty referenda, one in 1980 and the second in 1995. These and other political facts are central to the cultural narrative and therefore I have augmented the government's story with two sources that focus explicitly on language politics in Québec (Martel & Pâquet, 2010; Oakes & Warren, 2007). The narrative I have outlined is also influenced by my engagement with Canadian and Québec studies. The result is not intended to be the definitive cultural narrative of Québec, but rather a credible one to form the basis for examining content chosen by textbook producers. I have divided it into the five decades that correspond to the five decades of textbooks investigated in this study in addition to one section including events before the 1960s and one section on themes that transcend the decades.

2.1 Before the 1960s: French from the Time of Colonization

According to the government of Québec publication, the story of the French language in Québec begins with the founding of Québec by Samuel de Champlain in 1608 even though there had been significant French exploration in the 1500s by Jacques Cartier, which marked the beginning of the French presence in America. The next years included a number of 'firsts' including families, schools, visits from Jesuit missionaries, contact with indigenous people, and the arrival of women intended to help populate the new colony. Jesuit missionaries made up one strand of settlers, but the real adventurers were *coureurs des bois*, who lived, hunted, traded, and intermarried with the native people while pushing the boundaries of French settlement. The new way of life of these settlers resulted in their developing a unique Canadian identity and ultimately led up to the marking of a date in 1670 when the French settlers officially established their new identity as *Canadiens*. Most Québec histories emphasize the difference between this *Canadien* approach to settlement and that of the English. The former cultivated a new life and new identity by living off the land using the knowledge they gained from working closely with the indigenous people rather than trying to transplant their European lifestyles.

The path of settlement for the Canadiens took a negative turn with the victory of the English in North America over the French, and specifically the loss of Québec in 1759 and Montreal in 1760. In the treaty following the war, one part of New France became 'la Province of Québec' (written in English in the otherwise French language description in the document). English became the language of power and law, but French voices were not silenced in part because they so outnumbered the British. Under British rule, the Québec Act of 1774 gave official recognition to French, reestablished French civil law, and allowed the Canadiens to participate in the civil government in the colony. French was used in civil affairs and the interests of Francophones were debated. In this North American French-speaking society of *Canadiens*, the first novel appeared in French in Québec in 1837.

The gains made by Francophones were interrupted by the 1837 Patriots' Rebellion against the British, which resulted in a British commissioned report to study the causes of the uprising. The infamous Durham report of 1839 recommended uniting the provinces of Canada into one Canadian Province with a British majority population, which was done the following year. Lord Durham's report famously and memorably called for assimilation of the French Canadians into the British colony because, according to the report, they were a people without history or literature. The aftermath of this episode resulted in a large exodus of Canadiens to the USA, marking one significant wave of immigration of Francophones to the USA many years after the early French explorers.

For the Canadiens, however, such setbacks never seemed to mean defeat. In 1841 a law covering public instruction made available a network of French medium schools, and Laval was established as the first francophone university in Québec. However, despite the law, in provinces outside Québec, by the mid 1860s, French Catholic education was not well supported, and such schools were closing. In this time period, Québec emerged as needing to take responsibility for maintaining French in Canada. In 1867 the British North American Act created the Dominion of Canada by uniting Québec, Ontario, New Brunswick, and Nova Scotia. That act gave both English and French the status of official languages in parliament in Ottawa and in Québec even as the demise of francophone interests continued outside Québec, most dramatically demonstrated by the execution of Louis Riel, the Francophone founding father of Manitoba after he led an uprising in Manitoba in 1885.

In 1895 the *École littéraire de Montréal* [Montreal literary school] was founded with the goal of saving French by developing the national literature. Leaders in French Canadian society were concerned with improving the status of their language in view of the fact that English was used more and more in arenas of business, science, and modernization. Oakes and Warren (2007) described the linguistic situation at the end of the 1900s as extremely disadvantageous for the Francophones: French Canadians did not speak English, which was being used for high-status purposes across Canada; nor did they speak a high-status variety of French.

This situation was feared to result in Francophones shifting to English as a means of seeking higher-status education, jobs, and opportunities for their children. In response, the *Société du parler français du Canada* was formed in 1902 to increase the status of Québec French by raising awareness of its historical roots and conducting descriptive linguistic work. Over the next twenty years, a number of events helped to institutionalize the use of French in Québec including a provincial law stating that companies serving the public must serve clients in French or English, a congress on the French language in North America, a commission to establish French geographic place names, the first French radio station in Canada, and a federal law stating that civil servants placed in Québec must speak French. There were a few international milestones beginning in 1950 when the first international meeting of Francophone countries was held, Québécois songs were first recognized in France, Radio Canada's television began broadcasting in French, and the Québécois film industry began to develop. Such international connections and recognitions are an important part of the cultural narrative, which portrays this time period as a time of struggle at the hands of English speakers, who, the story goes, had no interest in speaking Québécois French.

In 1959, just before the cultural transformation of the 1960s, the first reference to *joual* was noted as the term referring to the colloquial variety of French used in informal settings in Québec. In a 1960 book entitled *Insolences du Frère Untel*, the *Frère* argued that the French language needed to be protected from the corruptions it endured in colloquial use and from the influence of English (Desbiens & Lurendeau, 1960). Moreover, he argued that since language is a public good, it is the responsibility of the state to protect it. In retrospect, his message forecasted the core of Québec's cultural narrative as it unfolds throughout the next five decades.

2.2   The 1960s: The Quiet Revolution

The period of modernization and social change, *la revolution tranquille* [The Quiet Revolution], in Québec began in 1960 with the election of the Liberal government of Jean Lesage. Among the changes was the opening of the Office of the French language in 1961 by a government that was preparing to be the guardian of the French language, replacing the Catholic church in its role as the keeper of Québécois identity. Québec's government set out to improve conditions for French speakers in Québec. At about the same time, the Canadian government convened a commission to investigate the status of bilingualism and biculturalism in Canada. The finding released in 1965 exposed the poor working conditions and earning power of French Canadians relative to those of English speakers. The experience of social injustice felt by Québécois citizens fueled nationalist sentiments, which in Québec refers to allegiance to the separatist movement. These feelings led to the formation of the Parti Québécois in 1968 with René Lévesque as its leader. The goal of the party was Québec's sovereignty. The same year, Pierre Elliott Trudeau, leader of the Liberal party in Canada, took office as Prime Minister in Canada. His goal was Canadian unity, and one of his methods for accomplishing a unified Canada was through the Official Languages Act which established Canada's policy of official bilingualism in 1969.

With Québec nationalism on the rise, French President, Charles de Gaulle, made a visit to Montreal in 1967 on the occasion of the world fair, Expo '67. There he made his infamous speech in which he, the foreign president, called for Québec's independence. 'Vivre le Québec libre' are the words that are remembered both in Québec and in the rest of Canada. The Québec government publication did not include this inflammatory event, but the publication does mark 1967 as the birth of the identity 'Québécois' based on a resolution adopted in Montreal stating that the people of Québec wish to be called Québécois rather than French Canadians. The irony that they had to abandon their ancestors' identifying name, Canadien, to the rest of Canada in order to maintain their collective identity is not lost on many Québécois today. The following year a school district in Montreal (Saint-Léonard) eliminated bilingual classes for immigrants, requiring them instead to take classes taught in French. The same year, *le joual*, which had been criticized so definitively by Frère Untel, was recognized in cultural events as an expression of Québécois identity. The decade ended with Québec's law to promote the use of French (Bill 63), and the Canadian official languages law recognizing both English and French as the official languages of all of Canada.

2.3   The 1970s: The Charter of the French Language

The Québec government had established its own commission to study the state of the French language and language rights in Québec (Commission Gendron) years earlier, but their report recommending that French be made the only official language in Québec was released in 1973. This led the way for Bill 22, which acted on the recommendation by making French the official language of Québec, requiring use of French on public signs, limiting government contracts to businesses that were moving toward conducting business in French, and setting strict eligibility requirements for attending English medium schools. In 1977 the iconic language law, the *charte de la langue française (loi 101)* [Charter of the French Language (Bill 101)], made French the official language of

Québec, asserting the significance of a language for expressing the identity of a people, and assuring that French would be the normal language of work, learning, communication, and business.

Throughout this political process of attaining a legal status for French, there was also serious applied linguistics work underway because of the need for a variety of French that would actually express the Québécois identity. The pronunciation of Québec French is distinct; some people draw an analogy between Canadian French and American English relative to their European counterparts. The vocabulary of Québec French may contain borrowings from English, as well. The work on standardization of Québec French raised difficult issues. The colloquial variety (*joual*) was not a candidate, but similarly, there was little, if any, interest in attempting to adopt the foreign variety of French spoken in France. There was interest in promoting a variety considered to be international, but as Oakes and Warren (2007) noted, 'international' French is an abstraction rather than a concrete variety of French that can be targeted for adoption. Ultimately, the linguistic work was done to describe a Standard Québec French, which is not *joual* and is not adopted from another region. This work took many years, but it got an important boost in 1977 by the Québec Association of French Teachers, who advocated the teaching of '*le francais d'ici*' [the French from here]. In 1979, with the Québec French standardization project underway, a first milestone was reached for the creation of feminine forms for the names of professions in 1979—a feature that would mark Québec French.

2.4   The 1980s: The First Sovereignty Referendum

The French language was a central unifying force in Québec as the Parti Québécois put forward the 1980 sovereignty referendum in Québec. René Lévesque, the leader of the Parti Québécois delivered on the party's promise to put forward a referendum, but the people of Québec voted it down by a significant margin (60 % to 40 %). The suspense and drama surrounding the Parti Québécois taking power, the lead up to the vote, and then the outcome were sufficient to penetrate the media in the USA, which is typically all but silent on Canadian politics. The defeat of the referendum was a significant blow to the movement, but it did not impede the work to increase the status and standardization of Québec French. Québec's international relations continued to be emphasized, and in 1987 the second summit of the international organization of French-speaking countries was held. In 1988 Québec started receiving television broadcasts from all of la francophonie, thereby connecting the French-speaking world.

2.5   The 1990s: The Second Sovereignty Referendum

The Québec government document cites one single issue for the 1990s: immigration. By the 1990s, family size in Québec had become very small relative to the period before the 1960s. This demographic, in addition to increases in immigration, created new linguistic challenges for the French language in Québec. The most serious problem for French was the fact that many immigrants to Québec wanted their children to learn English, a situation that has required ongoing diligence on the part of the government to assure that laws are in place to keep immigrants out of English medium schools while keeping English medium schools within reach for Québécois Anglophone families, as required by federal law. Immigrants were in the spotlight in what was again a dramatic scenario when a second referendum was put forward. The sovereignist Parti Québécois had been returned to power after two failed attempts at negotiation with the federal government for appropriate accommodations for Québec's aspirations (the Meech Lake Accord and the Charlottetown Accord). The 1995 referendum was defeated by a fraction of a percent, along with speculation that the votes of some of the immigrants had been decisive. There was talk of yet another referendum coterminous with continued negotiations with the federal government until the Parti Québécois lost power to the Liberals in 2003.

The role of French in this complex political narrative remains important because the Parti Québécois, the Party of René Lévesque, claims French as its issue as if candidates affiliated with other parties are equivocal in their support of French language laws. However, the fact that French is the language of Québec and is central to Québec identity is undisputed by any viable political party in Québec.

2.6   The 2000s: Continued Expanded Global Presence

In 2000, a commission was again established to study linguistic issues in Québec, with particular attention to the mastery of French. This intense level of preoccupation with the quality, status, and future of French continued both internally and figured in the foreign policy agenda of the Liberal government of Jean Charest, Québec's premier, beginning in 2003. The US-Québec policy included the promotion of French in North America as indicated by the statement on the government website:

> Ensuring the long-term viability of the French language in the Americas is a central focus of the Government of Québec's efforts. As North America's only majority francophone society, Québec is committed to fostering the use of French and the teaching of the language beyond its borders. The existence of francophone communities across North America also helps to further the use of French. As the cradle of French in North America, Québec is strongly committed to protecting and promoting the French language. To that end, the Government offers a variety of resources—programs, courses and online content—and undertakes initiatives with a number of organizations. (Ministry of International Relations, 2010)

International work continued through the first decade of the 2000s through Québec's support of UNESCO's statement on the right of governments to promote cultural diversity in 2007. In 2008, Québec celebrated the 400th anniversary of the settlement of Québec City by French settler, Samuel de Champlain, as a tribute to the perseverance of the Québécois, against all odds, to maintain, standardize, elevate the status of and promote Québec French.

2.7   Enduring Themes

The national motto of Québec is 'Je me souviens' [I remember]. It appears on the license plates for vehicles in Québec. This can hold many meanings, but most centrally it refers to the national memory of the cultural narrative of endurance of the Canadiens-Québécois in the face of seemingly insurmountable odds. Endurance refers to the maintenance of linguistic and cultural distinctness as a people over 400 years. The theme of memory manifests in the French textbooks as well as in conversation with people of all ages in Québec, who express their sense of pride for being part of a resilient force. Québécois are proud of their heritage and central to their heritage is their French language.

Part of the cohesive bond that secures Québec's collective identity is the constant external threat instantiated by forces poised to weaken the power or status of Québec French. This force consisted of the British after what they refer to as the conquest in 1759, and so the Canadiens needed to achieve solidarity in moving their French and Catholic agenda forward in whatever ways were possible. The external force remained the British through the Patriot's rebellion and Lord Durham's report. However, after the 1867 North American Act when Louis Riel, the francophone founding father of Manitoba, was executed by the government of first prime minister, Sir John MacDonald, in 1885, the threat of the British seemed to evolve into the threat of the English Canadians and has remained so since then. More recently, in a postmodern turn, the threat is diffused across the immigrants, who come from many different places, but who have to be legislated away from English medium education for their children. In this sense, the threat might be seen more generally as the English language rather than certain groups of people. The need for constant vigilance of the Québécois people has helped to reinforce their collective identity and reminds them of their collective past.

The third theme that flowered within the period of change in the 1960s was the conflict over the value of a bilingual versus a unilingual language policy. By the end of the 1960s, the federal government led by Pierre Elliott Trudeau and the Québec government led by René Lévesque were on opposite sides of this dispute, and for the most part still are today. Trudeau's solution of a national bilingual policy was intended to counter Québec's aspirations for sovereignty or separation by ensuring equal treatment and access to opportunity for French Canadians under the law. In Québec, bilingualism was seen as opening the door for the certain demise of the French language in North America. Without protection for French in Québec, it seemed that the situation would again deteriorate and French would disappear, just as it has in many places outside Québec, including the USA. The Charter of the French Language requires that French be used for business and in all other facets of society in order to eliminate the choice to use English. This standoff between Ottawa and Québec regularly raises questions that go to the supreme court for adjudication and sometimes result in modifications to Québec's laws.

3   Québec's Cultural Narrative and French Textbooks

My brief sketch demonstrates the centrality of the French language in Québec's national cultural narrative and reveals a gold mine of potential content for textbook producers wishing to include important historical and political content in their textbooks. It is a story of mystery and intrigue about how the French language has survived against all odds in Anglophone North America. It is fuelled by the passion of the Canadiens for their language and way of life despite their diminishing numbers. It encompasses holy and unholy alliances across government and church, the birth of at least one political party, and the near death of religion. The story connects occasionally to the USA, and it regularly engages with the rest of Canada. It has political sides, but no unequivocal winners and losers—just compromises that sustain ongoing peace and continued political action. It is the central narrative that underlies the interpretation of all that transpires in Québec and some of what happens in the rest of Canada.

This material is plentiful in academic and public resources such as libraries, museums, and websites. Because it is both Canadian and Québécois content, versions of the material can be found in both English and French. Nevertheless, I noticed years ago that students studying French on my campus did not seem to have any knowledge of Québec. Recalling that I had not learned about Québec in my university French classes in Michigan in the 1970s, I looked into *The Modern Language Journal* for any insight on this issue. What do students in beginning French classes learn about Québec? I found a commentary in *The Modern Language Journal* in 1989 in which the author reported his observation that the variety of French spoken in Québec was not a welcome topic in

French classes. 'Teachers have admitted openly to teaching their students to censure Québec French … Study abroad advisers recognize that few of their advisees want to visit, study, or live in Québec. A second year student whom I advised to spend his junior year at Laval [in Québec] told me bluntly, "I couldn't go there because, really, I don't understand anything they say"' (Salien, 1989, p. 96).

I would expect the public to be challenged to make sense of language varieties, but my students did not even seem to know that French was spoken in Québec. I decided to investigate. I conducted a study of first-year textbooks used in beginning French classes at large universities in the northern region of the USA. I found that at least some Canadian content appeared in all of the textbooks studied, although the amount and type of content differed substantially. From a quantitative perspective, it provided results about the number of textbook sections containing Canadian content, but the extent of the content within each section was not investigated in that study. I concluded, 'The quantitative analysis produced by the present study provides results with broad strokes and leaves aside a detailed analysis of the nature of the Canadian linguistic and cultural content in the textbooks that were examined.' (Chapelle, 2009, p. 149)

These results prompted me to look more carefully at the nature of the Canadian content in textbooks and at the chronology of its appearance. To what extent is the provocative cultural narrative of Québec communicated to students as they are beginning to learn French? How does the sample of textbooks that I gathered from a survey of large universities in the northern region of the USA reflect the population of such textbooks nation-wide? The population of textbooks of interest in the previous study was clearly specified (as those in use at certain universities), but it is unknown what the relationship is between this population and the larger population of beginning-level French textbooks used in the USA. Moreover, in view of the complex production of textbooks, a more adequate analysis would need to take into account the evolution of Québec in French textbooks. Both the views of language teaching professionals and the actual status of French in Canada have evolved over the past century in ways that are relevant to what appears in textbooks today.

4   Methodology

The questions this study addresses are issues in foreign language teaching broadly rather than questions of evaluation particular to selection of a textbook for a specific class. The methodology therefore had to be designed to yield knowledge of interest to the field.

The research design draws upon the pragmatic philosophy underlying mixed-methods approaches to research (Creswell and Plano-Clark, 2011). It combines quantitative and qualitative approaches to yield credible results about an important practice-based question. In this chapter, I am concerned primarily with issues typically associated with quantitative research: defining the population of interest and presenting the logic of the sampling plan to obtain a relevant sample of textbooks; identifying the Canadian and Québec content in the textbooks and quantifying the content. These steps are necessary to address the research questions posed in this chapter as well as to sustain the interpretability of the textbook analysis by providing a basis for making sense of the relationship of the textbooks investigated to all the textbooks in the domain of interest. Moreover, interpretation of the qualitative results in the following chapters requires the description provided in this chapter.

4.1   Population and Sampling Plan

Populations and samples are fundamental concepts in empirical research because they provide the basis for interpretation of results. Populations and samples are typically associated with quantitative research but are equally important in planning and interpreting qualitative research. In both quantitative and qualitative research, observations are made using a sample. In order to interpret the findings beyond the actual observations in the sample, it is necessary to specify the target population to which interpretations are intended to apply and the way that the sample was selected from the population. The population in this study refers to beginning-level university textbooks for teaching of French published for use in the USA. More precisely, I am interested in the textbooks that were seen by the profession as important and sufficiently valuable for the profession to take note of during the time period when they were available for use in the five decades beginning in 1960 and ending in 2010.

I identified the population as the beginning-level French textbooks that had been reviewed in the major professional journal for French language teaching in the USA, the *French Review*. This definition of the population was credible in view of the fact that book reviews of beginning-level textbooks for university students were abundant in the *French Review* across the period of interest. The lists of textbooks obtained from searching the reviews section of all issues of the *French Review* for the five-decade period provide a good indication of the ones of interest in the profession during these time periods. Because one of the questions in my study addresses chronological change in textbook content, the population needed to be subdivided, and I did this by decade in order to maintain a sufficient number in each subsample to show chronological trends. By subdividing the population into groups by decade, I was able to make interpretations of results based on the decade in which the book review appeared and report results according to decades.

The number of first-year texts in the decade subpopulations ranges from thirteen in the 1960s to forty-one in the 1980s. Factors contributing to these differences undoubtedly include the number of books actually available on the market and editorial policies for book reviews. Shifts in the numbers of students enrolled in French may also have contributed to a big jump in numbers of textbooks in the 1980s. Data from the MLA enrollment statistics (Goldberg, Looney, & Lusin, 2015) show a jump of over 100,000 between 1960 and 1968. By 1980, when the next data were available, the numbers had dropped somewhat, but text book production may have blossomed in the 1970 in response to the increased enrollment through the 1960s and possibly into the 1970s. Then, enrollments were up again somewhat in 1995 before dropping back to hover around the 200,000 mark for the next couple of decades. The number of textbooks in each of the subpopulations appears in Table 2.1, which shows a sufficient size of subpopulations to address questions about chronological trends in the profession.

My plan for sampling was to obtain the entire subpopulation of textbooks for each decade, but my plan met the reality of actual availability of textbooks. To obtain the textbooks, I searched on *Amazon.com*, a web source that automatically taps into a wide range of used book sellers. I bought the textbooks in the population that were available, ending up with various percentages of each of the subpopulations in each subsample, as shown in Table 2.1. The subsamples consist of approximately half of the textbooks identified in each of the subpopulations, but the actual percentages differed ranging from as high as 85 % of 1960s books to as low as 33 % of 1990s books.

I treat the textbooks that I could not obtain as missing data, as a survey researcher would do, recognizing that the sample is incomplete. Critical to the survey researcher is an explanation of why some of the data were missing because if data are missing systematically (e.g., all of the people angry about an issue decide to return the survey), the interpretation of the results is necessarily affected. The sample is a biased reflection of the population. Similarly, one should ask whether or not the missing textbooks had not shown up in the used book outlets for a systematic reason that would lead to biased interpretations of the results. One might speculate that those that were used by the most students would be most plentiful today, but I am treating the books I could not obtain as random missing data for the purposes of interpretation of results.

Knowledge of the size of each subsample of textbooks relative to its respective subpopulation (i.e., the percentage of textbooks in each subsample)

Table 2.1 Summary of the population, sample, and percentage of representation of the books in the study

Decade	Number of first-year university textbooks in the book reviews section of the *French Review*[a]	Number of identified textbooks included in the sample	Percentage of the identified textbooks included in the sample (%)
1960s	13	11	85
1970s	23	11	48
1980s	41	23	56
1990s	27	9	33
2000s	20	11	55
Total	125	65	52
Mean	24.8	13	52

[a]If two editions of a textbook appeared within a single decade, only one of the editions was included in the population

comes into play in appropriate interpretation of results. For example, the sample for the 1960s warrants strong confidence in the statements about textbook content in that decade, whereas findings about textbook content in the 1990s need to be treated as more tentative because of the 33 % coverage of the subpopulation for that decade. Figure 2.1 shows the number of books in the subsample for each of the five decades relative to the number in its respective subpopulation. In Fig. 2.1, the amount of the population showing behind the lightly shaded sample area indicates the degree of tentativeness that should accompany any interpretations about results for a particular decade. The small dark area above the 1960s contrasts with the larger one above the 1990s.

4.2   Types of Content

Canadian and Québec content consisting of both text and image were identified and counted. The textual content was tabulated as consisting of one of three types as summarized in Table 2.2: contexts, culture notes, or

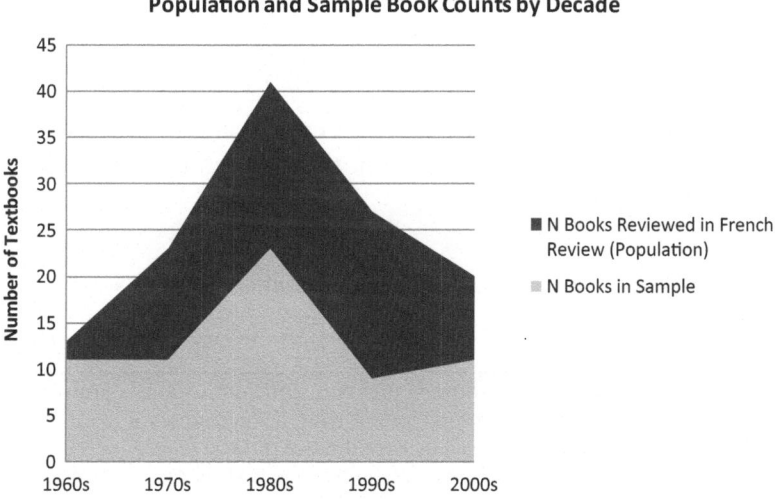

Fig. 2.1 Graph showing the sample of textbooks in the study in relation to the population

single words and sentences. Contexts refer to reading passages, dialogues, and other textual presentations that are used as part of the language that students are exposed to in various demonstrations and activities of French. Such texts in textbooks need to be about something, and when a text is about Canada or Québec in these textbooks, the text was counted as a 'context' from which students might possibly learn something. A second type of presentation appears in foreign language textbooks explicitly labeled with an expression such as 'culture notes.' They appear in specially marked sections of the text to signal that they are an aside or extra information for the readers. They are used throughout the textbooks to provide information about culture as a sideline to the explanations of grammar and exercises. Their function as a carrier of content is signaled, particularly in more recent textbooks, by the fact that they often are presented in English. A third type of textual presentation mentions an aspect of Canada or Québec in a word, phrase, or sentence without providing any additional information to help learners understand the context. These instances are found in explanations of grammar or vocabulary and exercises containing sentences that are disconnected semantically such as, 'Les Grands Lacs sont au sud du Canada' [The Great Lakes are south of Canada] (Hendrix, 1961, p. 12).

Images include maps, line drawings, cityscapes, landscapes, famous people, Canadian characters introduced in the textbooks, and scenes depicting cultural icons and events. In Chaps. 4 and 5, I describe some of the different types of images, but in this chapter, I report the overall quantitative analysis.

Table 2.2 Quantitative indictors of textual presentation of Canadian and Québec culture

Code	Definition	Language
Context	A segment of the text that is sufficiently long to convey some content even if the primary purpose is to illustrate the use of language	French
Culture note	An inserted box or section of the text whose primary purpose is to introduce students to specific aspects of culture	English or French
Word/sentence	Linguistic examples of one word or sentence making reference to Canada or Québec	French

4.3   Procedures for Analysis

The analysis required for describing the Canadian and Québec content of the textbooks quantitatively consisted of identifying and coding relevant content and then counting each category of content. The sample of sixty-five books was searched by a research assistant who had studied French and had taken a course on language policy in Québec. She found the textual Canadian and Québec content, which was then transcribed into an electronic file and coded. The codes relevant to the analysis in this chapter were unambiguous because 'cultural notes' were explicitly labeled with an expression that set them out from the lesson, single 'words and sentences' contained one sentence or less, and 'contexts' consisted of more than one sentence. I worked with the student closely when she started the process, and checked the codes after she had completed them. The texts and their codes were entered into *Nvivo*, which was then queried to obtain counts of each of the three categories of text.

In a second review of the sixty-five textbooks, the images of Canada and Québec were identified by the same undergraduate student of French and were checked by me to verify that they met the criteria of depicting Canada or Québec. My review of the selections verified that all of them that the student had made were indeed appropriate for inclusion. In addition, I found several images that should clearly be included so I added those, but there were a few images that were not clearly labeled and had not been identified by the student, so I did not include them in the data for analysis. I counted each of the images identified in each book, keeping the counts separate by the decade subsamples. The analysis was conducted to address two questions for each of the decade subsamples, one about quantity and the other about variation for the images.

5   Quantity of Canadian and Québec Images

The number of images of Canada and Québec is summarized in two ways. First, I provide data summarizing the numbers of images for each of the five decades, and then I discuss the variation among the books in each of the decades. These results shown by subsamples provide an over-all view of change in the amount of visual representation of Canada and Québec over the five-decade period.

5.1   The Number of Images by Decade

The numbers of images of Canada and Québec that appear in the text-books over the five decades are summarized in Table 2.3. Three ways of summarizing the image counts are provided. The third column shows the total number of pages with images of Québec and Canada in the subsam-ple for each decade. The change is dramatic across the five decades, with only one image in all of the texts of the 1960s, then a gradual increase into the 1970s, 1980s, and 1990s, with a big jump in the 2000s. The total number of images (column five) shows a similar trend slightly more dramatically, with a total of 188 images in the books of the 2000s. These raw counts do not take into account that the number of books in each decade subsample is not the same, and therefore in columns four and six the weighted counts are presented, showing the average numbers of pages with images and average numbers of images, respectively.

Table 2.3 Summary of data showing images representing Canada and Québec across five decades

		Descriptive summary statistics of Canadian and Québec images					
Decade	Number of books	Total number of pages with images	Average number of pages with images per book	Total number of images	Average number of images per book	Range of number of images in books	Number of books with no images (%)
1960s	11	1	0	1	0	0–1	10 (91%)
1970s	11	13	1	24	2	0–14	4 (36%)
1980s	23	41	1	54	2	0–17	11 (48%)
1990s	9	38	4	45	5	0–18	4 (44%)
2000s	11	153	14	188	17	6–43	0 (0%)

The average numbers of pages with images and average numbers of images per book (columns four and six) are plotted in Fig. 2.2, which depicts a dramatic change in the visual representation of Québec in the textbooks across this time period. In the eleven books from the 1960s, only one image shows Canada. This sketch of a map showing the French possessions in North America, the only one in all eleven textbooks, leaves the average pages with images and image counts per book less than 0.5, which was rounded to zero. The images in the 1960s textbooks for the most part show images of people and places in France.

In the following three decades, the number of images of Québec increased—slightly in the 1970s and 1980s and to a greater extent in the 1990s. The big jump occurred in the 2000s, with averages of fourteen pages with images and seventeen images per book. These increases are shown as average numbers per book in each respective part of the subsample in Fig. 2.2. The big jump from the 1990s needs to be interpreted in view of the relatively small sample in the 1990s. It may be that with 33 % coverage of the population of textbooks, I did not happen to have the textbooks containing a greater amount of Canadian and Québec content. Nevertheless, the finding of dramatic increases in the presence of Canada and Québec in textbook images from the 1970s and 1980s to the 2000s stands.

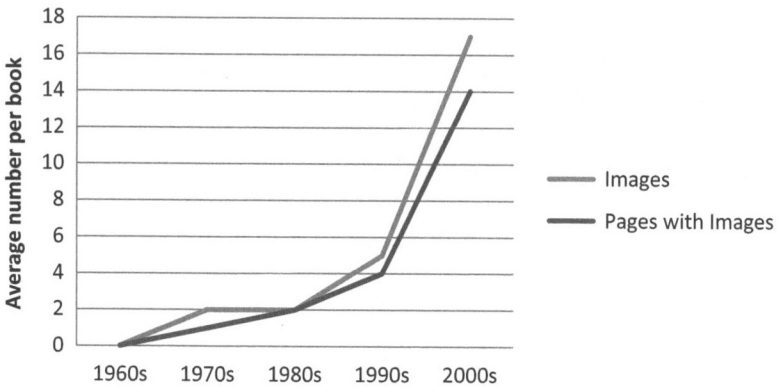

Fig. 2.2 Average number of images and pages with images per book in each decade

5.2   Variation in Images Across Textbooks by Decade

The summary of totals and averages across each subsample is useful for looking at trends but they can be misleading when variation exists in the subsamples. The 1960s subsample contained virtually no variation except for the one textbook with one image. For the other subsamples, measures of variation are needed because they provide an indication of how well average numbers accurately summarize the characteristics of the subsamples. One way to look at variation in the amount of visual representation is in the ranges shown in column seven in Table 2.2. With only one image in one book, the range in the 1960s is essentially zero, meaning that the textbooks in the sample are homogeneous in their lack of images of Canada and Québec. In the 1970s, 1980s, and 1990s, the ranges of numbers of Québec images in each of the decade subsamples indicate that at least one book in the decade subsample contained as many as 14, 17, and 18 images of Québec, respectively. However, there were also books in each of these decades with no images of Canada and Québec. In other words, despite the appearance of Canada and Québec in images beginning in the 1970s, students may or may not have any exposure to Canada and Québec in textbook images, depending on the textbook used in their class. In the 2000s, one book contained as many as forty-three images of Canada and Québec whereas one textbook contained only six. The plot of the maximum numbers of images per book in Fig. 2.3. has a shape similar to the one with the average in Fig. 2.2.

The other end of the range statistics indicates that there were books in each decade subsample except for the 2000s containing no images of Québec. The final column in Table 2.3 shows the numbers and percentages of books containing no images of Québec in each of the subsamples, and the percentages are plotted across the decades in a graph in Fig. 2.4. The graph shows dramatic changes in the addition of Québec images across the five decades, with 91% of books containing no Québec images in the 1960s and all books containing some Québec images in the 2000s. The increase to 100% is sudden in the 2000s, however, with almost 50% of books containing no images of Québec through the 1970s, 1980s, and 1990s subsamples.

The changes in the visual presentation of Canada and Québec in textbooks over this period undoubtedly stem from changes in multiple factors. The shift toward a polycentric view of culture in foreign language teaching is the factor typically cited. However, changing technologies dramatically affected the publishing industry during this period, providing more access to images and expanding flexibility in publishing. Moreover, the change in the status of French in Québec during this period, as described in the cultural narrative in the first part of this chapter, heightened awareness of Francophone culture in Canada by outsiders. These numbers, however, only tell part of the story. To examine how Canada and Québec were represented in the textbooks, it is necessary to examine what was in the images. To address this question in Chap. 4, I add to this picture with a qualitative analysis of the images. Before doing so, however, I examine the amount and types of meanings in the text about Canada and Québec in the rest of this chapter and the following one.

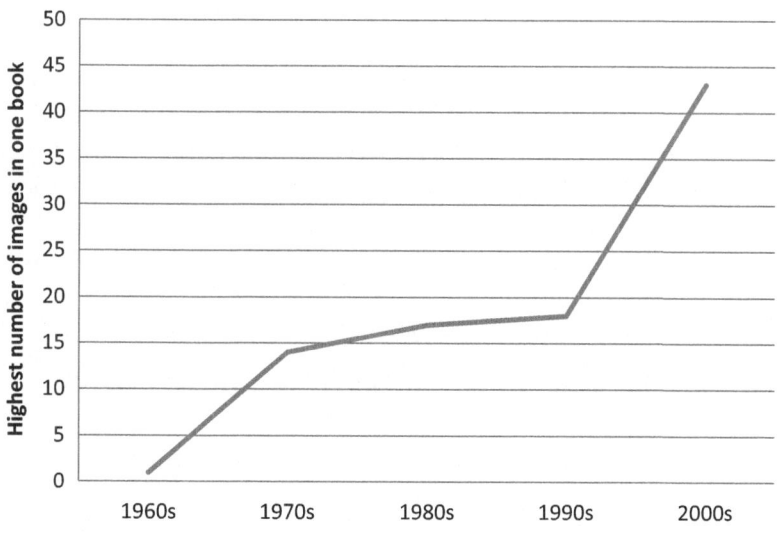

Fig. 2.3 Maximum numbers of Canadian images appearing in one book in each decade

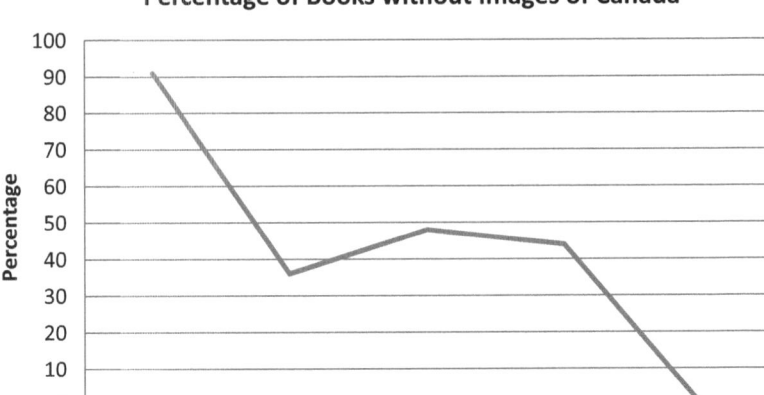

Fig. 2.4 Percentage of books in each decade with no images of Canada

6   Quantity of Written Text

The quantity of written text about Canada and Québec was summarized by calculating total counts, averages, and indices of variation. First, I provide summaries of the three types of textual content for each of the five decades, and then I discuss the variation among the textbooks in each of the decades. These results shown by subsamples provide an overall view of change in the amount of textual representation of Canada and Québec over the five-decade period.

6.1   The Number of Instances of Textual Content

The quantitative analysis of cultural content in text shows the amount of each of the three types of Canadian and Québec content that appeared in French textbooks over the five decades. The results in Table 2.4 show both the total counts of each of the three categories of content appearing in the texts and the average numbers of appearances of each type of content per book in the sample. The average numbers allow for comparisons across the five decades because they take into account the differing numbers of books in each of the decade subsamples.

The most important categories are the contexts and culture notes because they may provide opportunities for students to learn aspects of cultural narrative. The level of appearance of these two categories progresses through three periods. First, in the 1960s and 1970s, they appear on average fewer than one time per book in the sample. This means that the chances for students of beginning French to be introduced to Canadian and Québec culture through their textbooks were extremely small. The few cases where Canada is mentioned are like Text 2.1, from *Beginning French: A cultural approach,* which illustrates a brief context presented as part of a dialogue in which someone in France aspires to take a trip to North America. The context is created as a conversation about the desired trip. In the dialogue, language expressions such as 'faire un séjour' and future conditional forms of the verbs ('I would love to go' and 'It would be wonderful to spend') are taught. To teach the language, the context is needed. The context creates an image about the closeness of Canada and the USA—from the perspective of the French speaker considering a trip to the new world.

Table 2.4 Summary of data showing numbers of contexts, culture notes, and single sentences across five decades

Decade	Number of books	Total counts			Average per book		
		Contexts	Culture notes	Single sentences and words	Contexts	Culture notes	Single sentences and words
1960s	11	9	3	57	0.82	0.27	5.18
1970s	11	10	9	87	0.91	0.82	7.91
1980s	23	43	85	235	1.87	3.70	10.22
1990s	9	17	26	82	1.89	2.89	8.55
2000s	11	93	94	140	8.45	8.55	12.73

Text 2.1

Projets de vacances

...

-Si c'est possible, j'aurais envie d'aller en Amérique. Ce serait merveilleux de passer quelques jours au Canada, de faire un séjour à Québec, de voyager aux États-Unis, de rester huit jours à New York, et de voir la Californie. (Hendrix & Meiden, 1961, p. 205)

The few contexts in the 1960s refer to Canada as a distant land, either geographically or historically as a place of exploration for the French. In the 1970s, in contrast, the perspective is closer up, as illustrated in the dialogue in Text 2.2 between two French tourists who are actually in Canada, at a hockey game.

Text 2.2

Les sportifs

Michel et Danielle sont des touristes français au Canada. Ils assistent, avec des milliers d'autres spectateurs, à un match de hockey sur glace. Danielle ne dit rien, alors que tout le monde crie. Elle est assise, alors que tout le monde est debout. Elle a l'air de s'ennuyer, alors que tout le monde a l'air de s'amuser follement.

Danielle : Mais qu'est-ce qui se passe ? Pourquoi tous ces gens crient-ils comme ça ? Ils ont mal aux dents.

Michel : Qu'est-ce que tu dis ?

Danielle : Pourquoi est-ce qu'ils crient si fort ?

Michel : Parce que l'équipe de Québec vient de marquer un but ! Je t'en prie, fais un effort pour comprendre. Ne te décourage pas si facilement !

Danielle promet d'essayer. Elle regarde avec attention les mouvements des joueurs, mais ils se lancent la rondelle si adroitement qu'elle a peine à suivre. Au bout de quelques minutes, elle en a vraiment assez.

Danielle : Pourquoi se précipitent-ils comme des fous derrière ce petit machine ? Ils ont peur de le perdre ?

Michel : Écoute, sois gentille ! Si tu n'aimes pas ça, n'en dégoûte pas les autres !

Danielle : Bon ! Moi, je m'en vais. Je vais faire un tour en voiture. Je te retrouverai après le match. Passe-moi les clés, s'il te plaît.

Michel : Tiens, les voilà. Ne me les perds pas, surtout !

Danielle : Ne t'en fais pas ... Je ne suis pas complètement folle. (Clarke & Holt Editorial Staff, 1974, pp. 306–307)

In the 1980s and 1990s, with an average of almost two to four instances of Canadian or Québec content in textbooks, chances were somewhat greater for a student to encounter Canada and Québec in the textbooks. Text 2.3 from *Allons-y, le français par étapes* illustrates a letter written to a *québécoise* woman from Michel, a *franco-ontarien*, who is in France. Michel makes reference to aspects of Québec culture, such as the snow in winter, skiing, Québec French, and dealing with English speakers and American culture. This and other examples from the 1980s begin to show an engagement with the people, issues, and identities in Canada and Québec that was not present in the previous decades.

Text 2.3

Lettre à une Québécoise

Ma chère Louise,

Un gros Joyeux Noel! Je t'envie dans ta maison québécoise au fond de la campagne. Ça doit être blanc partout! Mais, franchement, après une jeunesse passée à pelleter des bancs de neige à n'en plus finir, je ne me plains pas. Ici, j'ai échangé ma pelle contre un parapluie!

Qu'est-ce qui t'arrive par les temps qui courent? Fais-tu souvent du ski de fond? As-tu fait tes cipâtes et tes tourtières? Je t'imagine en train de passer un dimanche tranquille à écouter ton Vigneault et à te demander si ton bizou va partir lundi matin. Laisse-moi savoir ce qui se passe chez toi!

Par ici, ça va pas mal. Je veux surtout te parler de la présentation que j'ai faite aux étudiants de la classe de français la semaine passée: « Qu'est-ce que le Canada français ? » Eh bien, j'ai essayé de leur faire comprendre (dans 45 minutes!) la différence entre un franco-ontarien comme moi, et une Québécoise comme toi. Ça n'a pas été facile, je te le jure. Pour eux, le Canada français est tout à fait uniforme. De toute façon, comment leur parler d'une culture exclusivement « canadienne »—francophone ou anglophone—quand on est inondé par les média américains du matin au soir? Je leur ai donné quand même les grandes lignes. En plus, pour finir, je leur ai lu du Tremblay. Ils ont bien peu compris mais, tout en riant, ils ont vite constaté que le joual n'est pas du tout la langue de Racine, pas plus que le « cockney » est celle de Shakespeare.

À part cet épisode, il n'y a pas grand chose à raconter qui vaille la peine. La fin du semestre approche, et je me prépare pour les examens. Ecris-moi au plus sacrant! À la revoyure !

Michel (Bragger & Rice, 1988, pp. 442–443)

Text 2.4 shows an example of a 1990s culture note from *Entre Amis: an Interactive Approach to First-year French* which describes geographic and demographic information about Québec in an encyclopedic fashion. Following the description are questions. The first two are comprehension questions and the third asks for students' opinions about why Montreal has an underground infrastructure for transportation, shopping, and so on.

Text 2.4
Montréal

La ville de Montréal est le centre de la francophonie en Amérique du Nord; deux tiers (2/3) de la population parle français comme langue maternelle. Montréal, où habitent vingt pour cent de la population québécoise, se situe sur une île. C'est la deuxième ville du Canada, après Toronto. Et c'est la deuxième ville francophone du monde, après Paris. Chaque année, beaucoup de touristes visitent Montréal, une ville à la fois moderne et historique. Au centre de la ville, le Vieux-Montréal est un hommage au passé. Ses églises, ses restaurants et ses vieilles maisons attirent beaucoup de visiteurs. Mais Montréal est aussi une ville très moderne. Sous les gratte-ciel du centre-ville existe toute une ville souterraine de restaurants, boutiques, cinémas, cafés, et même un métro !

À vous. Repondez.
1. Quelle est la plus grande ville francophone du monde ? Et la deuxième ?
2. Est-ce qu'il y a un métro dans votre ville ?
3. Imaginez la raison pour laquelle il existe une « ville souterraine » à Montréal. Est-ce qu'il y a des magasins et des restaurants souterrains dans votre ville ? (Oates, Oukada, & Altman, 1991, pp. 142–147)

In the 2000s, a notable increase in the instances of Canadian and Québec content occurred in the culture notes and contexts with almost nine instances per book on average. The passage in Text 2.5 about the Canadian author, Gabrielle Roy, a seminal Francophone author in Canada, appeared in *Paroles* in 2007. In this case, the authors made a strategic content choice so as to be able to introduce students to this famous Canadian author, whose name appears in the list of artistic figures students should know according to the recommendations of the American Association of Teachers of French. The textbook producers also included a photograph of Roy, which may signal to students the importance of the content. They provided focus and explanation of the linguistic point so the presentation serves both the linguistic and content-related goals. One of the linguistic objectives is to illustrate the use of verbs in the *passé composé* that take *être* as the auxiliary verb—verbs to do with a life story contain the *passé composé* (e.g., she was born, she became, she came back, she published and she died).

Text 2.5
Gabrielle Roy est née en 1909. Elle a fait ses études au Manitoba, et elle est devenue institutrice. Puis, en 1937, elle est partie pour l'Europe et elle a commencé à écrire en France. Ensuite, elle est rentrée au Canada et, en 1945, elle a publié son premier roman. En 1950, elle est retournée en Europe et elle a continué à écrire des romans. Gabrielle Roy est morte à Québec en 1983. Elle a eu une vie assez discrète. C'est une très grande romancière. (Magnan, Berg, Martin-Berg, & Ozzello, 2007, p. 193)

Figure 2.5 shows a graphic representation of the changes in the amount of Canadian and Québec content that appears in the textbooks over the five decades. All three types of content increased throughout the five decades, with the exception of 1990, when slight decreases were apparent. The 1990s was the decade for which the subsample of texts was the least robust, however, with only 33 % of the subpopulation represented in the subsample. The knowledge of the relationship between the sample and population by decade indicates that the finding from that decade should be the least reflective of the population. The fact that the subsample was degraded by more missing data needs to be taken into account in interpreting the results, which are inconsistent with an otherwise upward trend in the amount of Canadian and Québec content over the five decades. Overall, the data suggest that the 1990s results should be questioned, and that the statement of an overall upward trend can be made.

6.2 Variation in Instances of Textual Content Across Textbooks

The results showing total and mean content counts per book provide one form of summary, but they need to be interpreted in view of the variation that occurs within and across the subsamples as well. For example, in the 1980s, on average, French books contained two instances of short

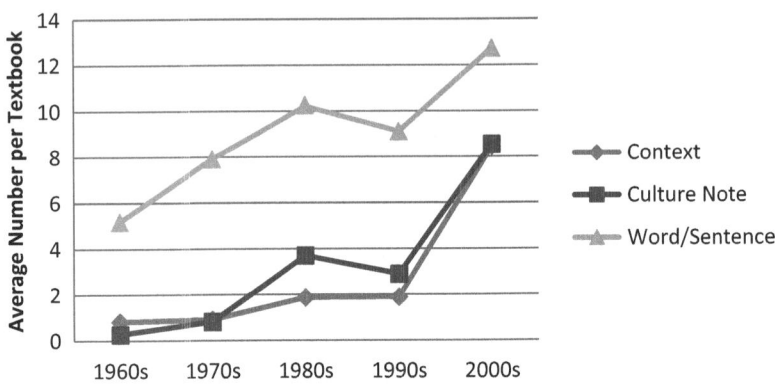

Fig. 2.5 Quantitative results showing increases in Canadian content of three types

texts that provided some contextualized information and almost four culture notes about Canada or Québec. Does this mean that every student studying beginning French in the 1980s should have been at least minimally exposed to culture in Canada and Québec? The data showing variation in the subsamples indicate that even though at least one book contained five contexts and twenty culture notes, there remained books in the sample that contained no contexts or culture notes about Canada and Québec. As shown in Table 2.5, until the 2000s, there were books that did not provide any context or culture notes about Canada and Québec.

The right side of Table 2.5 shows the numbers and percentages in each of the subsamples that contained no instances of each of the three categories of content. Of the books in the subsample, 30% contained no contexts and 43% contained no culture notes about Canada and Québec. The percentages, which are graphed in Fig. 2.6, show the downward trend in the percentage of textbooks with none of each of the three types of Canadian and Québec content. This graph shows dramatic differences in contexts and culture notes between the 1960s and the 2000s. In the

1960s, nine of the eleven books (82%) had no culture notes and seven of the eleven books had no contexts about Canada and Québec. Three of the books in the 1960s (27%) contained no single word or sentences about Canada or Québec.

The changes in the amount of Canadian and Québec content in samples between the 1960s and the 2000s showed slow but steady decreases in the numbers of books without any Canadian or Québec content. In the 1970s, the decade when the Charter of the French Language was adopted and preparation for the 1980 referendum vote was underway, the number of books without any contexts or culture notes about Canada and Québec remained substantial. Seven of the eleven books had no contexts (64%, which was the same as in the 1960s), and six out of eleven books (55%) had no cultural notes. In the 1980s, seven out of twenty-three books (30%) were without any contexts and ten out of twenty-three (43%) had no culture notes about Québec or Canada. In the 1990s, when Québec's struggles had been in the news for over ten years, and efforts were underway for another referendum, there were still books containing no Québec contexts and culture notes. Four out of the nine in the 1990s subsample (44%) did not have any contexts about Canada or Québec and three out of nine in the sample did not have any culture notes about Canada or

Table 2.5 Summary of data showing variation within subsamples of contexts, culture notes, and single sentences across five decades

Decade	Number of books	Range of counts of content			Number (%) of books with no textual content		
		Contexts	Culture notes	Single words and sentences	Contexts	Culture notes	Single words and sentences
1960s	11	0–3	0–2	0–15	7 (64%)	9 (82%)	3 (27%)
1970s	11	0–6	0–3	0–38	7 (64%)	6 (55%)	2 (18%)
1980s	23	0–5	0–20	0–33	7 (30%)	10 (43%)	3 (13%)
1990s	9	0–6	0–7	0–29	4 (44%)	3 (33%)	2 (22%)
2000s	11	0–17	5–21	1–43	1 (9%)	0 (0%)	0 (0%)

Percentage of Books without Canadian Cultural Content

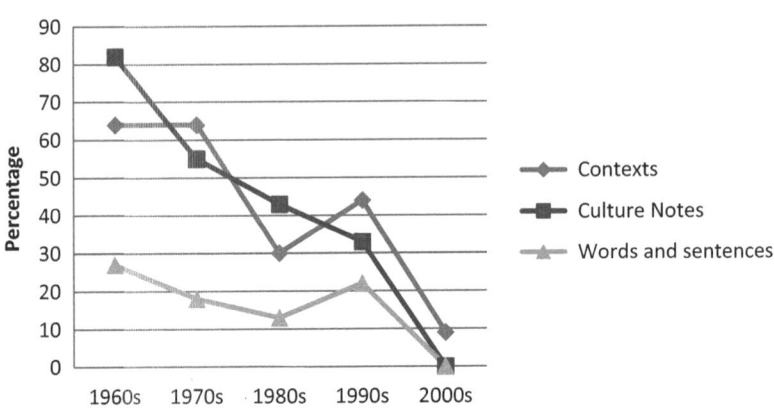

Fig. 2.6 The percentage of books in each decade containing no Canadian or Québec contexts, culture notes, or single words and sentences

Québec. Throughout this period, there was always at least one textbook in the sample (two in the 1980s) with no mention of Canada or Québec.

These figures summarizing both the averages and variation in the content in the textbooks underscore the importance of describing a sample of books with reference to the population of interest. If the population can be quantified, as it was in this study, the potential for appropriate interpretation of results increases. When textbook analysis examines textbooks whose relationship to a population of interest is unknown, it is not possible to know how the results should be interpreted. The examples of text I showed in this chapter give a glimpse of the way that cultural topics are presented. They illustrated that Canadian and Québec topics can be included without necessarily revealing aspects of cultural narrative. Characters in dialogues talk about visiting Canada, tourists attend hockey games, and Francophone authors are introduced without connecting their lives to the narrative that their work helped to compose. In the next chapter, I have been more deliberate in the choice of textual examples to provide only those showing aspects of Québec's cultural narrative as it is outlined in the first part of this chapter.

7   Conclusion

The cultural presentations in text and image in beginning-level French textbooks serve as one part of language and culture pedagogy in the course. They therefore provide a window on the degree to which students might have been exposed to Canada and Québec culture during each of the decades investigated. The textbook presentation of culture is instrumental in creating meaning for students through a process mediated by the teacher, other aspects of the course, and each student's past experience. Such assumptions about how meaning is created are based on a social-semiotic perspective to meaning-making, which will be elaborated in the next chapter as it pertains to the study. As for me, I do not remember the textbook I used in my beginning-level class in 1975, but the results of this study suggest that my inability to remember any Canadian or Québec content from my beginning-level French class at Michigan State University is probably because there was none. I did not become a French teacher, but my peers in French classes in the 1970s who continued to become teachers of French were also probably not exposed to Canada or Québec in their first-year courses.

As for the commentary on teachers' negative attitudes toward Québec French published in *The Modern Language Journal* in 1989 (Salien, 1989), the results in this chapter indicate that teachers of first-year French may have been exposed to Québec for the first time in the 1980s. This is the first decade when a sufficient number of textbooks contained Québec content that teachers would be likely to encounter French in Québec as they reviewed textbooks for possible adoption. Twenty years later, my study of French textbooks found Canadian and Québec content in the textbooks being used in first-year courses at universities in 2005, but concluded that in view of the importance of Canada and Québec to the USA, the amount of coverage was relatively small. These results can now be interpreted in view of the relative coverage of Québec and Canada chronologically. The amount of Canadian and Québec cultural content in the textbooks increased gradually from 1960 through the 1990s, and more dramatically, relatively speaking, in the 2000s. In the 2000s, the last decade of the study, the recent increases in Canadian and Québec content suggest that change may be underway. Such changes may be finally reflective of the changes in the status of Québec French that have been underway since the 1960s.

The results of the study also need to be interpreted in view of the methodological decisions that were made. The population of interest in this study was defined as all of the beginning-level textbooks used in university French classes in the USA whereas the previous study (Chapelle, 2009) investigated only those books that had been selected for particular universities. The results from the current study can be used to make interpretations about practices in the profession. In view of the division of the sample into chronological subsamples, results expressed as percentages are also interpretable across decades. The division of the sample into subsamples across the five decades also allows for meaningful metrics of variation to be reported for textbooks within each decade, as well as across the five decades. An understanding of the intended (sub) population, the degree of coverage of the (sub)sample, and the variation within and across subsamples are all essential for interpreting the counts of content provided in this chapter as well as the nature of the content in the next three chapters. Also critical for interpretation of the Canadian and Québec content in the following chapters is the cultural narrative outlined in the first part of this chapter. With this groundwork laid, the following chapters can move beyond the quantity of cultural content to look more specifically at what and how Canadian and Québec content is included. Doing so will provide the opportunity to examine the extent to which cultural narrative is included in the textbooks.

References

Bragger, J. D., & Rice, D. B. (1988). *Allons-y! le français par étapes* (2nd ed.). Boston: Heinle & Heinle.

Chapelle, C. A. (2009). A hidden curriculum in language textbooks: Are beginning learners of French at U.S. universities taught about Canada? *The Modern Language Journal, 93*(2), 139–152.

Clarke, K. M., & Holt Editorial Staff. (1974). *À la française*. New York: Holt, Rinehart and Winston.

Creswell, J. W., & Plano-Clark, V. L. (2011). *Designing and conducting mixed methods research* (2nd ed.). Thousand Oaks, CA: Sage Publications.

Desbiens, J. P., & Laurendeau, A. (1960). *Les Insolences du Frère Untel.* Montréal, QC: Les Editions de L'homme.

Goldberg, D., Looney, D., & Lusin, N. (2015). *Enrollments in Languages Other Than English in United States Institutions of Higher Education, Fall 2013.* Retrieved from http://www.mla.org/pdf/2013_enrollment_survey.pdf.

Gouvernement du Québec. (2008). *La langue française au Québec: 400 ans: quelques repères.* Retrieved from http://www.spl.gouv.qc.ca/fileadmin/medias/pdf/400ans_quelquesreperes2.pdf.

Gray, J. (Ed.) (2013). *Critical perspectives on language teaching materials.* New York: Palgrave Macmillan.

Hendrix, W. S., & Meiden, W. (1961). *Beginning French: A cultural approach.* Boston: Houghton Mifflin.

Kramsch, C. (1988). The cultural discourse of foreign language textbooks. In A. J. Singerman (Ed.), *Towards a new integration of language and culture* (pp. 63–88). Middlebury, VT: NCTFL.

Magnan, S. S., Berg, W. J., Martin-Berg, L., & Ozzello, Y. (2007). *Paroles* (3rd ed.). Hoboken, NJ: Wiley Custom Services.

Martel, M., & Pâquet, M. (2010). *Langue et politique au Canada et au Québec: une synthèse historique.* Montréal, QC: Les Éditions du Boréal.

Ministère des Relations Internationales et de la Francophonie. (2010). *Québec: Promoting the French Language.* Retrieved from https://www.mrif.gouv.qc.ca/content/documents/en/BR_USA_Francais_ANG.pdf.

Oakes, L., & Warren, J. (2007). *Language, citizenship, and identity in Québec.* New York: Palgrave Macmillan.

Oates, M. D., Oukada, L., & Altman, R. (1991). *Entre amis: An interactive approach to first-year French.* Boston: Houghton Mifflin.

Singerman, A. J. (Ed.) (1996). *Acquiring cross-cultural competence: Four stages for students of French.* Lincolnwood, IL: National Textbook Company.

Spolsky, B. (2004). *Language policy.* Cambridge, UK: Cambridge University Press.

Salien, J. (1998). Quebec French: Attitudes and pedagogical perspectives. *The Modern Language Journal, 82*(1), 95–102.

3

Québec Content in Text

The significant role of content in language instruction is recognized by the abundant discussion of language and content in the professional literature. The connection between language and content was once the concern of only teachers of English for specific purposes, but the connection between language and content is now a domain of interest for all professionals in foreign language teaching and research. Moreover, all courses are language courses because they require students to learn to use the language of the discipline and eventually to become a professional in the field through their use of the discipline's language. As a consequence, even educators in various content areas need to concern themselves with language teaching. Most language teachers and researchers would agree that content does not become integrated only in courses on science, math, or history, or in the advanced levels of language study. Despite the importance of content at all levels of language study, applied linguists have provided little guidance to teachers and materials developers on critical questions about selection and development of content for language learning materials.

This chapter builds on the idea that culture serves as an important source of content in beginning-level textbooks. In particular, it

© The Editor(s) (if applicable) and The Author(s) 2016
C.A. Chapelle, *Teaching Culture in Introductory Foreign Language Textbooks*, DOI 10.1057/978-1-137-49599-0_3

⸓   ⸲es how Québec's cultural narrative has been used as content ⸲eginning-level French textbooks for five decades beginning in the 1960s. Such an examination requires a means of analyzing cultural topics, on the one hand, and linguistic structures and words, on the other. The first section of this chapter describes the approach to conceptualizing the integration of language and content, which builds upon the social-semiotic linguistic perspective taken by Byrnes, Maxim, and Norris (2010) in their German curriculum revision at Georgetown University. My analysis of textbooks in this chapter extends this approach to analysis of beginning-level textbooks. I then describe my approach to identify Québec cultural narrative content in the textbooks and the quantitative results showing the extent of use of the narrative by textbook producers. From these results, I identify and quantify the genres of texts used to express the cultural narrative, and then I examine the language as it is used to create these genres. The chapter provides concrete examples of cultural narrative in beginning language materials and shows the central role of genre in understanding the important dimensions of language integrated with such content.

1   Conceptualizing Content and Language Integration

Content in language courses needs to be selected and developed by the language professionals responsible for decisions about curriculum and materials. The importance of content in language courses and the fact that it requires decision-making by professionals is evident in the MLA (2007) report, which refers to students' learning basic history, politics, and literature of the people whose language they are studying. The MLA report conveys the message that these are the basics underlying loftier goals of cross-cultural understanding. However, at the basic level content needs to be recognized as important because of the integration of language and content. The language presented and practiced at the beginning-level affects what students can say and do as well as who they can be in the target language. The integral connection between content and language is not developed in the MLA report, which appears to suggest that a solution to curriculum issues in language teaching should come through better connections with area studies. Referring to the statements in the MLA report, Byrnes et al. (2010) point out, 'there is a great temptation to frame language study overwhelmingly in terms of cultural study and then nearly to divorce that cultural study from language as a semiotic system' (p. 18).

The apparent sidelining of language is particularly problematic for my analysis of beginning-level textbooks, in which authors have gone to great lengths to select and create language on the basis of its appropriateness for learning at the beginning level. Byrnes et al. (2010), whose goal was to develop a four-year German curriculum taking into account both the content and language, provide a lucid explanation of the problem with reliance on content alone for foreign language curriculum and materials. The emphasis of the MLA (2007) report on translingual and transcultural competence as well as cultural narrative exacerbates the existing problem of cultural learning being relegated to the advanced levels, without hinting at an approach for analyzing how a curriculum design might scaffold students to the advanced levels of language required for them to achieve the proposed goal.

'The report's (MLA, 2007) lack of acknowledgement of what is involved when content and language are to be linked over a multiyear progression of articulated learning becomes troubling inasmuch as the deeper problem remains to be apprehended even in its major contours' (Byrnes et al., 2010, p. 21). A means of analyzing learning goals and materials cannot be limited to advanced-level goals and materials; it needs be productive for analysis across 'a continuum from the very beginning to the end point of the desired high-level ability' (Byrnes et al., p. 21). Byrnes et al. assert the need for the profession to conceptualize how language is used in particular cultures of interest to create oral, written, and multimodal texts and how instruction can be developed to help students learn from such texts. The meaning of text as including all forms of communication—oral, written, and multimodal—is significant here because it is the range of texts that create and express the cultural meanings that students are to learn.

1.1   Content in the Texts of Beginning-Level Textbooks

Beginning-level textbooks are full of texts that have been carefully selected to present aspects of cultural information while providing examples of language use. My sample of sixty-five French textbooks contained examples of texts conveying Canadian and Québec cultural content such as the one in Text 3.1, which was introduced in the previous chapter. It is about the francophone author from Canada, Gabrielle Roy. It includes sentences about her life in chronological order. At the same time, it illustrates the use of verbs in one form of the past tense (*passé composé*). These are particularly important verbs to teach at the beginning level because some of them are formed with the verb 'be' (*être*) as the auxiliary verb rather than the more frequent auxiliary verb, 'have.' Semantically, the verbs all have to do with a life story *passé composé* (e.g., she became, she came back), and so capturing them in Gabrielle Roy's life story simultaneously presents the verbs in a coherent manner along with cultural content, which according to recommendations of the American Association of Teachers of French (Singerman, 1996) should be taught.

Text 3.1
Gabrielle Roy est née en 1909. Elle a fait ses études au Manitoba, et elle est devenue institutrice. Puis, en 1937, elle est partie pour l'Europe et elle a commencé à écrire en France. Ensuite, elle est rentrée au Canada et, en 1945, elle a publié son premier roman. En 1950, elle est retournée en Europe et elle a continué à écrire des romans. Gabrielle Roy est morte à Québec en 1983. Elle a eu une vie assez discrète. C'est une très grande romancière. (Magnan, Berg, Martin-Berg, & Ozzello, 2007, p. 193)

[Gabrielle Roy was born in 1909. She did her studies in Manitoba and she became a teacher. Then, in 1937, she left for Europe and she began to write in France. After that, she came back to Canada and in 1945, she published her first novel. In 1950, she returned to Europe and she continued to write novels. Gabrielle Roy died in Québec in 1983. She had a rather discrete life. She is one of the great novelists.]

In selecting the Gabrielle Roy text, the textbook producers made a strategic content choice so as to be able to introduce students to this famous Canadian author. The authors also included a photograph of Roy, which provides a form of emphasis and detail that may signal to students the importance of the content. They simultaneously provided focus on and explanation of the linguistic point (the *passé compose* with *être*), so the presentation serves both the linguistic and cultural-content goals. From this perspective the text serves as a kind of container into which the cultural content and the linguistic forms cohabitate synergistically, as illustrated in Fig. 3.1.

This example demonstrates how language and cultural content are integrated in pedagogical materials at the beginning level. However, on both the culture and the language sides of the connection, the analysis requires more substantial grounding if materials are to be developed on the basis of these culture-language connections. On the culture side, we have to ask to what extent this particular exposition on Gabrielle Roy helps to build the cultural schema of the cultural narrative that is so important for developing students' basic understanding of Québec. I would argue that the chosen text presents Roy's life in a manner that does not explicitly reveal the cultural narrative even though Roy lived through and engaged with the cultural narrative as laid out in the previous chapter. On the language side, the past verb forms were judiciously chosen; how were they chosen? What other grammatical aspects of the text should students be looking at so that they can increase their language ability to eventually understand more grammatical aspects of texts and even produce texts? Byrnes et al. (2010) demonstrated that if language analysis takes into account its integration with content, text cannot be considered as simply the container into which authors place language and content. The text itself needs to be analyzed as the critical connection between the two. Byrnes et al. submit that the notion of text, as I have

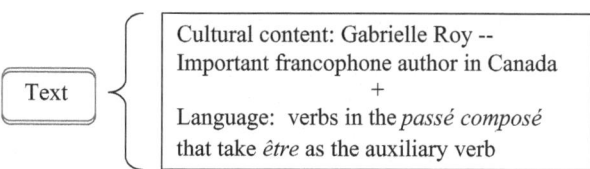

Fig. 3.1 Schematic diagram of a text as a container for cultural content and language

used it above, is 'too broad to be able to serve as a workable foundation (p. 42)' for curriculum and materials development. Instead, they work with the concept of genre, which refers to a text that is defined in terms of the communicative function it performs within a particular context.

1.2   Text as Genre

Any individual text such as the one about Gabrielle Roy is an instance of a genre of texts that perform the same function. Genres play a central role in organizing language to enact the cultural meanings such as telling the life story of an important author. Genres select the language needed to convey particular meanings. This integrated culture-text-language perspective, as illustrated in Fig. 3.2, is different from the text-as-container perspective shown in Fig. 3.1. Figure 3.2 shows the text about Gabrielle Roy, providing students access to cultural information through language. The genre of text is a historical biography. By reading this historical biography, students can learn how such a text uses the *passé composé* and the type of verbs in a life story that use *être* as the auxiliary.

The revised role of the text shown in Fig. 3.2 depicts the richer conceptualization of 'text' as it is theorized by the social-semiotic linguistic theory, systemic functional linguistics. Systemic functional linguistics provides both a general orientation useful for materials developers to re-vision the texts selected for textbooks and other materials in terms of their communicative roles within a cultural narrative. It provides an

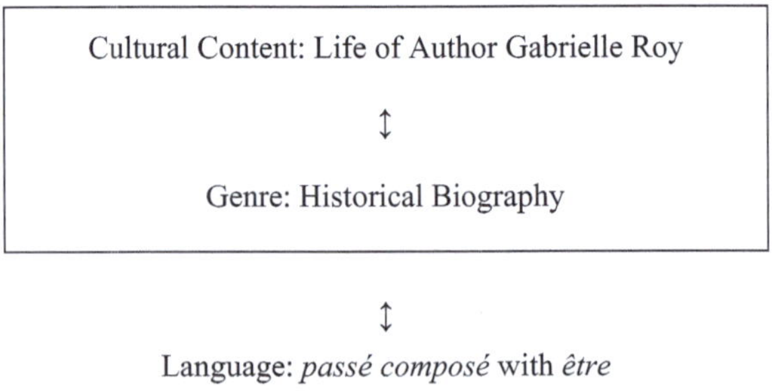

Cultural Content: Life of Author Gabrielle Roy

↕

Genre: Historical Biography

↕

Language: *passé composé* with *être*

Fig. 3.2 Schematic diagram showing text genre as central to expression of culture through language

analytic framework for examining key aspects of contexts and texts that draw upon specific aspects of language. An analysis that includes all three levels is essential for making decisions about the cultural content to be introduced, the texts needed to make such introductions, and the language critical to the functions the texts perform. It is the language in the texts that is taught. This general schema for analysis is shown in Fig. 3.3.

The rest of this chapter demonstrates the use of this three-layer approach to the analysis of the culture-language connection in French textbooks. The following section looks at the aspects of cultural narrative that have appeared in textbooks over the fifty-year period. Next, I examine the genres that have been used to present aspects of this cultural narrative. Finally, I show the types of linguistic features that are used to perform these genres.

2   Cultural Narrative

Québec's cultural narrative in the previous chapter affords the basis for investigating how important aspects of culture are presented in the French textbooks. With that as background, the textbook analysis identifies

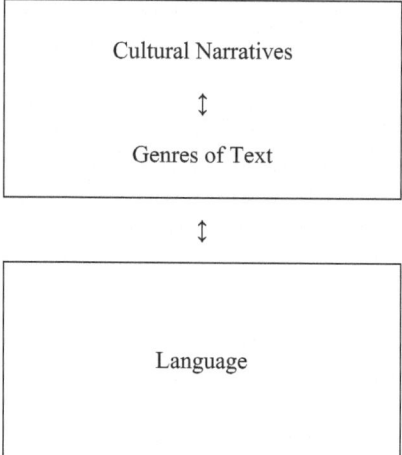

Fig. 3.3 Schematic diagram of the interconnections among cultural narratives, genres of texts, and language

Canadian and Québec content in the textbooks to assess their depiction of cultural narrative. For this analysis, aspects pertaining to the cultural narrative needed to be identified and other mentions of Canada or Québec not pertaining to the cultural narrative needed to be eliminated. In this section, I describe how I identified the cultural narrative content in the textbooks and present the quantitative results showing the numbers of textbooks in each decade that included aspects of Québec cultural narrative.

A summary of the amount of Québec cultural narrative appearing in the textbooks was produced in a three-step process: identifying and coding all Canadian and Québec content in the textbooks, screening the content that had been coded with certain labels to identify texts with cultural narrative genres, and counting the number of textbooks in each decade with Québec cultural narrative texts.

2.1   Identifying and Coding Canadian and Québec Content

The description of the sample selection and coding process is available in Chap. 2, but this section provides more detail about the codes used to identify the types of Canadian and Québec content that were found in the textbooks. The topic categories were created through a process of examination, review, and consultation with two coders to select codes that were sufficiently descriptive of specific aspects of content but general enough to encompass the considerable variety in the detail presented in the textbooks. When we began the process, we did not know exactly what topics would be found, so the codes were developed according to procedures of open coding, which allowed for the process of developing the codes through a process of repeated review of the content in the textbooks. After developing and reviewing the codes and the coding of content from several of the textbooks, the remaining textbooks were coded by one coder, an advanced undergraduate student of French who had taken a study abroad course on language policy in Québec. This qualitative process of establishing codes and reviewing their use is consistent with the types of overlapping codes that were needed to describe most of the content. For example, many of the textbooks contain a single historical text with the Québec story, which includes something about the Quiet Revolution,

Canadian history, and Québec identity. Rather than attempting to decide which of these themes is the best descriptor for the text, we would code it as containing each of the themes. The process departed from practices in quantitative content analysis, which requires the content to be segmented in a way that is amenable to assigning one primary code to each. Instead, the coding process took the analysis into a qualitative methodology of using expert judgment, review, and discussion to assign codes that would capture the important content even though in most instances a text contained content that was coded with more than one label. The codes and definitions of each of the subcategory code labels are shown in Table 3.1.

These codes were used to count the number of occurrences of each of the topics and results are described by Chapelle (2014). Table 3.2 summarizes those findings, which indicate an increasing appearance of all of the topics across the five-decade period. Table 3.2 shows that there was not even one instance per textbook on average of any of these topics in the early textbooks. Only in the 1980s did the topics of Québec culture and bilingualism appear in the textbooks at a rate of at least one per textbook on average. In that decade, the topic of Québec identity appeared on average two times in the textbooks. The 1990s saw the rate maintained of one instance per book on average on the topics of Québec culture and bilingualism. In addition, Canadian history appeared at least

Table 3.1 Code labels and definitions for content connected to Québec's cultural narrative in the French textbooks

Code label	Definition
Canadian history	Content referring to historical information about Canada and Québec, such as the founding of Canada by Jacques Cartier
Quiet revolution	Content making reference to the themes associated with the cultural revolution of the 1960s—that is, themes of the change to assert the authority of the French-speaking population in Québec
Québec identity	Reference made to the sense of pride French Canadians and Québecers feel for their heritage and the commitment they have for maintaining their language and culture
Québec culture	Specific references to symbols of Québec culture such as historical figures, artists, and landmarks
Canadian French	Explicit teaching of Canadian French expressions or reference to Canadian French language as distinct
Bilingualism	Reference to the bilingualism policy or bilingualism in practice in Canada or Québec

Table 3.2 Content pertaining to Québec's internal linguistic and cultural evolution

Content about...	1960s	1970s	1980s	1990s	2000s
Canadian History				gray	black
Quiet Revolution					gray
Québec Identity			black		black
Québec Culture			gray	gray	black
Canadian French					black
Bilingualism			gray	gray	

Note. No shading indicates fewer than one instance per textbook; *gray shading* indicates at least one instance per textbook; *black shading* indicates two or more instances per book

one time per textbook on average. In the 2000s, all topics are represented in the textbooks at least once on average and four topics—Canadian history, Québec identity, Québec culture, and Canadian French—appear at least twice on average. This summary of the amount of appearance of Canadian and Québec content is important because it summarizes the breath of the content that was available for inspection as I screened the texts for cultural narrative content.

2.2   Screening the Content for Cultural Narrative

I screened all content marked with the six content codes defined above to identify which of the texts included content that would be considered Québec's cultural narrative as I outlined it in the previous chapter. This was a qualitative process of searching the database for each of the texts and reading them to determine whether or not they qualified for inclusion. The large majority of the texts did, but in some cases, the content had been correctly coded but did not include the cultural narrative. Such cases included texts about Canadian history that did not touch upon Québec, Québec's cultural figures whose lives were not connected to the narrative, and description of Canadian French with no reference to difference and identity. Judgment calls were made to identify the relevant texts for additional examination.

2.3   Counting of Textbooks with Québec Cultural Narrative

At this point, in keeping with the attention to careful description of the sample, the numbers of textbooks that contain texts that I judged to reflect cultural narrative are shown in Table 3.3. Column two contains the total number in each decade subsample as given in the previous chapter. Column three shows the number of books in each decade and the last number shows the percentage of the books in each subsample that contains Québec's cultural narrative. The percentages allow for comparisons across decade samples, which indicate a steady growth in the number of textbooks containing Québec cultural narrative. In the 1960s and 1970s only around a third of the books contained anything about Québec's cultural narrative. In the 1980s and 1990s, that proportion increased to about half of the books in each decade's subsample. In the 2000s, all of the textbooks contained some mention of aspects of Québec's cultural narrative. These texts containing aspects of Québec's cultural narrative varied in which aspects they contained, the genres that they used to convey cultural narrative meanings, and the language that they used to do so. The specific cultural narrative aspect, genres, and language are described in the following sections.

Table 3.3 Number and percentages of textbooks containing aspects of cultural narrative content

Decade	Number of books	Number of books with cultural narrative content	Percentage of books with cultural narrative content
1960s	11	4	36
1970s	11	3	27
1980s	23	12	52
1990s	9	5	56
2000s	11	11	100
Total	65	35	54

3   Genres of Texts

If genres are the key to linking cultural narrative with language, then a definition of genre is needed that will allow teachers to analyze the texts appearing in their textbooks and those available to them for teaching from other sources, particularly the Internet. The linguistically based definition of genre that Byrnes et al. (2010) adopt has substantial theoretical grounding, which allows it to serve as a tool for analysis of genres rather than as a static and finite classification system. Martin and Rose (2003, 2008), who have substantial experience in analyzing the texts of textbooks and those produced by students, define genres as 'staged, goal-oriented social processes. Staged, because it usually takes us more than one step to reach our goals; goal oriented because we feel frustrated if we don't accomplish the final steps…; social because writers shape their texts for readers of particular kinds' (p. 6). With this basic conception of genres, researchers have set out to describe how particular genres are staged to accomplish particular goals within particular social contexts. To illustrate how this line of research can be applied to the goal of language learning, I first illustrate how textbook texts can be analyzed and summarize Byrnes et al.'s conception of genre in language learning, and then look at the genres used for Québec cultural narrative in the sixty-five textbooks.

3.1   Genres and Québec Cultural Narrative

Because cultural narrative includes the story of people, the most likely genre for cultural narrative is one of the genres that expresses past stories. These can include biographical and autobiographical recounts, historical recounts, and historical accounts (Coffin, 2006). In a 'recount,' the purpose is to tell a story as it happened with an emphasis on the chronology of events. The text about Gabrielle Roy from *Paroles* (Magnan et al., 2007, p. 193) is an example of a biographical recount because it states the chronology of events in Roy's life from the time she was born. She was born in 1909 and then studied in Manitoba. After that, she became a teacher, and then she went to Europe and began to write, and so on. The steps in the biography are anchored in time.

A historical 'account,' rather than only telling what happened as a chronological narrative, attempts to include an account of why things happened. The 'why' of the text is evident in Text 3.2, where the military campaigns and diplomatic moves are the causal explanation for France's maintenance of the territory in North America. The Act de Québec was responsible for the people retaining their right to speak French. The resentment of the English caused the formation of the *Parti Québécois*, and so on. Rather than using time as the method of organization, as was done for the biography of Gabrielle Roy, this explanatory genre of historical account is constructed through a combination of time and causal expressions that connect events in linked chains, showing motivations and motivated events in a coherent story.

Text 3.2

Je me souviens

France once maintained a vast territory in North America, called la Nouvelle-France. Britain, through a series of military campaigns and diplomatic moves, eventually took control of la Nouvelle-France by the mid-eighteenth century. Through l'Act de Québec (1774), the French retained rights to their language, civil law, and religion in what was to become the province of Québec. Today Québec is the largest of the ten provinces in Canada in terms of area, and the second largest after Ontario in population. French is also spoken in parts of New Brunswick, Ontario, and Manitoba.

Much of the industry and natural resources of Québec have been traditionally in the hands of English-speaking Canadian and US corporations. Access to high-paying jobs was often denied to French Canadians. The resentment toward the Anglo-Saxon dominance in economy, politics, and culture culminated in the formation of le Parti Québécois in 1968. In 1974 the provincial government voted to make French the only official language, and le Parti Québécois pledged to seek independence for Québec. The language legislation, especially as applied to commerce and education, has resulted in the departure of some large corporations, as well as part of the English-speaking population. Recent polls have shown a decline in support for the separatist movement. The New Charter of Rights, formulated as part of the new constitution of Canada (1982), conflicts with the economic and political interests of several provinces, especially Québec. The Québec provincial government has yet to accept the Charter entirely since it would make the language law invalid. (Hagiwara & De Rocher, 1985, pp. 190–191)

Table 3.4 summarizes the aspects of Québec's cultural narrative that are expressed through particular linguistic means in the text. Linking between the content and language through the historical account genre is what needs to be understood for a textbook analysis that is informative for both culture and language learning.

Texts often express more than one genre, as in the case of Text 3.3, which combines historical account and a historical factorial explanation, the latter referring to a text that explains reasons for an event. Text 3.3 appeared in *Connaître et se connaître: a Basic Reader for Communication* (Jarvis, Bonin, & Birckbichler, 1980, p. 175). Text 3.3 begins with a historical account similar to the one in Text 3.2 in which the time of an event (the 1960s) marks an event (the French Canadians begin to question English dominance and their isolation from the rest of Canada). The following sentence refers to the event with 'ainsi' (from this). From this questioning came the following events: the French in Canada became French Canadians, then Québecois. « Vive le Québec libre » became the rally cry of the Québécois and « Je me souviens » became their official motto. Gilles Vigneault's song « Gens du pays » became the national anthem of Québec. The next part of the text shifts to a factorial explana-

Table 3.4 Connections between aspects of cultural narrative and language through historical account text (Text 3.3)

Aspects of cultural narrative	Genre	Example of genre-relevant language used to express the aspects of cultural narrative
Colonization of North America by France Québec Act (1774)	Historical account	Cause-effect (through a series of military campaigns and diplomatic moves)
Domination by the English		Abstract noun phrases (Access to high-paying jobs)
Resentment of the English by French speakers		Nominalization (resentment; formation)
Formation of the Parti Québecois		Time expressions (in 1968)
Québec's interests are in conflict with Canadian Charter of Rights and Freedoms		Generic nouns (economic and political interests)

tion in which the idea that Québecois are different from other Canadians is explained by enumerating the reasons that they are seen as different.

Text 3.3

C'est pendant les années soixante que les Canadiens français ont commencé à mettre en question la dominance anglophone et leur isolement du reste du Canada. Ainsi, les Français du Canada sont d'abord devenus Canadiens français, puis Québécois. « Vive le Québec libre » est devenu le cri de ralliement des Québécois et « Je me souviens » leur devise officielle. Une chanson de Gilles Vigneault, « Gens du pays », est devenue l'hymne national du Québec.

Mais en quoi les Québécois sont-ils différents des autres Canadiens et pourquoi un certain nombre de Québécois demandent-ils leur indépendance ? D'abord, parce que leurs traditions, leur style de vie et leur système de valeurs viennent de leur héritage français, mais ils vivent dans un pays à dominance anglophone. Ensuite, les Québécois sont tradiontionnellement catholiques dans un pays généralement protestant. Sur le plan économique, les Québécois se sentent désavantagés aussi. Depuis longtemps, la plupart des compagnies sont contrôlées par des anglophones qui donnent la priorité aux gens qui parlent anglais.

C'est peut-être dans le domaine linguistique que les Québécois se sentent les plus isolés. Comme a dit Pierre Trudeau, l'ancien premier ministre: « Le Québécois veut être partout chez lui au Canada, et seul un Canada bilingue lui permettra de se sentir à l'aise de Vancouver à Saint-Jean » (Jarvis et al., 1980, p. 175)

Table 3.5 summarizes the connections between content and language that appear in Text 3.3.

These genres for expressing history lend themselves well to the presentation of cultural narrative. By explaining the reasons for the events and actions, they summarize for readers the national rationality and its origins in a way that a chronological listing of events cannot do. But historical genres are not the only texts in which elements of the national cultural narrative appear.

Text 3.4 is a brief excerpt from a lengthy dialogue depicting American students conversing as they embark on a car trip from the USA to Québec. After arriving in Québec City, they take a ride in a horse drawn carriage (which is a normal tourist activity there). The excerpted lines of conversation

Table 3.5 Connections between aspects of cultural narrative and language through a historical account and factorial explanation text (Text 3.4)

Aspects of cultural narrative	Genre	Example of genre-relevant language used to express the aspects of cultural narrative
French Canadians question domination by the English	Historical account and factorial explanation	Time expressions (c'est pendant les années soixante que) Cause-effect (sont devenu) Abstract noun phrases (la dominance anglophone) Nominalization (isolement) Specialized lexis (Gens du pays)
Symbols of independence and memory		Numeratives and connectives for ordering factors in the text (D'abord, ensuite, sur le plan économique)
Distinctness of Québecois: French heritage, Catholic religion, and linguistic isolation		Reasons expressed through contrasts (héritage français mais dominance anglophone; catholiques dans un pays protestant)
Economic disadvantage for francophones		Negative lexis (contrôlées par des anglophones... donnent la priorité au gens qui parlent anglais; se sentent isolés)

are between one of the American students, Bill, and the carriage driver, who later we learn is a student at Université Laval. This conversation does not include the historical genres' explanation so the cause and effect development of the narrative with explanations is absent. Instead, the students talk about their own identities using more concrete language of casual conversation.

Text 3.4
Bienvenue dans la Belle Province
Bill: Est-ce que vous pensez que vous êtes un peu français?
Le cocher: Est-ce que vous pensez que vous êtes un peu anglais? Non, bien sûr. Nous sommes complètement québécois, et vous êtes complètement américains! Mais nous n'oublions pas nos origines. (Lenard, 1977, pp. 269–275)

Unlike Texts 3.1–3.3, Text 3.4 uses the present tense of the relational verb 'be,' personal pronouns, and questions to create conversation. Statements are made without using the linguistic resources of time and reason. The interlocutors are talking about themselves. Because one of the interlocutors is Québecois and the other one had enough content and linguistic knowledge to ask a question, an important aspect of Québec's national narrative was included in the dialogue. Table 3.6 summarizes the linguistic features that express cultural content about pride of identity and memory of the heritage.

These examples illustrate how cultural narrative is included in beginning-level foreign language textbooks. They also show how the choice of genres affects the language that students have the opportunity to read and study. The language and culture are not added to what is chosen as an instructional text. On the contrary, the genre of each text selected by the textbook producers in turn chooses the language that students are exposed to. The central question about the way culture is depicted in texts in foreign language textbooks then becomes what genres have been used to express aspects of Québec's cultural narrative and how they serve in language learning.

3.2   Genres in Language Learning

The texts in foreign language textbooks are intended to help students learn the language by providing samples of how language works in texts

Table 3.6 Connections between aspects of cultural narrative and language through casual conversation (Text 3.4)

Aspects of cultural narrative	Genre	Example of genre-relevant language used to express the aspects of cultural narrative
Pride of identity and memory	Casual conversation	Questions (Est-ce que vous pensez que vous êtes un peu français?) First and second person pronouns (Vous, nous) Relational verbs (êtes) Present tense

to create meanings. Texts used as input for students' language learning at the beginning level are typically texts that have been created for other purposes, or simulations of such genres. They show students how people use language to accomplish a variety of communication goals. However, not all genres are equally accessible to beginning-level learners and therefore textbook analysis requires a means of distinguishing the accessibility of genres that are used in language textbooks as Byrnes et al. (2010) have done. Their continuum of accessibility is summarized in Fig. 3.4.

Byrnes et al. (2010) recommend a progression of genres in language learning based on the idea of continua of accessibility of the language each genre uses. Based on the continuum shown in Fig. 3.4, learners are first able to handle the dialogic language that occurs in conversation about people, things, and events. As they develop, they are able to interpret and produce monologic texts about more abstract topics. Byrnes et al. identified twenty-three genres that were included in their first-year courses in the curriculum that was planned to systematically develop literacy of their German learners. They grouped the genres into three types: primary discourses consisting of casual conversations, picture stories, cartoon strips, personal narrative, and recipe; secondary discourses consisting of texts such as information texts, TV reports, and newspaper feature articles; and blurred discourses which include literary works and other artistic forms. The faculty of this program selected these genres in

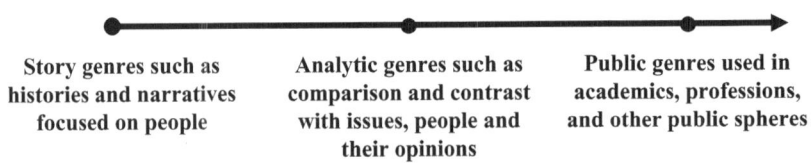

| Story genres such as histories and narratives focused on people | Analytic genres such as comparison and contrast with issues, people and their opinions | Public genres used in academics, professions, and other public spheres |

Fig. 3.4 Continuum of accessibility of genres for language learners at three levels. Summarized from 'Realizing advanced L2 writing development in a collegiate curriculum: Curricular design, pedagogy, assessment,' by H. Byrnes, H. H. Maxim, & J. M. Norris, 2010, *The Modern Language Journal*, *94*, p. 64

view of their theorized appropriateness in meeting the linguistic goals for students at the beginning levels.

The substantial theoretical grounding of the Georgetown University German curriculum has produced a rationale for curriculum progression that is relevant for examination of the way that genres are used to convey cultural content through language in beginning-level textbooks. It is not clear whether or not their particular genres were also motivated by particular aspects of cultural narrative that had been identified as important for the students to learn in conjunction with their language study. Cultural topics that are discussed may fit into a cultural narrative. However, the method of analysis that recognizes genres as the analytic link between content and language is useful for examining any content and language. This means that an analysis of how Québec's cultural narrative is taught does not end with an examination of cultural content. Instead, it begins with an identification of cultural content but then asks what genres have been chosen to convey the content and what the linguistic means for doing so are.

3.3   Genre Analysis of Cultural Narrative in Textbooks

What genres are employed over the fifty-year period to represent the cultural narrative of Québec? In the previous section, I described the process of identifying texts conveying Québec's cultural content which resulted in finding the fraction of the original textbooks containing elements of Québec's cultural narrative. I then read all of the texts which I had determined to be relevant to identify their genre. To name the genres, I used the common sense terminology that should be recognizable by teachers and materials developers.

Table 3.7 shows the numbers of textbooks containing Québec cultural narrative by decade along with the number of texts summed across the textbooks and the number of unique genres. The number of texts totaling 104 is the number of texts that I analyzed to classify them according to genre. In some cases, the textbook gave a genre-like description, which I used if I could agree with the description (e.g., newspaper report). Many of the texts were simply given a title referring to the topic and I examined

Table 3.7 Number of textbooks and texts containing aspects of cultural narrative content and number of unique genres by decade

Decade	Number of books with cultural narrative content	Number of texts containing cultural narrative content	Number of unique genres by decade
1960s	4	7	3
1970s	3	8	4
1980s	12	47	13
1990s	5	14	5
2000s	11	28	7
Total	35	104	13*

Note. *This is the total number of genres identified in the sample rather than the sum across decades. The 1980s total is the same as the total identified because each of the genres is represented in the books of the 1980s.

what the text was doing to arrive at a description that would be useful for capturing its purpose and comprehensible to teachers, materials developers, and other textbook analysts. In assigning genre labels to the text, I found that many textbooks had multiple examples of a genre. This fact is reflected in the final column of Table 3.7 showing the number of unique genres per decade. Such an analysis makes evident the increase in the variety of presentation in the 1980s, but other observations require a closer look at what the genres are and how they are distributed throughout the five decades.

The genres identified in the 104 texts were classified according to groups that would be useful for analyzing the connection between their content and language (Table 3.8). The most numerous genres for presentation of Québec's cultural narrative for beginning-level students were the history genres. As Byrnes et al. (2010) pointed out, history genres, especially those about people (autobiography and biography), are candidates for beginning-level texts because the language of narrative with concrete actors can be most accessible to learners. However, other forms of historical narrative are less accessible because of their use of abstract noun phrases and causal language which is not always explicitly marked. These genres are important for cultural narrative and they will be discussed in the next section.

Conversation genres also appear regularly in foreign language textbooks. Like some of the history text genres, the language of conversation can be accessible to beginning-level students because it often refers to concrete objects, the people in the conversation, and it can be undertaken with relatively concrete language. In the example shown in Text 3.4, it was apparent that an important aspect of Québec's cultural narrative was also conveyed in the conversation. In the following section, some other conversations are examined to identify key factors that make them useful for conveying aspects of cultural narrative.

Table 3.8 Counts of genres used to express aspects of Québec's cultural narrative

Genres used to express content about Québec's language politics	1960s (n=11)	1970s (n=11)	1980s (n=23)	1990s (n=9)	2000s (n=11)
History genres					
Historical text (with questions/ activity)	4(2)	1	17(8)	6(4)	14(5)
Personal narrative with questions			1		1
Picture story with questions			1		
Conversation genres					
Conversation (with questions/ activity)		1(1)	6(2)		4
Newspaper reports and letters					
Newspaper article			1		
Letter			2		
Artistic genres					
Literary text with questions			1		
Song lyrics	1		1		
Poem			1		
Invented genres for language learning					
List of facts			4		1
Statement	2	4	7	1	2
Activity prompt	1		4	3	4
Curated genres around a topic					
Mixture of genres		1	1	4	6
	7	8	47	14	28

Note. The number in parentheses indicates the number of texts followed by questions or other activities intended to engage students with the content of the text. For example, there were four historical texts in the 1960s books, and two of those included questions.

Genres recognized in the real world such as newspapers, letters, literary texts, song lyrics, and poems have appeared occasionally for conveying cultural narrative in the textbooks. However, at the beginning level, they are outnumbered by invented genres for language learning such as lists of facts, single statements, or prompts for activities for students. These language learning genres are increasingly mixed with other genres across the five decades. In the 2000s sample, in particular, aspects of cultural narrative were presented through curated collections of genres. An example of one such multigenre text is shown in one of the case studies in Chap. 5. What remains in this chapter is to look at the way that the genres connect aspects of cultural narrative with language.

4   Language

Canadian and Québec content may have been selected for the textbooks with primary concern for the topics or for the grammar. In this section, I have highlighted some of the lexico-grammatical features of the texts that come to light when such texts are analyzed in a more content and language integrated approach. Analysis of the language builds upon the cultural narrative outlined in Chap. 2 and the genre analysis introduced in this chapter. The linguistic analysis stems from the approach Martin and Rose (2008) demonstrate in the linguistic resources that people use to create meaning in texts. To bring the grammatical concepts into usable language for teachers and materials developers, I have again relied on the types of descriptions that Byrnes et al. (2010) present from their work with a group of teachers undertaking curriculum development together.

4.1   The Language of History Genres

To begin to look at the linguistic characteristics of texts in the history genres, I rely on the analysis conducted by Coffin (2006), which is also summarized by Byrnes et al. (2010). Coffin's analysis is the result of her study of writing in history, whose goal was to characterize the way that historians use language to construct meaning through the genres for expressing meanings about past people and events. Coffin identified multiple subgenres of historical discourse, as shown in Fig. 3.5, some of which are represented in the beginning French textbooks for conveying aspects of cultural narrative. In the French textbooks analyzed, these historical genres represented the largest proportion of all text types used to convey cultural narrative meanings. The analysis is complex, but not incomprehensible, and it is particularly useful for the purpose of language learning because it coheres with the idea of a continuum of linguistic accessibility summarized in Fig. 3.5.

Factors affecting difficulty for any individual are more varied than what can be captured in a single continuum like this, but linguistic accessibility is something that can be controlled by materials developers in their selection and adaptation of texts and therefore it is a dimension worthy of attention. Moreover, each of these genres contains particular linguistic features which should be considered in terms of what students can learn linguistically from reading, understanding, and using the text. Therefore, in an important sense they form the basis of both the language and cultural narrative that the textbook can be used to teach. Elements of each of these genres of history appear in the collection of textbooks, and the texts provide examples of the way that the choice of genres affects the language that is presented and can be taught. Each of the following examples was selected first because of its content, which conveys an aspect of cultural narrative through a history genre, and second through its exemplification of the history genres identified by Coffin (2006). They show the linguistic features that naturally occur in each genre.

The first example, the autobiographical recount, comes from a text in *Connaître et se connaître: A Basic Reader for Communication*, Second

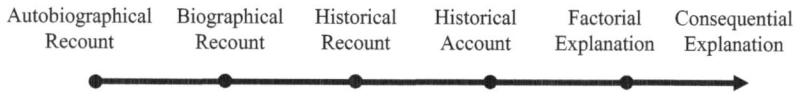

Fig. 3.5 Progression of likely linguistic difficulty for historical genres (Coffin, 2006)

edition (Jarvis, Bonin, Corbin, & Birckbichler, 1980). This text was selected for inclusion in the sample containing cultural narrative because it mentions the discovery of Canada by Jacques Cartier. The first person story is about a teacher from Québec who has traveled north to teach to the indigenous (i.e., First Nations) people, the Inuits of northern Canada. In the excerpt shown in Text 3.5, Fancine is introduced, and then she begins her autobiographical account. Like the biography of Gabrielle Roy, the autobiographical genre affords the opportunity to use verbs in the past tense, and in this case, two of them form the past tense with the auxiliary verb *être* (*sommes arrivés* and nous *sommes installés*). However, this autobiographical account includes the author's observation that the first permanent snow was falling (*tombait*) when they arrived, which provides an opportunity to use the past imperfect aspect. In addition, the observation that '*là-bas tout est lent*' (Out there everything is slow) uses the present tense to indicate an observation that remains true according to the autobiographer. The text is organized by the chronology of the story, using the date as one time expression, but then switching the connectors to show the progression of time from the perspective of the text. The text uses the first person pronoun, *nous* (we) as the predictable subject of the sentences, making the grammar relatively transparent.

Text 3.5
L'École dans le Grand Nord
  Francine, une Québécoise, enseigne dans une de ces écoles. Elle raconte ses impressions.
  Nous sommes arrivés le 10 septembre. Le *lendemain*, **la première neige** permanente tombait. **Nous** pensions commencer à enseigner tout de suite. C'était une erreur: *là-bas* tout est lent. *D'abord*, **nous** nous sommes installés dans notre maison. Puis **nous** avons fait la connaissance du principal et du comité de parents d'élèves. (Jarvis et al., 1980, pp. 210–211)

The second example, Text 3.6, is a historical recount that appeared in *Thème et variations: An Introduction to French Language and Culture* (Hagiwara & De Rocher, 1985). The historical recount, like the (auto) biography, is expressed using past tense verbs and time expressions. The actors, however, are named as people. The people as well as the things and places are expressed in the third person. This example recounts the chronological progression of the French arrival in North America that is the beginning of the cultural narrative.

Text 3.6
Les Français en Amérique
  Vous savez déjà qu'on parle français au Canada, surtout dans la province de Québec. Quand est-ce que les Français sont arrivés en Amérique du Nord ? L'histoire du Canada français remonte loin, au seizième siècle. Entre 1534 et 1541 **Jacques Cartier** a fait trois longs voyages au Canada. Pendant son deuxième voyage, **il** a découvert le Saint-Laurent. **Il** a planté une grande croix sur une colline et il a nommé la colline Mont Réal. **Un autre explorateur**, Samuel de Champlain, a exploré le golfe du Mexique, la Nouvelle-Angleterre, et ensuite l'est du Canada. Il a établi des colonies françaises en Acadie—aujourd'hui les provinces maritimes canadiennes de la Nouvelle-Écosse et du Nouveau-Brunswick—et **il** a fondé la ville de Québec en 1608. **Québec** est ensuite devenu la capitale de la Nouvelle-France, un vaste territoire française en Amérique du Nord.
  Le dix-septième siècle a été la période la plus active de l'exploration de l'Amérique…
  L'exploration a continué au siècle suivant… (Hagiwara & De Rocher, 1985, p. 208)

The example of a historical account is excerpted from a text giving an account of Québec's cultural narrative in *Entre amis: An Interactive Approach to First-Year French* (Oates, Oukada, & Altman, 1991). The historical account is organized through a combination of historical chronology (time) and cause-effect, which can be marked explicitly with cause-effect markers such as 'En consequence' or lexically through the use of words that hold the meaning of causality such as taking possession of the new world, which affects what can happen next, including the possessors' (the French) building on the new possession (Canada).

Text 3.7
L'histoire du Québec: Découverte et colonisation
  C'est en 1535 que **l'explorateur français Jacques Cartier** découvre le fleuve Saint-Laurent et la terre qui l'entoure. **Cartier** prend possession de

cette terre nouvelle au nom du roi de France. En 1608, **Samuel de Champlain** construit une habitation sur un roc qui forme une citadelle naturelle près du Saint-Laurent. C'est la première communauté française en Amérique du Nord, et **Champlain** est le fondateur de la Nouvelle-France. Cette première ville s'appelle Québec.

En conséquence de la guerre de Sept Ans en Europe, **les Anglais** font la guerre contre les Français au Canada. En 1759, **l'armée anglaise** est finalement victorieuse sur les plaines d'Abraham à Québec. **Montréal tombe** aussi quelques semaines plus tard. En 1763 **la France** signe le traité de Paris et abandonne à l'Angleterre ses colonies situées à l'est du Mississippi. En plus, **les Anglais** obligent un grand nombre des Français qui habitent la Québec et l'Acadie (aujourd'hui, le Nouveau-Brunswick) à quitter le Canada. **Beaucoup de ces francophones** s'installent en Louisiane, une autre colonie française. Ce sont les descendants de ces Acadiens-là qu'on appelle aujourd'hui les « Cajuns ». (Oates et al., 1991, pp. 144–145)

Time is marked in a historical account, as it is in a recount, but the language and positioning of information add an additional layer of meaning, which is the account. A recount tells what happened, but an account adds why these events happened as well. Figure 3.6 summarizes the combination of time and cause-effect relations that are in Text 3.7.

In Text 3.7, the time expressions are used to express organization, but in addition, events are more highly interconnected than a chronological list because they are depicted as a chain of causes and effects. There is one clear causal expression, En conséquence de la guerre de Sept Ans en Europe (As a result of the Seven Years War in Europe), that begins the second paragraph outlining the critical events of the mid 1700s. The other cause-effect relationships shown in Fig. 3.6 are stated more implicitly through the use of the meanings conveyed as the actions: Cartier taking possession causes other settlers to come to the new world so that francophone communities are founded; the English winning in Québec and Montreal falling results in the demise of the French rule and power in the new world. The actors appearing as subjects of the sentences are concrete proper nouns referring to people and places (e.g., Cartier and Montréal) or the more generic 'les Anglais' (the English) or 'Beaucoup

Time	Time			Time	Time
1535	1608			1759	1763
Cause →	Effect	Cause →	Effect	Cause →	Effect
Cartier took possession of the new world for the king of France.	Champlain founded the first francophone community, Québec.	The seven-year war in Europe.	The English were at war with the French in Canada.	The English army won in Québec and Montreal fell a few weeks later.	France handed over the new world colonies to England. The English forced the evacuation of many francophones, many of whom went to Louisiana.

Fig. 3.6 Historical account using time expressions and causal language in Text 3.7

des ces Francophones' (a lot of these Francophones). The verb tense used throughout this text is the present, which illustrates this characteristic of historical narrative in French: once the time is established through other signals, the verbs can use the simple present. Other characteristics of this genre that are important for the narrative are the specialized lexis, which in this text appear as geographical names.

An example of a factorial explanation appeared as one part of a text called 'La politique culturelle au Québec' in the textbook *Débuts: An Introduction to French* (Siskin, Williams-Gascon, & Field, 2007). The longer text, of which Text 3.8 is one part, provides parts of the cultural narrative of Québec. Text 3.8 shows the author's use of a factorial explanation to present the factors that precipitated the adoption of the Charter of the French Language by the government of Québec. In this very short text, seven factors, which are highlighted in the text, are presented as causal factors leading up to the Charter as the result in the final paragraph.

Text 3.8

La situation en 1971

En 1971, **beaucoup de Québécois** parlaient français et anglais. Mais **le bilinguisme** mène à l'assimilation, et **presque toutes les communautés francophones de l'ouest du Canada et de la Nouvelle-Angleterre** sont devenues progressivement anglophones.

L'anglais était la langue des affaires et de l'industrie au Québec. **Les anglophones** étaient souvent à la tête des entreprises. **Les immigrés** préféraient envoyer leurs enfants dans les écoles anglophones. En 1971, **79% des enfants des immigrés** étaient dans une école anglophone. Depuis la Conquête, **le français canadien** adoptait beaucoup de mots anglais. Dans les régions anglophones, **on** avait peu de respect pour le français nord-américain. À Toronto, à Vancouver, même dans les écoles anglophones du Québec, **on** apprenait généralement le français de Paris.

1977: La charte de la langue française

La «charte de la langue française» était un acte de politique culturelle unique au monde. **Son but** était d'assurer à la langue française le premier rôle dans la société québécoise et de permettre au français de survivre en Amérique du Nord. (Siskin et al., 2007, pp. 457–459)

Figure 3.7 shows the factorial organization of the text, which is not marked with clear structural signals such as 'many factors led up to the adoption of the Charter' or 'one of the factors... another factor.' Instead the factors develop a theme of negativity about the situation which prompted a change. Moreover, reading the negativity requires the reader to take the point of view of the francophone in Québec. One signal, 'mais' at the beginning of the second sentence needs to be understood as the shift from what most readers would see as a positive—a lot of people in Québec spoke French and English—to what is framed as a negative in this text—that bilingualism leads to assimilation. The following factors leading to the Charter are expressed with language showing negativity: it conveys the message that there is little respect for North American French. The other factors need to be understood as negative in the context of French in Québec in that time period, linguistic discrimination, and fear of the loss of the heritage language.

Factors	Result
Bilingualism leads to assimilation (as has happened in New English in the United States and in the West of Canada).	
English was the language of business and industry in Québec.	
English speakers were usually the heads of the businesses.	The Charter of the French Language was adopted to assure the place of French in Québec society
Immigrants preferred to send their children to Anglophone schools.	
French Canadians were adopting a lot of English words.	
French Canadians were not respected.	
French learners were learning the French of Paris.	

Fig. 3.7 The factorial explanation of Text 3.8 about factors leading up to the Charter

The time of the text is marked as a snapshot of one year, 1971, with three mentions of 1971, and then the final paragraph is about the Charter in 1977, which is marked in the heading for that part of the text. The verb tense and aspect used throughout is the imperfect past, which indicates a continuing state or action in the past (e.g., Many Québecois spoke French and English; English was the language of business). Some of the noun phrases used as subjects are concrete or generic, as seen in the previous examples, but this text also contains the abstract noun 'bilingualism' as a subject as well as the complex noun phrase, 'almost all the francophone communities in the west of Canada and in New England' (*presque toutes les communautés francophones de l'ouest du Canada et de la Nouvelle-Angleterre*) also appear in this text. The place-holding subject 'on' also appears as the subject.

An example of a consequential explanation appeared in *En route: Introduction au français et au monde francophone* (Valdman, Barnett,

Holekamp, Laronde, Magnan, & Pons, 1986). This text, shown as Text 3.9, outlines the consequences of the Quiet Revolution.

Text 3.9
Le Québec
  <u>Vers 1960</u> **les Québécois francophones** ont connu ce qu'ils appellent « la révolution tranquille. » Il s'agit d'un grand développement économique accompagné de changements sociaux et politiques profonds. **L'Église catholique**, qui a dominé la vie québécoise pendant des siècles, joue <u>maintenant</u> un rôle moins important. **Le gouvernement québécois** a établi un système de mesures sociales très ambitieux. **Il** a entrepris la nationalisation de quelques secteurs, par exemple, l'énergie et les soins médicaux. **Le gouvernement** a aussi essayé d'encourager le développement et la diffusion de la culture québécoise à travers la littérature, le théâtre et la chanson. Enfin, **il** a donné une grande important à la langue française en faisant des lois pour insérer le français dans la vie économique—les banques, les bureaux, les usines. (Valdman et al., 1986, p. 540)

The time in this text is introduced as the time period around 1960 (vers 1960), when the Quiet Revolution occurred. The Quiet Revolution is defined as being about economic development with profound social and political change. The consequences are forecast and linked to the definition through the expressions 'economic development' and 'social and political change.' Each of the consequences provides detail on these areas, as outlined in Fig. 3.8.

The consequences are expressed using verbs primarily in the *passé composé* to denote past events and actions; one verb is in the present with the adverb 'now' (*maintenant*) to indicate 'now in this time period the church plays a less significant role.' Factors expressed the particulars that cohere lexically with the definition of the event, and one overt marker of listing 'finally' (*enfin*). The nouns serving as subjects are concrete and generic expressions.

To summarize the ways that the historical genres have been used in French textbooks to express aspects of cultural narrative, Table 3.9 pres-

Event	Consequences
The Quiet Revolution: Great economic developments accompanied profound social and political changes	The Catholic church plays a less important role. The Québec government established an ambitious system of social measures. The government undertook nationalization of energy and health care. The government tried to encourage development and diffusion of Québec culture. The government gave great importance to the French language.

Fig. 3.8 Consequential explanation using time expressions and causal language in Text 3.9

ents the connections among the three levels of cultural narrative, genre, and language in the historical genres in Texts 3.5–3.9.

Having examined the language of history genres in the examples, it should make sense to add these types of grammatical features to the genres that Byrnes et al. (2010) placed on a continuum of accessibility, as shown in Fig. 3.9. Byrnes et al. (2010) see some history genres as good candidates for the types of actions, clauses, and relationships that would form the basis for early language learning. Examples of language with these characteristics can clearly be found in the corpus of texts expressing Québec's cultural narrative. This finding contrasts with the idea that cultural narrative can be introduced to students only after they have mastered the basics of the language. These examples show instead that the basics of the language are introduced through the telling of cultural narrative. In other words, these examples show instances where authors have created materials that can be used to teach language and culture to beginning-level students. Such a foundation in the actions, people, places, timing, and motives that make up Québec's cultural narrative is

Table 3.9 Historical genres appearing in first-year textbooks

Cultural narrative	Genre	Language
Jacques Cartier's discovery of Canada	Autobiographical recount	First person and concrete subjects of sentences Verbs in past tense and present tense Time expressions used to mark organization
French arrival in North America	Historical recount	Third person and concrete subjects of sentences Verbs in past tense Time expressions used to mark organization
The founding of Canada by the French and subsequent loss to the British	Historical account	Third person: both generic and specific participants Verbs in present tense, which expresses a narrative in the past Organization marked by both time and cause-effect relations Specialized lexis consisting of geographical names
The factors leading to the adoption of the Charter of the French language in Québec	Factorial explanation	Factors expressed as negative aspects of a situation Verbs describing the situation are in the imperfect indicating a continuing state in the past Time expressions mark the overall time of text A range of noun phrases including abstract, complex, and the impersonal 'on' meaning something like 'one' or 'people in general'

(continued)

Table 3.9 (continued)

Cultural narrative	Genre	Language
The consequences of the Quiet Revolution	Consequential explanation	Factors expressed as particulars that cohere lexically with the definition of the event, and one overt marker of listing, 'finally'
		Verbs expressed primarily in *passé composé* to denote past events and actions; one verb in the present with adverb 'now' to indicate 'now in this time'
		One time expression marks the overall time.
		The nouns serving as subjects are concrete and generic expressions.

needed for students to move into more analytic genres that use the basic knowledge to increase the complexity of the ideas and language of the texts they work with.

4.2   The Language of Conversation Genres

The written historical text genres were the most numerous for the overall sample of textbooks, but elements of Québec's cultural narrative also appeared in the conversation genres in the textbooks. As illustrated in Text 3.3, the carriage driver in conversation with an American has the opportunity to express his pride in his nationality in addition to his memory of his origins. He uses the plural pronoun to say, 'We are completely Québecois, but we do not forget our origins.' What is it about casual conversation that creates the opportunity for such revealing statements about social and collective identity to appear? Eggins and Slade (1997), who provide a thorough exploration of the genres of casual conversion, distinguish casual conversation from pragmatic conversation. Pragmatic conversation appears in first-year language textbooks to demonstrate to students how to get things done in the language (e.g.,

Beginning Level Texts

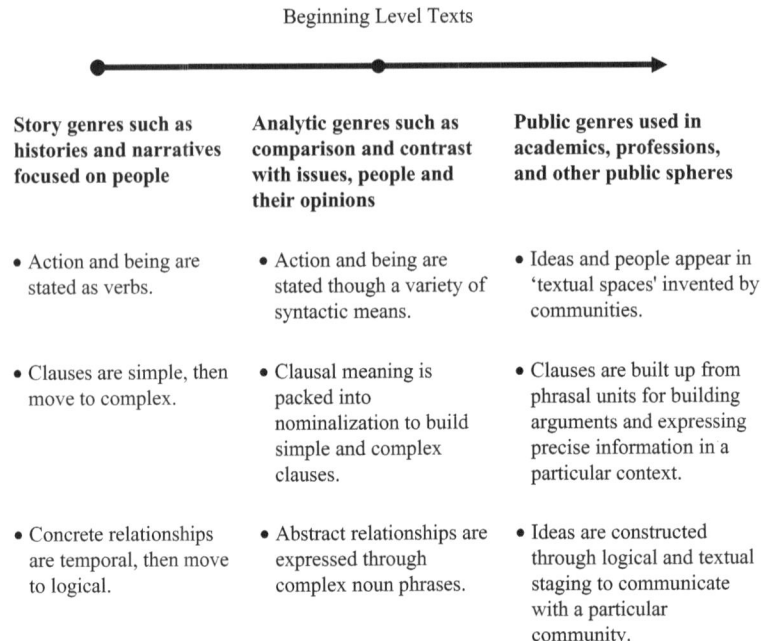

Story genres such as histories and narratives focused on people	Analytic genres such as comparison and contrast with issues, people and their opinions	Public genres used in academics, professions, and other public spheres
• Action and being are stated as verbs.	• Action and being are stated though a variety of syntactic means.	• Ideas and people appear in 'textual spaces' invented by communities.
• Clauses are simple, then move to complex.	• Clausal meaning is packed into nominalization to build simple and complex clauses.	• Clauses are built up from phrasal units for building arguments and expressing precise information in a particular context.
• Concrete relationships are temporal, then move to logical.	• Abstract relationships are expressed through complex noun phrases.	• Ideas are constructed through logical and textual staging to communicate with a particular community.

Fig. 3.9 Trajectory of text characteristics for students' development from the beginning through advanced levels as defined by Byrnes et al. (2010). Summarized from 'Realizing advanced L2 writing development in a collegiate curriculum: Curricular design, pedagogy, assessment,' by H. Byrnes, H. H. Maxim, & J. M. Norris, 2010, *The Modern Language Journal, 94*, p. 64

ordering in a restaurant, getting stamps in a post office, buying orange juice at a store, or inquiring about the time of the next train). Casual conversation, in contrast, appears to have no real purpose, on the surface. Instead, it seems to participants to be undertaken 'just for the sake of talking' (Eggins & Slade, p. 8). But there is a purpose. Eggins and Slade describe the purpose by noting that 'casual conversation is a critical site for the social construction of reality' (p. 16). Through collaboration in making meaning, interlocutors use language to represent themselves as members of groups and position themselves as individuals. Are students at the beginning level ready to be exposed to casual conversation?

According to Byrnes et al. (2010), casual conversation should figure significantly in the syllabus at the beginning level. In their Level I syllabus on the topic of education, it appears primarily in the context of informal communication at school that takes place as casual conversations between intimate participants concerned with individual experiences of school life (e.g., at the student cafeteria or in the school yard). The key linguistic features include reference to specific participants, use of the present perfect, and colloquial expressions (Byrnes et al., 2010). To analyze how it expresses cultural narrative, the analysis needs to take into account who the speakers are. Casual conversation takes place so that interlocutors can socially construct reality. Accordingly, the reality that can be constructed depends on the interlocutors. Eggins and Slade (1997) characterize successful casual conversation as advancing through developing a tension between, on the one hand, establishing solidarity through the confirmation of similarities, and, on the other, asserting autonomy through the exploration of differences. These tensions are apparent in the samples of textbook casual conversations, where in some cases they prompt information about Québec's cultural narrative.

The nature of the cultural narrative and the language used to convey it depend critically on who the participants are and what they know. Figure 3.10 shows a continuum of participant difference that affects the amount, quality, and expression of Québec cultural content based on findings from my sample of casual conversations. In the textbooks, characters at one end of the continuum are French speakers of unknown origins and knowledge. These speakers mention a key element of Québec cultural narrative, but are limited in their contribution. On the other end of the continuum are Québécois speakers who can reveal more, particularly in conversation with an interested and knowledgeable interlocutor.

All of the casual conversations are fabricated for the purpose of teaching French, but they are recognizable as casual conversation because the authors have crafted the language in a way that depicts conversation. In the first group of three dialogues, it is not clear who the interlocutors are or what they may know, but at one or more points in the dialogue, pieces of Québec's cultural narrative are presented.

French speakers of unknown
origins and knowledge

Québécois speaking with
someone with some knowledge
and interest in Québec

Fig. 3.10 Continuum of participant characteristics relevant to the appearance of Québec cultural narrative in dialogues

4.2.1   Interlocutors of Unknown Origin and Knowledge

The textbook *Appel: Initiation au français* (Ollivier, Morran, & Howard, 1983) contains a dialogue with students discussing what language to sign up for. The dialogue is titled 'Rayonnement de la France' [The influence of France]. The conversation turns to where French is spoken. Ken contributes the name of one of the characters in Québec's cultural narrative as shown in Text 3.10. The interlocutors consist of several students who appear to express solidarity by each contributing ideas about the scope of French language use in the world today. In this sense, they take turns expressing their unique knowledge of a particular area. Melissa, who is trying to decide about signing up for French states that aside from France the only place she knows of where French is spoken is Québec. In a move of affiliation Ken acknowledges Québec, and adds his knowledge that Jacques Cartier is connected to Québec. He does so emphatically, 'Qui n'a pas entendu' to express his certainty that this knowledge is so important that everyone knows it. The following turns by other students add information about other French-speaking areas of the world, and Québec is not mentioned again.

Text 3.10
Melissa: A part la France, j'en connais un, c'est le Québec.
Ken: Oui. Qui n'a pas entendu parler de Jacques Cartier ! (Ollivier et al., 1983, pp. 371–373)

Text 3.11 shows a dialogue from *Rendez-vous: An Invitation to French* (Muyskens, Omaggio, Chalmers, Imbarton, & Almeras, 1982) in which Corinne and Jacques, of unknown origin, talk about the early French explorers in Canada. In the textbook, the text's purpose is to provide examples of the past subjunctive verb tense and mood. The interlocutors express their solidarity through their agreement about the extraordinary feats of the *couriers du bois* and their addition of information about French colonization. They take turns making statements of fact about the early French explorers, each expressing positive appraisal of the actions of the explorers. Corinne begins the dialogue by stating that she envies the adventurers of the *couriers des bois*. Jacques shows solidarity with Corinne by emphasizing the extraordinary feats with the emphasis, 'Imagine!' in addition to a statement that there was not one single European in the Saint Lawrence before Cartier arrived. Corrine continues with an expression of affiliation, 'you know that' (*tu sais que*), using the informal form of the pronoun, and some additional information about the French exploration, and finally Jacques with a booster, 'I admire even more' (*J'admire encore plus*), contributes additional acts of the French explorers. The solidarity is built strongly through the agreement on positivity and the collective building of a pool of facts about the French in North America, which they state with certainty. Their expression of difference is in the uniqueness of the information each presents.

Text 3.11
Aventuriers français du Nouveau Monde
Corinne: Parfois, j'envie les aventures des coureurs des bois français avant que l'Amérique du Nord n'ait été entièrement explorée.
Jacques: Imagine! Il n'y avait pas un seul Européen dans le Saint-Laurent avant que Cartier n'y ait amené ses hommes...
Corinne: Tu sais que, bien que la Nouvelle Amsterdam ait eu un peuplement néerlandais dès 1626, c'est un Français, Pierre Minuit, qui en a été le premier gouverneur et qui a acheté Manhattan aux Indiens.
Jacques: J'admire encore plus ce coureur des bois Toussaint Charbonneau, qui a guidé Lewis et Clark jusqu'à qu'ils soient arrivés au Pacifique! (Muyskens et al., 1982, p. 443)

Text 3.12 shows the dialogue between two people from the textbook *Échanges: première année de français* (Comeau & Lamoureux, 1982). The moves in the dialogue are not headed with the names of the speakers, but readers can infer that one of them is George. Readers of the textbook may remember that George is Canadian from an earlier introduction in the chapter, but readers do not know if he is Québecois; moreover, his national identity is not important in this dialogue because he presents his information about Canada for his interlocutor by reading from a book. George speaks with another person of unknown origin, but who is clearly not Québecois. The background for the conversation is presented as follows: 'Jacques Cartier découvrit le Gaspé. La Louisiane fut un territoire français jusqu'en 1803. Cette année-là les États-Unis l'achetèrent.' [Jacques Cartier discovered le Gaspé. Louisiana was a French territory until 1803. That year the USA bought it]. The readers know that George and his interlocutor took a trip to Canada and are now back home talking about the French in North America. The dialogue opened using the language of solidarity, 'our visit,' 'George,' 'Do you know,' with the familiar form of you. The question also positions George as different and of higher status by assuming that he knows about the history of French presence in North America. George, in turn, affirms that he has a book on the subject from which he reads the critical piece of cultural narrative about Jacques Cartier's discovery of Canada in 1534. The solidarity and difference continues through the next two turns with another question and response read from George's book. The interlocutor's response to the information about the sale of the Louisiana purchase shows an affective engagement with a surprised repetition of the price of twenty-seven million dollars. Then, George continues to contribute to solidarity by agreeing with the statement that that amount of money was small by adding his own words of humor about Napoleon being a great general but a terrible businessman.

Text 3.12

- Notre visite au Canada, Georges, a piqué ma curiosité. Sais-tu de quelle période date la présence française en Amérique?
- J'ai justement à la main un petit livre sur le sujet, Ben. Je cite: « On vit la présence français en Amérique du Nord dès 1534, année où Jacques Cartier découvrit la péninsule du Gaspé, qui fait partie de la province actuelle de Québec. »

- Est-ce qu'il y a eu aussi en Amérique des colonies françaises en dehors du Canada ?
- Oui, Ben. Je continue: « De 1699 à 1803, la Louisiane fut un territoire français. Mais Napoléon vendit ce territoire aux États-Unis, qui l'achetèrent pour environ vingt-sept millions de dollars. »
- Vingt-sept millions! Mais ce n'est pas beaucoup pour un tel territoire!
- En effet, Ben. Napoléon état un très grand général mais un homme d'affaires abominable! (Comeau & Lamoureux, 1982, p. 447)

4.2.2 Dialogues with a Québécois(e) Interlocutor

The use of linguistic signals of affiliation and solidarity such as expressing grounds for agreement and asking questions reaps a greater benefit in terms of cultural narrative when one of the interlocutors in these textbook casual conversations is Québecois and the other has some knowledge and interest in Québec. Cultural narrative from the Québecois comes easily and predictably, but it comes in response to a statement about Québec or a direct question from the interlocutor.

Text 3.13 shows a brief dialogue in *Rendez-vous: An Invitation to French* (Muyskens et al., 1982). Marianne of unknown origin is speaking with Québecois Gilles about politics. The dialogue picks Québec narrative content to illustrate an alternative to the use of the past subjunctive verb. The alternative is presented as the use of 'hope that' (*espérer que*), which is shown in the final line of the dialogue: 'I hope that we will know how to recapture the political power that we deserve.'

Text 3.13

Séparatisme au Canada

Gilles: Nous Québécois, nous sommes fiers, mais il est bon de se rappeler que nous avons de bonnes raisons de l'être.

Marianne: Tu veux dire que vous avez toujours dû vivre entourés d'Anglais mais que vous avez pu garder votre langue intacte.

Gilles: Nous avons gardé intactes notre langue, notre culture et notre identité collective. J'espère que nous saurons regagner la force politique que nous méritons. (Muyskens et al., 1982, p. 447)

There is much more going on in the dialogue, grammatically speaking. Gilles aligns himself with the Québecois people, who are proud: 'We Québecois,' he begins the dialogue. He positively evaluated their grounds for being proud: 'We have good reasons for being proud.' Marianne's turn builds solidarity by elaborating on the reason for the well-deserved pride. She responds, 'You mean that you always had to live surrounded by the English but that you have been able to keep your language intact.' Gilles' turn affirms Marianne's statement in the strongest terms. He repeats the words in an affirmative sentence: 'We have kept intact our language.' He then adds to Marianne's statement about language, 'our culture and our collective identity.' He goes one step farther in the last sentence, again using an affirmative statement: 'I hope that we will know how to regain the political power that we deserve.' In Gilles, readers can see the persona of a passionate supporter of Québec's autonomy that is so important to the cultural narrative.

Text 3.14 shows a brief segment in *Langue et langage: Le français par le français* (Pucciani & Hamel, 1983) of a longer conversation in which a conversation takes place between two Francophones, one French woman (Mme Morin) and two students, one of whom is from Québec. Françoise from Québec and Jessica are visiting Paris with some other students. The Québecoise, Françoise, speaks about Québec culture in response to Jessica's statement assuming that in Canada Françoise would know the same crisis of culture that Mme Morin is complaining about in Paris. Françoise agrees that they face the same crisis, but then offers the critical observation that the external threat posed by the English speakers simply reinforces their conviction to maintain their culture.

Text 3.14
Au pays de Descartes
...

Mme Morin: C'est ça. La raison humaine, l'intellect, l'art... Mais avec bientôt un Disneyland aux environs de Paris, une pyramide dans la cour du Louvre, et la mahgrébisation de nos grandes villes, on se sait plus quoi penser !

Jessica (*à Françoise*): Chez vous, entre le Canada anglais et les États-Unis, vous devez connaître cette même crise.

Françoise: Oui, mais chez nous, cela nous renforce dans notre culture.

...

(Pucciani & Hamel, 1983, p. 637)

In Text 3.15 from *Langue et culture: A Basic Course in French* (Valdman, 1975), a dialogue between Pierre, who appears to be French, and Françoise, who is Canadian, raises the theme of bilingualism. This dialogue shows considerable language of interpersonal engagement because Pierre asks questions directly to Françoise. Pierre begins by using his knowledge of Canada to state that Françoise is lucky to live in a bilingual country. Françoise sets him straight by pointing out that only the French Canadians are really bilingual. Pierre continues by asking questions about the language spoken at the university, the colloquial language (called *joual*), and the language she speaks at home. This dialogue demonstrates that casual conversation genres afford the opportunity for students to see interpersonal language used to obtain more and more interesting information about current consciousness and practices that make up the cultural narrative at the present time.

Text 3.15

Pierre: Si, mais <u>vous</u> savez, aujourd'hui en Europe, dans tous les métiers la pratique de plusieurs langues étrangères est très utile et quelquefois même, indispensable. <u>Vous</u> avez de la chance d'habiter un pays bilingue.

Françoise: <u>Vous</u> savez, au Canada il n'y a que <u>nous</u> Franco-Canadiens qui soyons vraiment bilingues.

Pierre: Quelle langue est-ce qu'on emploie à l'université?

Françoise: Moi, je vais à l'université de Montréal qui est une université francophone. J'ai des amis qui vont McGill, qui est une université de langue anglaise.

Pierre: J'ai entendue parler du joual. Qu'est-ce que c'est exactement?

Françoise: C'est le français que beaucoup de gens parlent, surtout dans la région de Montréal. Ça vient de la prononciation locale pour « cheval ».

Pierre: Et vous parlez cette variété de français?

Françoise: Avec mes amis, bien sûr. Mais à la maison, comme Maman est française et que Papa a vécu longtemps en France, nous parlons le français de France. Maman est née dans le Midi, et comme elle a un petit accent méridional, nous la taquinons à ce sujet chaque fois qu'elle se plaint de la façon de parler des gens de Montréal. (Valdman, 1975, pp. 547–548)

4.2.3 Summary of Cultural Narrative in Casual Conversation

Aspects of Québec's cultural narrative are presented in some of the casual conversation included in the textbooks. The content is used in interaction that constructs social realities through the negotiation of solidarity and difference. Table 3.10 summarizes the aspects of cultural narrative that appear in the examples provided, but this summary is not intended to define the range of all possible cultural narrative content that could be brought up in casual conversation. Casual conversation can be about anything, and therefore the scope for possible cultural content is open to the many topics that dialogue writers can build into the conversations of the participants. The key factor affecting the quality of the conversations for Québec cultural narrative is participants' identity, interest, and knowledge.

4.2.4 Casual vs. Pragmatic Conversation

The analysis of casual conversation provides some insights for examining the cultural narrative potential in the conversations in first-year textbooks. The conversations examined in this section are casual conversations, but to get the complete picture, it is necessary to return to the broader characterization of conversation that includes both casual and pragmatic conversations. In the sample of textbook conversations above, none were pragmatic conversations. In pragmatic conversations, the topic is fixed upon accomplishing something, and therefore the probability of engaging in the activity of socially constructing the world is much less. The textbooks contain plenty of pragmatic conversations, but the national

Table 3.10 Summary of conversation genres and genre-relevant language containing aspects of Québec's cultural narrative

Text	Aspects of cultural narrative	Genres of casual conversation among	Example of genre-relevant language used to express the aspects of cultural narrative
3.10	Jacques Cartier	Students of unknown origin, location and relationships	Question used for emphasis: Who has not heard of?
3.11	The first French explorers who worked with the native people; Jacques Cartier	Unknown people	Statements of positive interest and first person: I envy, I admire even more (*J'envie*... J' admire encore plus...); events in past sequence: before [clause] (*avant que*...); specific people and places: Cartier, Saint Lawrence
3.12	Jacques Cartier marked the beginning of French presence in North America in 1543; the French had a substantial presence in North America beyond Canada.	Unknown people, one from Canada	Questions; first and second person: our visit, do you know, I have (*notre visite, sais-tu, j'ai*); third person and subordination from the book; multiple verb tenses/aspects; expressions: at hand (*à la main*), there were (*il y a eu*), businessman (*homme d'affaires*)
3.13	Québécois pride in maintaining French and hopes for attaining real political power	Two unknown people, one Québécois	Collective first person plural: We Québécois (*Nous Québécois*), our language (*notre langue*); first and second person singular: you mean (tu veux dire), I hope (j'espère); expressions: have good reasons to be (*avoir de bonnes raisons de l'être*)
3.14	The threat of English Canada and the USA strengthens French Canadians' culture.	French people talking to visitors to France, including a Canadian	First person and second person: we (nous), you (vous); expressions: at your place (chez vous)

(*continued*)

Table 3.10 (continued)

Text	Aspects of cultural narrative	Genres of casual conversation among	Example of genre-relevant language used to express the aspects of cultural narrative
3.15	Bilingualism in Canada and Québec Varieties of French, definition of Joual, acceptability of Joual as colloquial language, and the distinctiveness of Canadian French	Two students, one French and one Canadian	First, second, and third person; present and past tense verbs; questions using a variety of syntax; subordination; expressions: be lucky (avoir de la chance)

origin of the interlocutors is frequently not made evident. Based on these observations, I would suggest the conceptualization of textbook conversations as shown in Fig. 3.11.

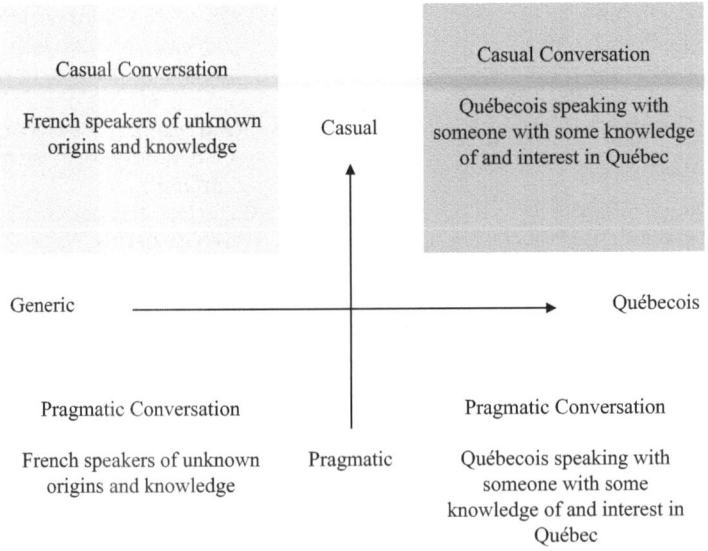

Fig. 3.11 Analysis of likely appearance of Québec cultural narrative in conversation based on conversational genre (casual vs. pragmatic) and interlocutors (*Note.* Darker shading predicts greater plausibility for detailed Québec cultural narrative)

It would be possible to create texts showing pragmatic conversations used to carry out cultural business, but none were found in the analysis. From a social-semiotic perspective, the conversation genres in the textbooks had not necessarily been chosen to show students the types of texts that are used in Canada and Québec to carry out important cultural practices.

4.3 Other Genres

The linguistic characteristics of historical and casual conversation genres can be seen in other genres whose purposes share some core features with both. For example, letters and journalistic reports are often written to both convey a historical narrative and engage with readers to construct social reality. Text 3.16 from *Vis-à-vis: Beginning French* (Amon et al., 2004) shows an example of a journalist's report on Montreal as a French-speaking city. In doing so, it begins with a question. Rather than choosing the conversational syntax for the question (Can you speak French…?), the newspaper engages the readership with a more general question (Is it possible to speak French…?). Because no relationship exists between writer and readers, the author's first move needs to capture the attention and interest of the reader. This is done textually by placing the provocative idea (Speaking French in a French environment in North America) first, and following with the syntactic work of making it a question (est-ce-que c'est possible?). The report genre does not wait for the readers to answer the question, but instead provides a response to the question immediately following the question. The report genre allows for some elements of historical texts, but can also bring in biographical language as well as conversational language with quotes. The options for presenting Québec cultural narrative with beginner-level language are rich.

Text 3.16
Reportage -Montréal: vivre en français
   Parler français, dans une ambiance française, mais sur le continent américain, est-ce-que c'est possible? Bien sûr!

> Il y a près de chez vous un territoire francophone. C'est la province de Québec, au Canada. Dans cette région, le français est la langue officielle des administrations, du travail, du commerce et des communications.
>
> Combien de membres représente cette communauté? Six millions de personnes. Très actives et passionnément francophiles, elles désirent protéger leur héritage culturel français.
>
> Étudiante américaine, Deborah étudie le français à l'université de Montréal pour devenir professeur. Tous les jours, elle lit 'Le journal de Montréal' ou 'La presse.' À la télévision, elle regarde des programmes français proposés par le Réseau de l'Information (RDI).
>
> Elle aime se promener dans les rues tranquilles de la vieille ville. «J'ai l'impression d'être en Europe» dit-elle. On comprend pourquoi: Montréal a été fondé par les Français en 1642. Ses origines sont évidentes dans son architecture, dans les noms des rues, dans le Vieux-Port. Mais surtout, à Montréal, on attache une importance essentielle à la beauté de l'environnement et à la qualité de vie. Exactement comme à Paris, à Rome, ou à Madrid. (Amon et al., 2004, p. 103)

Such combinations of syntactic characteristics are found in other genres which appear with less frequency in connection with Québec's cultural narrative in the textbooks. There are a few letters, which can also have some of the characteristics of historical narrative and casual conversation, depending on the topic. Artistic genres such as excerpts from literature, poems, and song lyrics which appear in small numbers similarly combine the two types of genres to create something unique.

Another genre that can be expressed and that can elicit a variety of types of language are those invented for language learning. Invented genres, particularly in the 2000s, take the form of new genres that have been curated from several different ones. Such mixing of genres is evident in the books of the 2000s, where it was impossible to give a single genre classification to many of the sections on Québec. I will return to an example of one such textbook in Chap. 5, where I examine in more depth the complete picture of Québec's cultural narrative in five of the textbooks.

5   Conclusion

This chapter offered substance to the idea of teaching language and culture at the beginning level through the use of textbook analysis. To gain a substantive, useable analysis, Byrnes et al.'s (2010) observation is that genres are essential for seeing the connection between language and culture. From this theoretical basis, I was able to transcend the limiting approach to content and language often taken for materials development in the first-year course.

Instead I was able to characterize the linguistic construction of aspects of Québec's cultural narrative for beginning-level French students. Two genres that are prevalent in first-year textbooks were examined through the use of examples from the textbooks. Such an analysis is particularly rich for materials developers hoping to sequence presentation of language in a manner that is appropriate for language learning. It is useful because of the linguistic analysis in systemic functional linguistics that provides a conception of grammar and grammatical development from the perspective of how language is used to create meaning. It is the meanings of cultural narrative that I was concerned with in this chapter, and I was therefore able to draw upon the systemic functional analysis of history texts (Coffin, 2006), as Byrnes et al. (2010) did in their analysis, and on meanings entailed in the social construction of cultural narrative in conversation by relying on the analysis of Eggins and Slade (1997). The systematic basis for analysis of how language creates meaning (Martin & Rose, 2003, 2008) provides a good foundation for understanding first-year textbooks. The same social-semiotic perspective informs the analysis of how nonlinguistic visuals make meaning in textbooks in the next chapter.

References

Amon, E., Muyskens, J. A., & Omaggio Hadley, A. C. (2004). *Vis-à-vis: Beginning french*. Boston: McGraw Hill.

Byrnes, H., Maxim, H. H., & Norris, J. M. (2010). Realizing advanced foreign language writing: Development in collegiate education: Curricular design, pedagogy, assessment. *The Modern Language Journal, 94*(Supplement), 1–221.

Chapelle, C. A. (2014). Five decades of Canadian and Québec content in French textbooks in the United States. *American Review of Canadian Studies, 44*(4), 415–432.

Coffin, C. (2006). *Historical discourse: The language, time, cause and evaluation.* London: Continuum.

Comeau, R. F., & Lamoureux, N. J. (1982). *Échanges: première année de français.* New York: Holt, Rinehart and Winston.

Eggins, S., & Slade, D. (1997). *Analyzing casual conversation.* London: Equinox.

Hagiwara, M. P., & De Rocher, F. (1985). *Thème et variations: An introduction to French language and culture* (3rd ed.). New York: Wiley.

Jarvis, G. A., Bonin, T. M., Corbin, D. E., & Birckbichle, D. W. (1980). *Connaître et se connaître: A basic reader for communication* (2nd ed.). New York: Holt, Rinehart, and Winston.

Lenard, Y. (1977). *Parole et pensée: Introduction au français d'aujourd'hui.* New York: Harper and Row.

Magnan, S. S., Berg, W. J., Martin-Berg, L., & Ozzello, Y. (2007). *Paroles* (3rd ed.). Hoboken, NJ: Wiley Custom Services.

Martin, J. R., & Rose, D. (2003). *Working with discourse: Meaning beyond the clause.* London/New York: Bloomsbury Publishing.

Martin, J. R., & Rose, D. (2008). *Genre relations: Mapping culture.* London: Equinox.

Modern Language Association of America. (2007). *Foreign languages and higher education: New structures for a changed world: MLA ad hoc committee on foreign languages.* New York: Author.

Muyskens, J. A., Omaggio, A. C., Chalmers, C., Imbarton, C., & Almeras, P. (1982). *Rendez-vous: An invitation to French.* New York: Random House.

Oates, M. D., Oukada, L., & Altman, R. (1991). *Entre amis: An interactive approach to first-year French.* Boston: Houghton Mifflin.

Ollivier, J., Morran, M., & Howard, C. M. (1983). *Appel: initiation au français.* New York: Harcourt Brace Jovanovich.

Pucciani, O. F., & Hamel, J. (1983). *Langue et langage: le français par le français.* New York: Holt, Rinehart, and Winston.

Singerman, A. J. (Ed.). (1996). *Acquiring cross-cultural competence: Four stages for students of French.* Lincolnwood, IL: National Textbook Company.

Siskin, H. J., Williams-Gascon, A., & Field, T. T. (2007). *Débuts: An introduction to French.* Boston: McGraw-Hill.

Valdman, A. (1975). *Langue et culture: A basic course in French.* New York: Macmillan.

Valdman, A., Barnett, M. A., Holekamp, E., Laronde, M., Magnan, S. S., & Pons, C. (1986). *En route: introduction au français et au monde francophone.* New York: Macmillan.

4

Québec Content in Images

One way that content is conveyed in foreign language textbooks is through the use of images consisting of photographs, line drawings, reproductions of paintings, and maps. Such images can convey important cultural meanings, but they also have a cosmetic value for the textbooks. Images break up the text, adding visual input of a different type and drawing students' attention to particular aspects of culture or other content. The images in the beginning-level textbooks across all five decades from 1960 to 2010 show people, places, and cultural symbols. These images were selected by textbook producers, but what kind of meanings did they choose to convey? How are these meanings intended to contribute to the language and culture learning of textbooks users? How have the meanings changed over time? This chapter addresses these questions by examining the use of images in French textbooks to convey Canadian and Québec content. It builds on the quantitative overview of images in the textbooks presented in Chap. 2 by examining what is presented in images, how it is presented, and how the presentation changes across the decades. This qualitative analysis draws upon a social-semiotic perspective of visual design (Kress & van Leeuwen, 2006), which provides an

© The Editor(s) (if applicable) and The Author(s) 2016

C.A. Chapelle, *Teaching Culture in Introductory Foreign Language Textbooks*, DOI 10.1057/978-1-137-49599-0_4

analytic framework for describing how images communicate certain messages and how they work together with text to create meaning.

1   Why Study Images?

Foreign language textbook producers and teachers today have access to unlimited quantities of images—still and video—on the Internet that they can use to create activities for students. The importance of such images in teaching culture predates this extraordinary supply. In the 1980s, Lafayette observed,

> Every modern-day textbook includes an abundance of attractive photographs taken in the target countries as well as illustrations of a variety of realia. There is often a higher incidence of culture in photographs and realia than in the printed exercises and texts found in the book. Unfortunately, these visuals are rarely mentioned in class and are almost never supported in the text by culturally related exercises and activities. (Lafayette, 1988, p. 53)

Lafayette (1988) suggested techniques that teachers could use to capitalize on the messages to be found in textbook images including questions that prompt students to engage in description, information gathering, and comparison.

These suggestions are useful for working with textbook images but the issue today extends beyond talking about images already placed in textbooks. Teachers and materials developers need sufficient knowledge to be able to exercise their agency in selecting images. However, as Risager (1991) observed, many language teachers are lacking in the fundamental knowledge and skills required for representing what she calls the socio-cultural (i.e., nonlinguistic) aspects of the language course in which images play a central role. Despite the importance language teachers place on the nonlinguistic aspects, 'the socio-cultural domain is characterized by amateurism. Normally, teachers and authors have not had the education and the materials needed to deal systematically with the sociological and anthropological field, and to clarify what themes and approaches are suited or necessary at the elementary level' (Risager, p. 182). The scope of Risager's observation extends beyond the selection of images for inclusion in language teaching materials, but images are clearly central in representation of the social and cultural world that is part of foreign language teaching.

Over the past twenty years, the need for sophistication on the part of the profession has grown with the expanding options for teachers and materials developers. However, it is difficult to find evidence that materials developers have cultivated their expertise in selection of visuals. A recent study of images in two EFL textbooks was equally critical of the textbook developers' use of visuals. Distinguishing between denotational and connotational meaning in images, Weninger and Kiss (2013) criticized the extensive denotational use of images and argued that images should play an important role in raising issues of cultural connotation and in promoting cultural reflection.

> Images need to be much more than mere visual reinforcement or space-fillers. They need to be utilized as icons or symbols of things in their own right, as the explicit focus of attention in a meaningful pedagogic task, and as entry points for critical discussion about students' cultural beliefs and stereotypes, complemented by task and text that foster awareness and reflection. This is all the more important given the fundamental role of images in (mediated) communication (Kress, 2010; Kress & Van Leeuwen, 2006). (Weninger & Kiss, 2013, p. 711)

The four examples they provided showed the missed opportunities for critical cultural reflection as images of food, housing, and characters in traditional national dress provided visual supports for the items in the text and the learning activities. The textbook producers had left the images themselves unexamined, as Lafayette (1988) had found over twenty years earlier.

Weninger and Kiss (2013) were looking for textbook images that prompt critical discussion about cultural beliefs, awareness, and reflection, but how are textbook authors and teachers to create such materials? What kind of cultural teaching work are images capable of contributing to? Can aspects of cultural narrative be expressed in images? If improvements in the profession's capacity for designing visual aspects of instruction are to be achieved, a stronger basis is needed for understanding past and current practice. Textbook analysis should be able to contribute to improving understanding if samples of textbooks are large enough, the textbooks are of sufficient quality, and the analysis adequate to the task at hand.

This analysis reported in this chapter contributes to this goal by pioneering the systematic study of language textbook images in a large sample of relatively high-quality textbooks extending over a period of time. The quantitative results presented in Chap. 2 show the variability in the quantity of textbook images within and across the decades. Like the qualitative analysis of texts in the previous chapter, the qualitative analysis of images needs to offer tools for explaining how meaning is conveyed through the combination of elements chosen by the textbook producer. The social-semiotic analogue to text analysis for images has been developed by Kress and van Leeuwen (2006). Their framework for analysis of meanings in images is used in this chapter to provide insight into how images of Canada and Québec make meaning in the French textbooks.

2   Theoretical Approach

In the previous chapter, I was able to draw upon the work of Byrnes, Maxim, and Norris (2010), who had applied social-semiotic analysis of text to the concrete issues of curriculum and materials development. Their use of social-semiotics, and specifically systemic-functional linguistics, yielded a wealth of concepts and formulations that were directly applicable to my textbook analysis and beyond. In the analysis of images, in contrast, I need to start at a point that is farther removed from the problem because researchers have not yet offered such a systematic approach in applying theory to practice for analysis of culture in foreign language textbook images. I therefore need to begin with a description of the perspective and basic tools to be used for the analysis. These are drawn from a more complex presentation of Kress and van Leeuwen's framework in their 2006 book entitled *Reading Images*, which Wodak and Meyer (2009) situate within the trajectory of critical discourse analysis as a framework that provides a means of analyzing the contribution of non-linguistic resources in making meaning.

Kress and van Leeuwen (2006) developed their social-semiotic methods for analysis of images by extending social-semiotic linguistic theory to the nonlinguistic to describe the way that nonlinguistic visual signs make meaning. From this perspective, the authors and editors who select and create images do so because they have a particular interest in representing meaning. Such meaning is expressed by what Kress and van Leeuwen refer to as the 'criterial aspect of the object' (p. 7). The 'object,' in fact, can be an actual object, but alternatively, it can also be an idea, concept, or message. With respect to images of Québec in the textbooks, the interest may be in showing the attractive historic distinction of the old city in Québec. The majority of the authors and editors that included Canadian images in the textbooks had such an interest. Many chose the Château Frontenac as the criterial aspect of the old city. The pictures are not identical because there are many different ways that facets of the building can be shown in a picture, but the criterial aspect of the historically charming old city is recognizable. This process of making meaning with images from Kress and van Leuveen's perspective consists of the process as shown in Fig. 4.1. The arrows can be read as 'results in' so that the figure says, 'The interest of the textbook producer results in selection of a criterial aspect of an object, which in turn results in representation of that aspect through the use of an image appearing in a textbook.'

This theoretical conception contains elements useful for the diachronic analysis of the images because it looks beneath the images to their core meanings (criterial aspects) and the motivation for the selection of the criterial aspects they are intended to represent (interest). Like a grammatical analysis of language that might describe noun phrase complexity

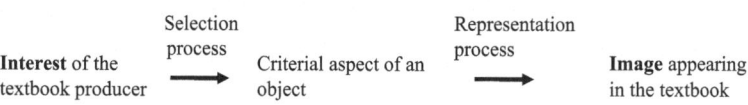

Fig. 4.1 Theoretical conception of the meaning making process resulting in textbook images

or verb tense, the image analysis can examine criterial aspects of objects in images. Consistent with social-semiotics, images do not have meaning but rather they are used to create meaning within a certain context (i.e., meaning is constructed socially). As Kress and van Leeuwen (2006) put it, 'In our view signs are never arbitrary, and "motivation" should be formulated in relations to the sign-maker and the context in which the sign is produced, and not in isolation from the act of producing analogies and classifications' (p. 8). The diachronic questions then can be posed about not only changes in the images, but also changes in criterial aspects, and interests of textbook producers. The whole image may contain many parts and aspects of design, but it is selected for its representation of what the designer sees as criterial. All the rest of the detail comes along with whatever is the criterial object. This perspective emphasizes the agency of the creator of images and the context in which they are created and interpreted.

In analyzing the images, however, it is the concrete elements of detail that need to be examined, and therefore a method of analysis has to provide a way of interpreting specific aspects of the detail in addition to identifying the criterial aspect. As an extension of systemic-functional linguistic theory, Kress and van Leeuwen (2006) are concerned with three types of functional meanings that can be expressed through image, as summarized in Table 4.1. Ideational meanings are about the identity of people, objects, and locations, the activity they are engaged in, as well as the locations and manner of their activity in the image. The ideational analysis examines the identity of people and places and the activity of the people. Interpersonal meanings express their proximity to each other in the picture and with the reader as indicated by their gaze, eye contact, distance from the camera, and camera position. Proximity includes engagement and attitude of people in the image, reflecting the extent to which the viewer remains an outsider looking at the other culture from a distance, or as someone invited into the world of the image. Textual meanings are those created by the coherence of elements within an image in addition to the coherence of the images to the visual and linguistic context of the page and the textbook as a whole. Table 4.1 summarizes the three types of functional meanings and presents the guiding questions they motivate for the analysis of the images.

Table 4.1 Types of functional meaning, potential aspects for analysis, and guiding questions for the qualitative analysis of images

Types of functional meaning	Potential aspects for analysis	Guiding questions
Ideational: What is going on	The identity of people, objects, and locations, the activity they are engaged in, the locations and manner of their activity	Who and what is pictured in the images? What are they doing? What locations are shown?
Interpersonal: The relationships and attitudes involved	The attitudes of people and their proximity to each other in the picture and with the reader as indicated by their gaze, eye contact, distance from the camera, and camera position.	What do the spatial positions of the people relative to each other and to the camera suggest about their relationship to each other and to the viewer? What do the eye contact of the pictured people and camera angle indicate about the engagement of the viewer with the picture (offer vs. demand)?
Textual: The internal and external coherence	The meaning created by positioning elements in the image in addition to the placement of the image on the page and its accompanying text	How do elements within the image cohere and guide the viewer's attention? How does placement of the image on the page with other images and text create meaning? How does the image work with the text on the page (including the image caption) to create meaning?

Conducting such an analysis of foreign language textbooks requires knowledge on the part of the analyst. Ideational meanings are about the identity of the people, places, and activity in the target culture. These ideational meanings in many cases are created multimodally through the use of both image and text, but in many cases an analysis of the significance—or triviality—of what is presented requires knowledge of what is culturally important. In the examination of the cultural content of Canada and Québec, for example, significant expressions of identity are presented by the textual identification of the people pictured in images as 'French Canadian,' 'Canadien,' 'Québécois,' or even as 'Canadian.' The significance of these different terms for identity is evident in the important events in Québec's cultural narrative. Images can display activity in everyday social situations, political events, or special performances and displays, for example, but recognizing the meaning of these requires cultural knowledge.

The analysis of interpersonal meanings also benefits from knowledge on the part of the analyst in addition to the three analytic categories Kress and van Leeuwen (2006) defined. The first is the degree of contact with the viewer that the people in the image display. People represented can engage in high contact with the viewer when they make eye contact with the camera. When a person in the image looks directly at the camera, Kress and van Leeuwen refer to the image as a 'demand' because the person in the image appears to be reaching out to engage with the viewer. With respect to presentation of culture in textbooks, such images may signify an invitation to readers to engage with the culture, come closer, or consider the identity and activity of the person in detail. In my analysis, therefore I consider high contact to be one indicator of high proximity of the image to the student reading the textbook.

Proximity is also indicated by the social distance of the images to the viewer, which is expressed through the distance of the camera to the photographed objects. Close social distance of people to the camera typically shows the face of one person, but can include more than one person. Medium distance shows more than the face and may contain other people in addition to possibly something in the setting. At medium distance the viewer can typically see what the people are doing and so the activity becomes part of the meaning of the image. A distant image shows primarily a landscape or setting, but can also contain people. The people are part of the setting, in this case, rather than being the criterial aspect of interest to the textbook producer.

A third aspect of interpersonal meaning is the subjective stance, which is expressed through the level of involvement of the photographer with the subjects of the photograph. The image shows a high degree of involvement when the image is taken as a frontal view. This view expresses the most proximate position for the viewer. The photographer's position indicates a low degree of involvement when the image is taken at an angle. An image taken at an angle expresses that the photographer (and therefore the viewer) is not in the same world as the people photographed, but rather is looking in at another world at a distance. The subjective distance between the photographer and the photographed creates a subjective distance between the viewer (the students reading the textbook) and the subjects of the photograph. The least proximity is expressed by what Kress and van Leeuwen (2006) refer to as an objective stance, which is typically seen in scientific-looking drawings that express facts. In the French textbooks, the most important of these are the maps that appear, particularly in the books of the 2000s, which show French speaking regions of the world. The three dimensions of interpersonal analysis used to assess the proximity of the images are summarized in Table 4.2.

My summary of Kress and van Leeuwen's (2006) seminal work moves directly from theory to analytic categories to be used in the analysis of images. In identifying the relevant categories, I have selected from what could be a much more complex analysis. For materials selection and development, the priority is to have useable categories that are relevant to cultural meaning in textbooks. These are summarized by the categories shown in Tables 4.1 and 4.2, which are provided to allow readers to refer back to the terms that are used throughout the analysis.

3   Qualitative Analysis of Image Content

A total of 312 images with Canadian or Québec content were identified in the 65 textbooks. This number creates a challenge for a qualitative framework for examining the semiotic potential of the images, but to make interpretations about change over the fifty-year period, it is necessary to begin with a sample rather than just a few images. I began the analysis by looking at all of the images to attempt to place them in categories based on the objects they represent. The collection consists of a variety of types of images including maps depicting Canada or Québec as

Table 4.2 Framework for analysis of the interpersonal meanings expressed by images containing people

Three dimensions of proximity	Options for each of the dimensions	Suboptions	Explanation of options
Contact with the viewer	High contact: gaze of the person(s) is directly at the viewer.		Person in the image looks directly at the camera. This is referred to as a 'demand' because the person in the image appears to be reaching out to engage with the viewer.
	No contact: there is no gaze at the viewer		The eyes of the people in the image are directed away from the camera.
Social distance from the viewer	Close-up		Proximity of the people to the camera shows the face of typically one person, but can include more than one person.
	Medium distance		Shows more than the face and may contain other people in addition to possibly something in the setting.
	Distant		Shows primarily a landscape or setting, but also contains people. The people are part of the setting, rather than being the focal element of the image.
Attitude expressed to the viewer	Subjectivity	Level of involvement	Ranges from <u>high degree of involvement</u> when the image is taken as a frontal view to a <u>low degree of involvement</u> when the image is taken at an angle.

(*continued*)

Table 4.2 (continued)

Three dimensions of proximity	Options for each of the dimensions	Suboptions	Explanation of options
		Degree of power	Ranges from <u>viewer power</u> when the image was taken from above to the contrasting <u>power of the photographed</u> over the viewer. Photographs can be taken at the same level, indicating equal power between the photographed and the viewer.
	Objectivity	Oriented toward action	A diagram, chart, or map often appearing as a front view showing how something works.
		Oriented toward knowledge	A diagram, chart, or map depicting theoretical knowledge reflecting omniscience.

Note. Summary developed from *Reading images: The grammar of visual design* by G. Kress and T. van Leeuwen, 2006, London, UK: Routledge.

a region where French is spoken, a variety of line drawing and sketches, scenes of streets sometimes with particular buildings, landscapes, people, iconic Canadian or Québec images, and political and historical images. This initial rough grouping of image content was a good orientation for me but too unprincipled to make sense of. Moreover, Kress and van Leeuwen's (2006) framework suggests an important distinction between images containing people, which have an important interpersonal dimension, and images of places which do not. For foreign language teaching, the interpersonal is clearly an important aspect of the meaning that one wants to be able to describe in an analysis. I therefore made two groups by distinguishing images containing people from those in which the criterial aspect is the place. There are people in some of the images where the cityscapes and landscapes are criterial, so the two groups are not mutually exclusive. I identified a third group containing images pertaining to Québec's cultural narrative, and these are examined in the following chapter.

4   People in Images

Textbook producers include images depicting the people who speak the language students are studying. Kress and van Leeuwen's (2006) analytic tools directed my attention to questions about who the people are, what they are doing, and where they are located. These three questions guide the ideational analysis, but I focus in particular on the first two features, the identity of the participants represented in the pictures and the activity they are engaging in. I focus on the faces and positioning of the people in the images with questions about their attitudes and proximity to each other in the picture and with the reader as indicated by their gaze, eye contact, distance from the camera, and camera position. In the 1960s, none of the textbooks contains images with people in Canada, but people are depicted in the images from the 1970s through the 2000s.

4.1   The 1970s

In the 1970s a total of twelve images across the eleven textbooks show people who can be recognized by viewers as Canadians or Québécois. Of the twelve images six come from one textbook, *Parole et Pensée* (Lenard, 1977), which is examined more closely in the final section of this chapter to look at their role in the text. In this section, I describe the characteristics of the images as a group in terms of their ideational, interpersonal meanings.

4.1.1   Ideational Analysis: Identity and Activity

The ideational analysis examines who the people are, what they are doing, and where they are. In only two of the images were the specific identity of the represented person named. In *C'est la vie* (Pimsleur, 1970), two images show the weight lifter from Québec named Claude Hardy, and his name is given in the caption of one of the images. It shows him with his son, who is practicing his weight lifting and the caption reads, 'Claude Hardy et son fils' (p. 33). The images accompany a short vignette in which Claude Hardy is in a conversation in a Tavern in Québec, and he is identified as coming from Château-Richer, which the reader presumes is in Québec. In one of the images in *Parole et pensée* (Lenard, 1977), an artist drawing a portrait is shown with a caption that identifies him as 'un artiste québecois' so his identity is named more specifically than in any other of the images in the 1970s textbooks. The criterial aspect of the Claude Hardy pictures is the specific person, but the criterial aspect of the picture of the artist is defined by what the person is doing rather than who the person is. In these pictures, however, the national identity of the pictured people is clearly marked as Québécois.

In contrast, none of the other images specifies the people as Québécois. Instead, in the other images, the criterial aspect is the activity the people are doing because what they are doing signals the roles they are playing in Canada. In two images, Canadians in appropriate uniform are playing hockey and playing in a marching band, respectively. The hockey game in black and white with no caption is not explicitly marked as to what teams are playing, but the accompanying dialogue between French tourists at the game makes reference to one team being from Québec. In another image, the marching band is clearly marked for nationality with a very large Canadian flag (red and white with a maple leaf) held high above.

The six images in *Parole et Pensée* (Lenard, 1977) include images depicting scenes from the tourist area of old Québec and displays of agriculture produced in Québec. Two of them show a horse drawn carriage available to tourists for transportation. The person most visible in these is the carriage driver. Another is the picture of an artist outdoors in Old Québec who is drawing the portrait of the child seated in front of him. The fourth pictures a soldier in costume with the regiment mascot, a goat, at the Citadel, a fort and museum that tourists can visit in Québec. As shown in Fig. 4.2, the people in the agricultural displays play the role of producers, standing behind their fabrics and apples, respectively.

Two images in *French Language and Lifestyles* (Hagiwara & De Rocher, 1985) show street scenes in Québec and Montreal, respectively. The picture of a street in Québec shows three women and a man who walks

Fig. 4.2 'Cet jeune fille vend des objets tissués à la main' (Lenard, 1977, no page number).

with his arms around two of the women. The caption reads, 'Des jeunes gens sur la rue Sainte Anne à Québec' (p. 183). The picture of the street in Montreal, also with people, does not refer to the people in the caption, instead identifying the picture as 'Le vieux quartier à Montréal' (p. 185). Although both of these images contain people, the criterial aspect is the place where the people are located rather than the people themselves.

4.1.2   Interpersonal Analysis: Proximity

The interpersonal analysis of these images reveals the degree of contact the image makes with the viewer, its social distance, and the attitude expressed—all of which contribute to the proximity of the image to the viewer. With respect to eye contact, none of the people in the images directs his or her gaze at the viewer. Instead, the represented participants are engaged in playing hockey, drawing a model, or lifting weights, for example. The lack of eye contact of the two Canadians standing behind their respective products, apples and fabrics, are particularly noteworthy. Their gaze is set off to the left so as not to detract from the criterial aspect of the image—the products of Canada. The caption of the image containing the apples expresses in language the message conveyed by the eyes of the producer: 'Le Canada produit des pommes en quantité' [Canada produces a lot of Apples.] The person represents Canada. The woman in the other photo has a similar stance, but the caption to the image says, 'Cet jeune fille vend des objets tissués à la main' [This young woman sells hand-made items.] The caption acknowledges her as a person in the picture, but she remains unnamed, her position is distant, and her gaze is into the distance. The lack of eye contact with Canadians in the 1970s texts positions viewers as observers of a distant culture whose people do not look our way to demand our attention or invite our engagement with their eyes.

The social distance depicted in the images similarly does not invite viewers too close to the Canadian and Québec characters represented. The single close-up in the images of the 1970s pictures is a close view of the horse's face while he gets a drink of water from a fountain. The humans are pictured in the background with sunglasses on. The horse, Bobby, plays a role in the dialogue given in the text, as does the carriage driver, whom we see at a distance in this and another picture. In all of the pictures the viewer's distance from the person pictured is sufficient to see what the people are doing, or what they have done in the case of the images of the products, and what they are wearing. In each case, the people are doing something that shows their role as a type of Canadian, a carriage driver, an artist, an athlete, and the minder of the goat mascot. Each of the latter three is wearing a uniform consistent with his role. Only the people walking on the street in the images in *French Language and Lifestyles* (Hagiwara & De Rocher, 1985) have the appearance of ordinary people on the street in Québec.

The attitude expressed to the viewer through the angle of the images suggests a moderate level of involvement. The hockey game picture in *A la française* (Clarke & Holt editorial staff, 1974) appears to have been taken from a frontal view, as does the image of the four people walking on the street. In each case, the viewer could be there, watching the game in the stands or greeting the people on the street as they walk toward the viewer. The other images are shot from an angle, placing the viewers in the position of observer of a world that he or she is not a part of. The other aspect of attitude, power, as depicted through the high, even, or low angle of the images, appears as neutral in most of the images. The exceptions are the images, of the producers, whom we see as distant but pictured from below with their products in the foreground. This lends an additional measure of distance to these images as the producers appear slightly above the viewer and their respective products.

4.2   The 1980s

In the 1980s, the ideational content expressing who the people are, what they are doing, and where they are located became somewhat richer. Across the twenty-three textbooks, twenty-three images contained people. However, thirteen of the images appear in one textbook, *Son et Sens* (Valdman, MacMillin, Lavergne, & Gahaka, 1984), and the other ten are spread across seven of the twenty-three textbooks.

4.2.1   Ideational Analysis: Identity and Activity

In contrast to the 1970s when the only authentic Canadian character pictured was the weight lifter Claude Hardy, in the 1980s, authors and editors began to include images of historical and political figures. One of the historical figures was Jacques Cartier, the French discoverer of Canada. Another significant French character was Charles de Gaulle, French president, whose appearance in Montreal in 1967 was a historical moment of cultural narrative because of his encouragement for the Québec independence movement. Both of these figures were French, but are recognized as playing an important role in Québec. The two other pictured people were Québécois, René Lévesque, the political leader whose party put forward the 1980 referendum on sovereignty and Gilles Vigneault, a singer and poet who was active throughout the Quiet Revolution and sovereignty movement in Québec. The caption under the picture of René Lévesque reads, 'René Lévesque, chef du Parti Québecois,' and the text that accompanies the image is a dialogue in which one character expresses a statement about identity, 'Nous Québecois, nous sommes fiers' (p. 447). The image of Gilles Vigneault in *Accent* (Mondelli, François, & Terry, 1984) names him directly as 'Le chanteur Québecois' (p. 304) (Fig. 4.3).

The 1980s textbooks introduce two other types of identities. One is a named individual who is introduced in the textbook, but is unknown as a public figure. Such ordinary people are the selection or invention of the textbook producer. *Allon-y!* (Bragger & Rice, 1988, p. 442), for example, shows Michel Paramas, introducing him by name in the caption. The lengthy caption also provides the information that he is from Nova Scotia, and that he is living in Ottawa, where he is studying for his doctorate and preparing to be a French teacher.

A second type of identity that appeared for the first time in the 1980s was in pictures of groups with historical significance in Québec's history. *Rendez-vous* (Muysken, Omaggio, Chalmers, Imbarton, & Almeras, 1982) contains a reproduction of a drawing named with the caption

Fig. 4.3 'Le chanteur Québecois' (Mondelli et al., 1984, p. 304)

'Coureurs des bois au Canada' (p. 444) with an explanation of the role of these 'French adventurers in the New World' (p. 444). In *Connaître et se connaître* (Jarvis, Bonin, Corbin, & Birchbichler, 1980), a cartoon sequence of several frames contains drawings of the French explorers accompanying Jacques Cartier and the indigenous Iroquois whom they met in Canada (p. 142). *Horizons* (Bennett, Bennett, Joiner, & Shinall, 1984) contains a page with two images, each containing a crowd whose identity is marked by the symbol that the people are holding. One image contains a group holding the Canadian flag with its maple leaf, whereas the second holds a poster with a map of Québec. The poster displays the slogan, 'prends ton pays en mains' [take control of your country] (p. 345). The two images are intended to show distinct identities of the two groups drawn along political lines, that is, one group that sees itself as Canadian and a the other as Québécois. The composition of this page is a rare instance of a visual display showing the controversy and political conflict surrounding the referenda in Québec.

Other Canadians shown in the 1980s remain unknown and unnamed. One image in *Horizons* (Bennett et al., 1984) shows two people standing in the snow (p. 344). This appears on the page with two other images and the title, 'Le Québec,' is the only language on the page with the images. The people are assumed to live in Québec. An image in *Appel* (Ollivier, Morran, & Howard, 1983) shows a man with sunglasses on a quiet street, where the only identity marker is a mailbox in the foreground stating in French and in English, 'Poste Canada' and 'Canada Post' (p. 403). The page contains a short text entitled 'Le Français au Québec' which is used as an exercise in forming negative sentences. The identity of the man, who is wearing sunglasses, is not given in the text. A similar type of scene is presented in *Echanges*, where viewers see a person on the street. This picture, however, has a caption, 'Une rue à Québec,' and in the background is the Chateau Frontenac, an iconic Québec symbol. In this picture and one in *Rendez-vous* (Muysken et al., 1982, p. 40), captioned 'Place Jacques Cartier à Montréal,' people are in the picture, but their identity is not what the picture communicates. The picture is about the place. In *Son et sens* (Valdman et al., 1984) a range of activities is shown across the many images. The activities include singing, attending a child's birthday party, walking on the street, shopping, engaging in political activity, and participating in a variety of entertainment and sports events.

4.2.2 Interpersonal Analysis: Proximity

The analysis of interpersonal meaning in the 1980s images shows slightly more engagement with viewers than the images of the 1970s, not through proximity of the camera, but through eye contact made in five of the images. In all of the images except five of the twenty-five, the people have their gaze set away from the camera, focused on what they are doing rather than on inviting engagement on the part of the viewer. The social distance in these images, except for one close-up of singer Gilles Vigneault, is in the mid-range or even distant. The one close-up does not make eye contact, but rather shows Vigneault engaged in his singing with his gaze pointed elsewhere (Fig. 4.3). People who appear to look directly at the viewer are pictured from a distance. In three of the cases, a careful look is required by the viewer in order to make a judgment as to whether or not the skier and the man walking down the street appear to actually look into the camera. Only two of the images show Canadians posed for full-length picture taking with their eyes on the camera.

The attitude expressed in terms of the level of involvement and degree of power through camera positioning varies throughout the 1980s collection of images. The front view of image is difficult to detect because of the various actions and possible points of the center front in each of the images where no single face with direct eye contact can be considered to mark the middle center of the image. The exception is the two images where the people make eye contact; in those the camera appears to be straight in front of the pictured people, reinforcing the high level of engagement through an appearance of involvement and equality. In the other images, the camera sits at various degrees of angular positioning. For example, the viewer looks up and at a slight angle to Gilles Vigneault and Charles de Gaulle, giving them less involvement and more power as stars on their respective stages. The image of de Gaulle actually shows the balcony from which he addressed the crowd in 1967, whereas Vigneault appears with only a microphone. The angle of the camera accomplishes the rest of the powerful effect. The many sports and entertainment events pictured in *Son et sens* (Valdman et al., 1984) show athletes and performers in action at various lateral angles as well as images from above or below. The overall effect is to portray these Canadian activities without strong attitudinal involvement and without a consistent message about power difference. Their number and variety in this text have a similar effect. Of the fourteen images with people in *Son et sens* (Valdman et al., 1984), the birthday party picture stands out because of a combination of its size and attitude conveyed. The camera is as close as may be possible to the center of the action, the child blowing out the birthday candles. Had the photographer taken an eye-level position, however, the viewer would have likely missed the engaged gazes of the several people attending the event. The slightly raised angle gives the viewer the maximum view of what is going on. And what is going on is notably different from the sports events, performances, and costumed performers in the other pictures. There is a real-life back yard in Canada that the viewer is shown as an observer.

Another interesting use of attitude resources appears on a page on *Horizons* (Bennett et al., 1984) where the message is about the defeat of the 1980 referendum on sovereignty. The intent of the placement of two pictures on the page is to depict two sides in the issue, the winning side carrying the flag with the maple leaf and the other side with sad faces and posters. The message is conveyed in a number of ways one of which is the angle of the camera, which is nearly straight ahead and at equal level with the crowd holding the maple leaf flag. This photo is the one that first catches the viewers' attention. The involvement is high, and the viewer is afforded just enough power, that is, height above the crowd, to see the immense size of the crowd. The support for this side is clearly large, viewers can see. The second photo on the page requires the viewer to look up and left (the opposite from the normal gaze for readers of English or French). The angle shown on the several people in the picture is clearly from the side. The protesters with their signs are not directly facing the camera. The angle does not invite involvement; is suggests that the viewers remain at a distance from what is going on there. These protesters carry a sign with a map and writing on it. They do not have a flag. Their message looks complicated and they look sad. Moreover, there are not very many of them. The viewer does not get the same angle of view as he or she sees in the other image so it is unknown how many people might be in this crowd. The contrasting happy/sad messages that appear on the faces of the people in each picture clearly express the intended meaning about the winning and losing side. The author and editors' selection of images with these particular subjective characteristics of attitude express the realities of the winners and losers in the 1980 referendum vote.

4.3 The 1990s

4.3.1 Ideational Analysis: Identity and Activity

In the 1990s, ideational content pertaining to known figures in Canada is limited to a single image of Brian Mulroney, a former Prime Minister of Canada, giving a speech at what appears to be a political event. The text does not reveal the significance of Mulroney for Québec or French, but a search on the Internet shows that he served as Canadian Prime Minister during some of the difficult, ultimately unsuccessful negotiations between the federal and Québec governments. He also earned his law degree at Laval in Québec and was completely bilingual; thus, a good example of the porous nature of what is portrayed elsewhere as the federal versus Québec divide.

Four images show close-up shots of people who are designated as Canadians, and one of these is a student at University of Montreal. He is reading a book, but the other three are simply being photographed. There is another photograph of students working in a laboratory at the University of Montreal. In nine of the images, the criterial element is the location, for example, the street, the campus, or the ice arena where the picture is taken rather than the people, so the people are going about their business of walking, sitting at a café, or playing sports. As shown in Fig. 4.4, one of the nine, *Voilà!* (Heilenman, Kaplan, & Tournier, 1989), shows the people stopped for a pose, a man and a woman, each standing with an instrument of snow removal in hand, with the backdrop of the snow-covered street in Montreal (p. 138).

Fig. 4.4 'Quel temps fait-il à Montréal en janvier? Montréal, Canada' (Heilenman, et al., 1989, p. 138)

4.3.2   Interpersonal Analysis: Proximity

The interpersonal analysis looks for eye contact with the viewer, which appears in three of the images. One is the picture of the snow shovelers who look directly at the camera for their picture (Fig. 4.4). A second is a gray bearded man, whose caption reads 'Le Québec.' What we see of him in the close-up picture is a heavy coat and a big hat. His gaze demands that the viewer look at him, but doing so raises questions for the viewer about who this unfamiliar person is and in why he has been chosen to represent Québec. The third one is a drawing of a human dressed as a waiter with food in hand who looks directly at the viewer. Eyes are difficult to discern in all but four of the other images because of the distance where the people in the other pictures are positioned. In the four where the eyes are evident, three show people intensely engaged in what they are doing at the political event (Mulroney talking to a listening audience) and at the university (eyes on the experiment in the lab or on the book being read). In the fourth, the Canadian's gaze is focused on an unknown distant object to the left of the camera.

The social distance is close for four of the pictures, as indicated above, but overall the images depict a great deal of variety in terms of social distance.

Of the seventeen images containing people, four are close-ups, four are shot from a medium distance, and the rest are at a distance. In the images shot at a distance, the criterial subject is the place rather than the people, and in the 1990s viewers see places populated with people rather than Canadians in unknown or imprecisely named places (e.g., a street in Québec). The places shot at a distance in the 1990s include the campuses of the Université Laval and McGill University, Terre des Hommes in Montreal, and Vieux Montreal, and the winter carnival (which takes place in Québec City). In these distant photographs of places in Québec, the viewer can see people walking, browsing, or experiencing the place, but the people are not the criterial aspect of the image. The image is about place.

The level of involvement varies across images in the 1990s, with the highest involvement in two of the images where eye contact is made. In each of these, including the drawing of a server at a restaurant who invites viewers in, the camera looks straight at the person. In all of the other images, the level of involvement varies with camera angles that keep the viewer in the position of a tourist and outsider looking in at places and people who do not connect with the viewer directly. The angles, however, vary from the street at the Université Laval where the viewer could step onto the snowy street and walk toward the people to one of the street scenes where the angle allows only for viewing the street, where distant people sit at charming cafés.

The viewer is given power particularly in some of the touristic scenes, where in order to see what is going on, the viewer needs to be elevated above the normal eye level. The viewers look down upon the winter carnival, the ice-skating on the river, and the shoppers in Vieux Montreal. Other photos do not use height to make an expression of power with the exception of Brian Mulroney at a political event. Mulroney stands above the camera, which views him from the side. The power is his, and the involvement is low. The viewer is watching—not invited to participate in—this Canadian political event.

4.4   The 2000s

In the 2000s, the overall number of images reached 188 in the sample and half of these included people, so the number of relevant images that could undergo qualitative analysis exceeded the desirable size for such analysis. Nevertheless, I examined all of the ninety-four images, drawing upon the same categories to attempt to detect any qualitative changes in the nature of the images. The greater number of images resulted in additional variety in both ideational and interpersonal meanings.

4.4.1   Ideational Analysis: Identity and Activity

In the 2000s, ideational content includes many images containing people engaged in the ordinary activities of walking on the street, shopping, sitting at cafés, and participating in sports. Many of these images are shot at a distance, and the locations are named so the viewer sees people filling their roles in particular locations. Still others contain the simple caption 'Au Québec' such that the viewer sees an example of what Québec looks like in some unknown location. The message is 'This is Québec.' In the 2000s for the first time literary figures appear among the small number of Canadians introduced through images. There are two instances of Gabrielle Roy pictured (in the same text, *Paroles*) and a picture of Ann Hébert. Singers Linda Lamy and Céline Dion are also introduced in photos as is a drawing of Felix Leclerc. Hockey hero Maurice Richard is also pictured in cartoon form and in a photograph. Historical figures, Jacques Cartier and Samuel Champlain, discoverers of Canada and Québec, respectively, are pictured. No political figures appear in the books in the 2000s.

In the 2000s, like in previous decades, many unnamed Canadian people appear in the images as well as a few people who are introduced. In *Débuts*, two lovers from 1939 who began as pen pals during the war are introduced with their pictures. Paul Tremblay and his family are introduced with his picture, a line drawing of this family, and some biography. In addition, the 2000s introduces another type of person through images, a Canadian who appears repeatedly through the text. In *Débuts* (Siskin, Williams-Gascon, & Thomas, 2007), the character is Hélène Thibaut, who plays the role of a journalist who is working on a story that keeps her reappearing throughout the textbook in images ten times. Hélène then accounts for nine of the twelve Canadian images in the text. The other three images are of the two lovers from 1939, and an image of a guide or teacher teaching a class in a park outdoors. In other words, despite the number of images counted and the apparent coherence created in the text by the story and repetition of Hélène's image, the images do not contribute to conveying ideational content about Canada and Québec.

Mais Oui (Thompson & Phillips, 2004) is the other textbook that uses character repetition, in this case through the multiple appearances of Isabelle from Québec. The exact same image is repeated nine times throughout the chapters as she (along with francophones from other countries) appears in the text and provides her perspective on a number of issues. The multiple appearances of Isabelle create cohesion for the reader, who becomes acquainted with not only the face of a québécoise person but also some of her interests and perspectives. The multimodal creation of meaning about an ordinary québécois(e) person appears for the first time in the 2000s. In *Mais oui!* (Thompson & Phillips), the introduction of Isabelle does not replace the appearance of other images of Canada and Québec. This text also contains some other images with cultural ideational meaning across multiple categories.

4.4.2   Interpersonal Analysis: Proximity

With the relatively larger number of images in the 2000s sample than in previous years, one might expect a stronger level of engagement through eye contact with the people, close social distance, and high involvement and equality of power. In fact, this expectation is met in *Mais Oui* (Thompson & Phillips, 2004) through the person of Isabelle (Fig. 4.5), who appears not only frequently but also in a close-up photo, taken straight on (not from an angle) and at the same level (not from above or below). Three other Canadian characters appear in the 2000s, two in *Espaces* (Mitschke, Tano, & Thiers-Thiam, 2007) and one in *Horizons* (Bennett et al., 1984), but these characters are not developed in the same depth as is Isabelle in *Mais oui!* (Thompson & Phillips). They are identified as Canadians and pictured.

The other people who make eye contact are distant in some ways that may limit the extent to which they can reach out to the viewer. One type of such people are the famous singer, Linda Lamy, authors, Ann

Fig. 4.5 Isabelle, a québécoise character in *Mais oui!* (Thompson & Phillips, 2004, p. 370)

Hébert and Gabrielle Roy, and hockey star, Maurice Richard. These stars appear in their photos looking at the camera, but the photos are from other times, places, and for different purposes. The people are too far removed to make genuine eye contact with first-year French students. Other photos which make eye contact across the distance of time are the photos of the 1939 young people who corresponded during the war. Their photos introduce their historic story of connection during a long ago war. The rather exotic-looking man with a gray beard and sheep skin coat and hat labeled as 'Québec' in *Chez nous* (Valdman & Pons, 1997) also makes eye contact, but this image raises more questions about his identity than it creates bonds of closeness. The other eye contact that appears in the 2000s is with characters with low modality (or realness); they are the line drawings of a protester for language rights in *Deux mondes* (Terrell, Rogers, Kerr, & Spielmann, 2005), the drawing of the Tremblay family in *Paralleles* (Foulerier-Smith & Zottee, 2000), and a whimsical overlay of le Bonhomme de Carnaval with the city behind him. These human-like figures make eye contact, but because of their own low modality the eye contact may have less effect in creating closeness with the reader.

With respect to social distance, the relatively large number of photos accurately predicts a variety of examples across the spectrum of social distance. Through the 2000s, viewers see Canadians pictured across the range of levels of social distance. At close range but without eye contact, viewers see Hélène Thibaut doing her journalism work, Céline Dion holding her baby, and Paul Tremblay, the father in a typical Canadian family, in a spontaneous-looking position. The viewer gets a close look without being invited in visually through eye contact. At mid-distance, viewers can see what people are doing. The activities are similar to those shown in the 1980s and 1990s including both the ordinary strolling through scenic city streets, sitting at cafés, and playing hockey as well as the exceptional participation in events at the winter carnival and performances. There are also plenty of examples of the people serving as the expected participants in a place which in the 2000s is often named. Places include La rue du Trésor à Québec and Petit Séminaire de Québec, École d'architecture, Université Laval.

Some of the images in the 2000s could be seen as high involvement as the camera appears to have been situated looking straight ahead so that the viewer can have the sensation of being there. The large majority of images, however, give the viewer a position of an observer with the camera at an angle so the viewer only watches Canada from the sidelines. The majority of images in the 2000s depict the representation of Canada with power equal to that of the viewer. There are some exceptions, however, when the viewer needs a bit of a lift to see the intended scene, such as the ones shown in *Espaces* (Mitschke et al., 2007, p. 427) of an independence protest, where the crowd is visible only from above, and the street in Québec, where the shops and their visitors are evident from a raised position. In such cases, the high vantage point allows the viewer the position of an outsider with the privileged view of what is happening. In some other cases, the people represented in the images have the position of power, particularly where images of performers are presented (Linda Lamy, Cirque du Soleil). Another case where the image is afforded higher power is one showing Québec flags carried by people in front of a government building in *Entre amis* (Oates & Oukada, 2006, p. 84). The camera appears to be slightly below the flags, which are clearly the focal elements in the image, and the messages conveyed by the images are about the power of Québec.

4.5   Summary of People in Images

The chronological analysis of the images with people shown in Table 4.3 reveals some changes that are useful for understanding the changing work that images have done in the textbooks over the five decades. In the 1960s Canada and Québec have no face at all. None of the pictures in the 1960s textbooks depicts Canadians. Canadians make their first appearance in the images of textbooks in the 1970s, when the people were pictured to represent Canadians performing institutional roles. The Canadians are kept at a distance from the readers, who observe what they are wearing and what they are doing, without the people pictured directing a gaze toward the viewer. The 1980s collection of images began to show more diversity of possibilities. Students are introduced to three important, historical characters (Jacques Cartier, Giles Vigneault, and René Lévesque) in addition to two people who pose for the camera as examples of Canadians. These two types of particulars—the famous Canadian and the example ordinary Canadian, are types of images that appear for the first time in the 1980s but continue through the following decades. In the 2000s, the ordinary Canadians are named and introduced in several cases. And the invented Isabelle in *Mais Oui!* (Thompson & Phillips, 2004) makes multiple appearances throughout the textbook so students can get to know her and her views (Table 4.3).

After the 1970s, the participants in the images begin to be shown in a variety of ordinary roles. People attend a child's birthday party, walk in the street, stroll the market, sit in the café, ice skate, and study at the university. Whereas in the 1970s, the largely unknown Canadians are playing institutional Canadian roles, beginning in the 1980s, students begin to see Canadians and Québécois in situ depicting activity accordingly. The proximity of people in the images also evolved after the 1970s to include more variety, showing some at a medium and far distance, and a few showing eye contact with the camera. In the 1990s, the social distance tends to be greater in many of the images and overall the places seem to be more important than the people's activity. In the 2000s with so many images, there is a wide variety in the way that the people are pictured. Still, only a few make direct eye contact with the camera, so the

Table 4.3 Summary of analysis of Canadian and Québec images of people

Category	1960s	1970s	1980s	1990s	2000s
Number of images	0	12	23	17	188
Identity		Primarily unnamed Canadians and Québecois	Four known figures and a character introduced in the text; others unknown	Unknown participants except one Canadian politician	Known artists figures introduced in text; unknown people; introduced fictional characters
Activity		Participants play institutional roles	Variety of activities: political, sports, every day activities	Every day activities: politics, sports, study, walking	Variety of activities
Proximity		Low proximity: no eye contact; no close shots; mostly angle vantage point	Variety of proximities: Several images with medium social distance; medium and far distance: shows what people are doing and who they are; a few with eye contact	Variety of proximities: A few images from medium and close distance; a few with eye contact, emphasis on place more than people	Variety of proximities: Some close-ups; one with eye contact

view of the student remains for the most part in the position of looking in at other people, a position that the student takes also for viewing places.

5   Places: Cityscapes and Landscapes

The second major group of images that appears in the textbooks is those showing places. These overlap to some degree with those containing people because images of people at a distance show them in a place. In many cases the criterial object is difficult to discern (people vs. place) because the people are pictured at a distance, but the place is not named or in some cases not even given a caption. Nevertheless, the potential for images of places may be to show students what important and ordinary places in Canada and Québec look like. In images of place, the participants can be people, streets, buildings, houses, restaurants, or other objects in the outdoors. My analysis in this section is concerned with ideational meaning, and specifically the identity of the places, the activity we can see in the places, and the proximity of the camera to the scene that is photographed. Each decade contains examples of both cityscapes and landscapes in the country, and the latter is considerably less frequent. I describe the scenes in terms of their identity, activity, and proximity for each of the decades beginning in the 1970s when these images began to appear.

5.1   The 1970s

In the 1970s eight of the images in textbooks showed places in Canada and Québec. One of these (13 %) was a country landscape and the other seven (87 %) showed city scenes. The identities of the images in the 1970s contain a range of general and unspecified places and specifically named places. Two (25 %) of the eight landscape images have no captions, but both are discernible to a knowledgeable viewer, one as the Québec parliament building with a decorative hedge with plantings spelling out 'Je me souviens', and the other as Place Jacques Cartier probably in Montreal. The captions in the other images identify some specific places pictured as,

'Le Château-Frontenac, La rue Saint-Anne à Québec, Le vieux quartier à Montréal,' the latter shown in Fig. 4.6. Other captions indicate what is in the picture, but with less precision. One with the caption 'Gaspé, Canada' shows a wide-angle landscape of a fishing village, and another shows a church that would not be recognizable except for the caption, 'Une église ultra-moderne à Québec.'

The activity in the 1970s cityscapes and landscapes is notably missing. Figure 4.6 shows the busiest of the Canadian and Québec images of the eight images. Rue Saint-Anne has people pictured as well, but Place Jacques Caritier is empty, as is the area in front of the Québec parliament building, the modern church, and even a picture of a border crossing point, where two cars are pictured, but they appear to be stopped and the viewer cannot see the people inside. The image with Le Château Frontenac shows an empty street except for a few cars, which may be parked. The image of Gaspé contains two tiny people standing still by their fishing boat, dwarfed by the hills rising above the water. Overall, the message from the pictures of cityscapes and landscapes is one of quiet.

Cityscapes and landscapes are almost by definition images that display a location at a distance. They provide an outsiders' view of a big picture.

Fig. 4.6 Image of Montreal street (Butturff & Coffman, 1976, p. 185)

Most of the pictures of places in the 1970s sample clearly qualify as providing such a view, although none shows a very distant cityscape. The exceptions are a few in the city, where the viewer sees people at a somewhat closer distance with the background of a city, as shown in Fig. 4.6, or where a certain building is the object of interest, such as the image showing the church.

5.2   The 1980s

In the 1980s, twenty-eight of the images in the textbooks showed places in Canada and Québec. Seven of these (25 %) were country landscapes and the other twenty-one (75 %) showed city scenes. Of the twenty-eight images, almost half contained no captions that would specify the identity of the object in the image for the students. Even the images that have captions, with a few exceptions, tend to identify the object(s) in a very general way, as shown in Fig. 4.7, for example. In this image, the iconic Château Frontenac appears in the distance, but is not named in the caption, which instead indicates that the viewer should interpret the image as a generic street in Québec. 'Une rue à Québec' the caption reads. Like the images

Fig. 4.7   'Une rue à Québec' (Comeau, & Lamoureux, 1982, p. 444)

in the 1970s, this street looks strangely quiet for a big city and the chosen view emphasizes the narrow street, the view eclipsed by the old building in the foreground, and the castle-like Frontenac at a distance. Other cityscapes in the 1980s are labeled as Québec or Montreal, for example, which provides more identification than the images with no captions, but not a lot of specification. Other images, however, are named specifically in the captions such as 'Statue de Samuel de Champlain devant le Château-Frontenac à Québec' in *Son et sens* (Valdman et al., 1984, p. 133), 'La Place Royale, un des quartiers les plus anciens de Québec' in *Theme et variations* (Hagiwara & De Roucher, 1985, p. 209), and 'Place Jacques Cartier à Montréal... Montréal, au Canada, est la seconde ville d'expression française dans le monde' in *Rendez-vous* (Muyskens et al., 1982, p. 40). One of the images showing a place outside the city specifies that it is 'La chute d'eau de Montmorency, un des beaux sites naturels de la province' in *En route* (Valdman, Barnett, Holekamp, Laronde, Sieloff Magnan, & Pons, 1986, p. 541).

Like the images from the 1970s, those in the 1980s tend to show places with very little human activity. Most of the places are either empty or very sparsely populated, like the one shown in Fig. 4.7, with one person seemingly alone on a long empty street. Only two images show any movement. One is the image of 'Place Jacques Cartier à Montréal' in *Rendez-Vous* (Muyskens et al., 1982, p. 40), which is lightly populated relative to the space shown in the image. The people are for the most part sitting. The ones in the foreground sit on the pavement and those at a distance sit on benches. Just a couple of people in the distance appear to be moving. A second image showing movement is one without a caption. A horse drawn carriage walks along an empty street in front of some historic-looking townhouses in *Horizons* (Bennett et al., 1984, p. 344).

The proximity of the cityscapes and landscapes to the viewer varies across the images. Most of them are at a distance where a scene is visible, like the one shown in Fig. 4.7. In the 1980s, however, there are also several panoramic and aerial views, particularly of Montreal and a couple that show a store front up close so that the French signage is evident to the viewer. Overall, the proximity varies more than in the previous decade.

5.3   The 1990s

In the 1990s, seventeen of the images in textbooks showed places in Canada and Québec. Three of these (18 %) were country landscapes and the other seventeen (82 %) showed city scenes. Seven of the seventeen images did not have captions to help identify the images for the viewers. This represents approximately 40 % of the images that were not identified. The ones that are identified vary in the level of specificity of the captions that they are given. They can be as general as 'Le Québec' which is used to show Le Château-Frontenac at a distance and the Saint Lawrence River in the foreground with a cruise boat in the water in *Chez nous* (Valdman & Pons, 1997, p. 142) to as specific as 'La cathédrale de Notre-Dame, Montréal' in *Entre amis* (Oates & Oukada, 2006, p. 145). Images without captions include a variety of views of Québec including aerial views of big cities, a frozen river with ice skaters, and the Université Laval campus.

In many of the images of the 1990s, despite the fact that the object pictured is a place, there tend to be people who are doing things in the places. For example, 'Le vieux Montréal' in *Chez nous* (Valdman & Pons, 1997, p. 142) is pictured at a medium distance with people walking around shopping and looking at things. An artist is at work drawing a portrait of a child, and the place looks alive. Another image with the caption 'La ville de Québec' in *Voilà* (Heilenman et al., 1989, p. 125) shows a street in Québec at a medium distance with people who are walking next to a busy street full of traffic, and another shows a soccer game underway in the foreground, with the backdrop of the campus of McGill University. There remains a solid collection of images showing places with no apparent activity such as the image of 'Le Château-Frontenac' in *Entre amis* (Oates & Oukada, 2006, p. 143) and a panoramic view of 'Saint-Siméon, Province du Québec' in *Voilà* (Heilenman et al., 1989, p. 125), as shown in Fig. 4.8.

The proximity of the viewer to the places pictured varies in the 1990s subsample. There are just a few panoramic and aerial views such as the view of Saint-Siméon shown in Fig. 4.8 and of unnamed cityscapes, which are probably Montreal. Most of the images, however, are taken from a medium distance such as the ones shown in Figs. 4.6 and 4.7. This

Fig. 4.8 'Saint-Siméon, Province du Québec' (Heilenman et al., 1989, p. 125)

medium distance view allows the student to see both the place and the activity that takes place there, where people are skating, walking to class, playing soccer, and shopping, for example.

5.4   The 2000s

In the 2000s, sixty-six of the images in textbooks showed places in Canada and Québec. Seven of these (11 %) were country landscapes and the other fifty-nine (89 %) showed city scenes. Of the sixty-six images, twenty-eight (42 %) were not identified with a caption. Unidentified images, like in the previous decades, represented a range of pictured objects, including areal city views, street scenes, and specific buildings such as Le Château-Frontenac. Other images contained captions, but their specific identity was not revealed. For example, the image shown in Fig. 4.9 is captioned 'Ici, on parle français.' Others are captioned simply with Montréal or Québec.

The shift toward more activity in cityscapes and landscapes that was evident in the 1990s blossoms in the 2000s subsample, as illustrated in

Fig. 4.9   Image from *Paralleles* (Fouletier-Smith & Le Zotte 2000, p. 57)

Fig. 4.9. The large majority of images showing places include people engaging in the activities relevant to those places, for example, enjoying the cafe culture, participating in outdoor sports, and engaging in touristic activities. Overall, Québec looks more populated and more alive in the 2000s subsample than in the earlier ones. This is perhaps in part a reflection of the fact that it is easier to obtain and publish images than it was earlier, but the material aspects of production alone could not account for the difference. There must also have been an increase in the interest of textbook producers in showing Québec.

The proximities of the images in the 2000s subsample also vary, but there is a greater tendency to see images at a medium distance rather than at the farthest distance because at the medium distance, the activity that people are engaging in is evident. The percentage of country landscapes, well suited to distant views, is smaller in the 2000s, which adds to the more populated nature of the sample.

5.5   Summary of Places in Images

Designation of the most pictured locations is difficult to do because of the variety of forms of identification that the books contained and the challenge of finding the right level for a unit of analysis. However, the one object that is the most pictured specific location across decades is the Château Frontenac in Québec City, with at least one representation in each of the decades from the 1970s through the 2000s. The Frontenac appears with every level of identification from no caption or reference in the text to the specific name of the hotel. The biggest change across the decades is the level of activity. In the 1970s and 1980s there were more landscapes showing the countryside than there were distant images of the cities. But in the 1990s and 2000s, the percentage of landscapes decreased, perhaps in favor of the activity of the city. The apparent increased interest in activity also resulted in fewer far distant images in the 2000s (Table 4.4).

The discussion of the place images has been somewhat brief in view of the fact that such images need to expand the lens to examine how the images are used in the contexts of the textbooks where they are placed. The many images that appear without any captions are particularly interesting in this regard. The images themselves are likely to be uninterruptable to students of French beyond a clue they might pick up through the positioning of the image on the page that is about Canada. If students do not pick up the clues about the identity of the image, images showing the cityscapes and landscapes of Canada and Québec are relegated to serving the role of artwork, enhancing the design of textbook pages but perhaps not adding to their knowledge.

6   Images for Multimodal Meaning Making: A Closer Look

So far, the analysis of images with people and places has concentrated primarily on individual images, except in the case of the identity analysis which often had to be constructed multimodaly through the use of the

Table 4.4 Summary of analysis of Canadian and Québec images of places

	1960s	1970s	1980s	1990s	2000s
Number of images	0	8	28	17	66
Identity		Named or identifiable places varying in degree of generality or specificity.	A range of levels identifiable from images with no captions (46 %) to some with specific names of places	A range of levels identifiable from images with no captions (41 %) to some with specific names of places	A range of levels identifiable from images with no captions (42 %) to some with specific names of places
Activity		Very little activity; empty-looking places	Very little activity; empty-looking places	A range of activity levels including places where people are doing things	Much higher level of activity evident in the places People shown doing many different activities suited to places
Proximity		Variety of proximities, but no extreme distance	Variety of proximities, including three with panoramic views of Montreal	Variety of proximities, including three with panoramic views of Montreal Most at a medium distance where activity is evident	Variety of proximities, but an emphasis on medium distant proximity, allowing for a view of activity

image caption as well. The 'textual' dimension of meaning, as introduced in Table 4.1, is constructed by positioning elements in the image in addition to the placement of the image on the page and its accompanying text. The questions that need to be addressed in such an analysis include the following:

How do elements within the image cohere and guide the viewer's attention?

How does placement of the image on the page with other images and text create meaning?

How does the image work with the text on the page (including the image caption) to create meaning?

Adding to these questions specifically for the analysis of images used in teaching, Weninger and Kiss (2013) pointed out, 'meaning potential is heavily contextual and depends on particular constellations of text, image and task' (p. 704). To take into account how images contribute to meaning making intended for learning, I look more closely at the use of the images in three of the textbooks, which are treated as three case studies. In case study research the critical sampling issue is how the cases are chosen from the pool of potential cases that one could choose to examine. I have sixty-five textbooks, over a hundred images, and considerable variability across textbooks, both within and across decades. How can I choose three for case studies? Should the selected textbooks be considered representative of the decade subsamples from which they are chosen? It would be efficient to be able to answer the questions by examining one book per decade, but in view of the variation within each of the decade subsamples, it is not possible to do that, so I needed a different strategy for selecting the cases.

In the interest of seeking the richest examples appearing in each decade subsample, I selected the textbook from each of the decades containing the most images. I wanted to include three cases, and in each of the decade subsamples for the 1970s, 1980s, and 2000s, there was one textbook that had far more images of Canada and Québec than the others in its subsample. These became the obvious choices for examining the multimodal meaning making in *Parole et pensée* (1970s) with sixteen images, *Son et sens* (1980s) with nineteen images, and *Paroles* (2000s) with twenty-seven images. I focused on the textual meanings through an analysis of the degree to which the meanings in the images were essential to the learning that appeared to be the goal of the readings and exercises in the texts. For the analysis, I created terms to express five levels of essentiality of the role of the images, with one indicating the most essential to language learning.

1. Task essential: The image is used as part of the learning task. The task could not be completed without the image because of a task requirement for the student to do something with the image.
2. Text enhancing: The image illustrates some specific aspect of the text making the text potentially more meaningful to the student. The image appears to have been selected precisely to cohere with and make more vivid an image in the text.
3. Generally orienting: The image plays a role in orienting the learner to the topic that will be developed in a section of the textbook.
4. Theme building: The image serves, typically with other images on the page or nearby pages, to contribute to building the meaning of a theme on a page or in a section.
5. Independent: The meaning of the image needs to be interpreted independently from the text of other images because there is no obvious connection to the texts or other images.

6.1   The 1970s: *Parole et Pensée*

The eleven books in the 1970s vary dramatically in their presentation of Canada. The book chosen, *Parole et pensée* (Lenard, 1977), has considerably more images of Canada than the others: sixteen relative to a maximum of two for any of the rest of the textbooks in the 1970s. All of the images of Canada are placed on four pages; one is a black and white reproduction of a painting and the rest appear on the center pages of the book, where a substantial collection of glossy color photos is placed. The images of Canada occupy the three final pages of this insert, which situates them in the lesson with the Canadian content. This section of images has a title of 'BIENVENUE DANS LA BELL PROVINCE,' and it directs readers to the page where the dialogue in Québec is.

Other than these images, the Canadian content consists of a narrated dialogue telling the story of five American students who decide to drive across the border from Maine into Québec for a short trip prior to their academic year of study in France. They make their way by car to Québec City, where they decide to take a ride in a horse drawn carriage. The carriage driver then gives them a tour and converses with them. In doing so, he uses some of the ideational language that appears in the images. Table 4.5 summarizes the degree of multimodality that is evident through the positioning of each image in the context of the others as well as the text. The dialogue text is the single text that coheres with the images, and six of the images enhance the language of the dialogue.

The images of the horse drinking from the fountain repeats the same ideational message as what is conveyed by the language of the dialogue: 'À chaque promenade, sa récompense, c'est de boire à cette fontaine, et il le sait' (p. 272). In this case, the author's interest in selecting precise criterial aspects resulted in representation of a horse drinking from the fountain while the carriage driver looked on from a distance. Other expressions in the text that are enhanced through the use of the images are the motto that the carriage driver introduces to the Americans, 'Je me souviens,' which appears in two of the images (five and six in Table 4.6). The image of the carriage with the horse and driver and the Château Frontenac enhance those aspects of the dialogue text. The image of the license plate (three) enhances the part in the dialogue where the customs agent welcomes the American students with 'Bienvenue à la Bell Province.' The other image that could be text enhancing if learners were given an explanation is the one with a military person in dress uniform with a goat. This scene would take place at the Citadelle in Québec, which the driver mentions, but the caption on the image would not allow the students to make that connection alone.

All of the other images in *Parole et pensée* (Lenard, 1977) work together (and with the text enhancing images) to build a theme about Canada and Québec in the several pages where they appear. It appears that the author's interest motivating the selection of these images was very general because it is not obvious why specific images such as the ultramodern church were chosen as objects to represent Canada and Québec. The

Table 4.5 Descriptions of images, their captions, and the degree of multimodality in their interpretation in *Parole et pensée* (Lenard, 1977).

Image description	Caption	Multimodality
1. Historic painting (p. 270)	ANONYME, L'esplanade à Québec (La Galerie nationale du Canada, Ottawa. Le Canada d'un autre temps. Il est bien différent aujourd'hui!	Theme building about Canada.
2. A Canadian flag	None	Theme building about Canada
3. A Québec license plate with the motto 'La Belle Province'	None	**Text enhancing:** The customs agent in the dialogue welcomes the American students with 'Bienvenue à la Bell Province.'
4. A photograph of the coat of arms with 'Je me souviens'	None	**Text enhancing:** The carriage driver explains that 'Je me souviens' is the motto of the city of Québec.
5. A photo of the Québec parliament with 'Je me souviens' spelled out with plants in the garden in the front.	None	**Text enhancing:** The carriage driver explains that 'Je me souviens' is the motto of the city of Québec.
6. A horse and buggy with a driver.	La caliche. Son cocher, et le cheval.	**Text enhancing:** An important part of the story told through the dialogue
7. Le Château Frontenac shown above the lower city of Québec	Le Château-Frontenac domine le fleuve Saint-Laurent. C'est un immense hôtel.	**Text enhancing:** Pointed out by the carriage driver in the dialogue
8. A nontraditional church	Une église ultra-moderne à Québec	Theme building about Canada

(continued)

Table 4.5 (continued)

Image description	Caption	Multimodality
9. An artist drawing a portrait in the open air	Un artiste québecois[a] examine attentivement son modèle	Theme building about Canada
10. A military person in dress uniform with a goat	La chèvre mascotte du régiment, accompagnée du sergent-major.	**Text enhancing:** The carriage driver mentions the Citadelle, where one would see the image, but does not make the connection.
11. Bushels of apples in the foreground with two producers in the background	Le Canada produit des pommes en quantité	Theme building about Canada
12. A dense collection of logs floating in water	Des troncs d'arbre flottent en masse sur une rivière près de Montréal.	Theme building about Canada
13. A sign advertising Coka-Cola with the message written in both French and English	Une affiche de publicité bilingue pour un produit consommé dans le monde entier.	Theme building about Canada
14. A table with hand-made fabrics in the foreground and a woman at the table in the background (Shown in Fig. 4.2)	Cette jeune fille vend des objets tissés à la main.	Theme building about Canada
15. A horse drinking from a fountain and people in the carriage in the background[b]	La récompense de Bobby, le cheval de calèche, après la promenade.	**Text enhancing:** The image presents the same message that is conveyed in the dialogue by the carriage driver.

Note. [a]This is the spelling of québécois used in the caption.
[b]The images without page numbers appear on a central unnumbered insert in the text.

textbook producer clearly was not interested in selecting all images that would enhance the text in the dialogue.

6.2   The 1980s: *Son et Sens*

In the 1980s, the twenty-three textbooks produced considerable variation in the use of images with nearly half of the sample (48%) showing no images of Canada at all. The text chosen for examination was *Son et sens* (Valdman et al., 1984), which had twenty-one images. This was much higher than the book with the next highest number of images, *Thème et variations* (Hagiwara & De Rocher, 1985), which had eight images on four pages. As Table 4.6 shows, of the twenty images, only one could be considered as task essential. The cartoon (number four) shows the daily life activities of someone who, the text indicates, lives in Montréal. Students are supposed to use the sequence to make interview questions for the person about what she does each day. Text is included in the cartoon, as well. Other exercises in the chapter cohere with the theme of everyday activities, but there is nothing of cultural significance about the fact that Marie lives in Montréal.

Five of the images are text enhancing because they provide specific illustrations that would help students to create meaning multimodally. All four of the text enhancing images are added to the meaning of a dialogue and accompanying text about a ski trip to Mont Tremblant in Québec. The first one (five) shows down-hill skiers in a full page at the beginning of the unit and accompanies the text introduction to Québec highlighting winter sports. Then, a hand-drawn map of Québec (eleven) contains geographical names that appear in the dialogue, allowing students to create a mental picture of the trip that the characters in the dialogue were making. Accompanying the dialogue, images 12 and 17 each picture skiers of the sort that might be found at Mont Tremblant and in images later in the chapter.

Ten of the images can be interpreted to contribute to building meaning of a section about Canada and Québec because they are in a unit that is about Québec and they add generally to the meanings with the other images and texts in that unit. Beginning with image 6 with the Chateau Frontenac in the background and a statue and people walking in the foreground, the images all help to build on a general theme of Québec. Many of the images in that section show scenes and activities in the winter, which best adhere to the overall topic and the topic of the dialogue, but even the images showing different seasons are counted as contributing to the general topic. The images extend though image 18 in Table 4.6, but within that span, there are some that contribute more precisely to the meaning of the dialogue, and I have included them in the group of five text enhancing images.

Three of the images are generally orienting for the theme that they are used to support, but in none of these cases was a Canadian image particularly needed or exploited to teach about Canada or Québec. The first (one) is one of many illustrations supporting a statement referring to 'a world where 75,000,000 people speak French every day.' The image showing a street in Montreal with the back of a bus in the foreground fits with the theme of transportation, the topic of a substitution exercise, which includes a line drawing of a bus as one of the objects students can say. The Montréal bus adds a dimension of reality to the topics, but the specific attribute of a Montréal bus is not exploited. Similarly, the color photograph of the hockey players is on a page with an exercise asking students to make statements about sports, but the hockey team from Québec is not part of the point. These types of multimodal interpretations do not enhance the cultural dimensions of the meaning in the images.

Two of the images need to be interpreted in terms of their own internal meaning making capacity because they do not appear to contribute to the textual meaning or any themes in the textbook in a particular way. Image 2 is a large image of a child's birthday party which has a caption indicating that it is in Québec. Without the caption, the birthday party could be almost anywhere. Similarly image 20 showing children in a tent is labeled to indicate that it is in Québec, but without the caption, it could be anywhere. These two images appear to respond to an interest to include everyday life in Québec, but the selection of specifically what to select as the criterial aspects of objects is not evident.

Table 4.6 Descriptions of images, their captions, and their connections with the text and activities in the text *Son et sens* (Valdman et al., 1984)

Image description	Caption	Multimodality
1. A scene at the winter carnival (p. 18)	None	General orienting: It is one of many illustrations supporting 'a world where 75,000,000 people speak French every day.'
2. Seven people and a dog attending a child's backyard birthday party (p. 9)	Bon anniversaire! (Au Québec)	None
3. A street in Montreal with the back of a bus in the foreground (p. 28).	A Montréal	General orienting: A line drawing of a bus appears as one of the objects that students can say as they participate in a substitution exercise.
4. Four-frame cartoon showing the daily activities of a person living in Montréal (p. 103)	Qu'est-ce qui se passe	**Task essential:** Students are supposed to use the sequence to make interview questions for the person about what she does each day. Text is included in the cartoon.
5. Down-hill skiers (p. 128)	None	**Text enhancing:** Accompanies the text introduction to Québec which highlights winter sports
6. A city scene with the Château Frontenac in the background and a statue, and people walking in the foreground (p. 133)	Statue de Samuel de Champlain devant le Château-Frontenac à Québec	Theme building about Canada
7. A welcome sign saying, Québec vous souhaite bienvenue | welcomes you, showing that it appears at Pointe-Fortune (p. 134)	None	Theme building about Canada
8. A child sitting on an ice sculpture at the carnival (p. 134)	Monument de glace pour le Carnaval à Québec	Theme building about Canada

(continued)

Table 4.6 (continued)

Image description	Caption	Multimodality
9. A clown (p. 135)	Clown de Carnaval	Theme building about Canada
10. The snowman, Le Bonhomme (p. 135)	Le Bonhomme de Carnaval	Theme building about Canada
11. A map of Québec (p. 135)	None	**Text enhancing:** The map contains geographical names that appear in texts and images later in the chapter.
12. A large group of skiers (p. 132)	Au Mont Tremblant	**Text enhancing:** Accompanies a dialogue about skiing at Mont Tremblant in Québec
13. A store front with a sign saying *galerie saint-denis* and *cadeaux Québec* (p. 139)	None	Theme building about Canada: Appears in a chapter with a lot of Québec content
14. A sign saying BOUTIQUE CHAMPLAIN CADEAUX (p. 139)	None	Theme building about Canada: Appears in a chapter with a lot of Québec content (and with #13)
15. Actors performing outside in the summer (p. 140)	Théâtre en plein air dans le vieux Montréal	Theme building about Canada: Appears in a chapter with a lot of Québec content
16. A traditional-looking stone house in the country (p. 140)	Vieille maison dans la campagne québécoise	Theme building about Canada
17. Cross country skiers in the snow (p. 143)	Le ski de fond au Québec	**Text enhancing:** A dialogue on the adjacent page refers to people in Montreal who go to Sainte-Agathe, 60 km outside Montreal for beautiful ski paths.
18. Tobogganers on a snowy hill (p. 143)	Une piste de toboggan	Text enhancing: The image appears in a section about winter sports.
19. People playing a game (p. 153)	A la foire à Trois-Rivières	Theme building about Canada
20. Hockey players on the ice in red, black, and white uniform (p. 155)	A Montréal	General orienting: The color photograph is on the same page as drawings of people playing sports, each labeled to show students how to talk about each.
21. Three children peeking out from a small orange camping tent (p. 330)	Québec: un magasin	None

6.3   *Paroles* in the 2000s

In the 2000s all texts contain images with Québec content, but *Paroles* (Magnan, Berg, Martin-Berg, & Ozzello, 2007) leads in the number of images with twenty-eight (Table 4.7). *Paroles* may also exemplify an important chronological advance in the use of images as essential for learning tasks. Eleven of the twenty-seven images in *Paroles* contribute meaning that is essential for task completion. Students are asked to try to figure out the meaning of the text on the business cards. Five business cards from Trois-Rivières in Québec are among the business cards that students are asked to try to interpret. Image 6 is a drawing of a red and white Canadian flag and is one of the seven flags used in an activity asking students to ask a question about nationality. The correct response is 'Ce sont des Canadiens. Ils habitent à Québec.'

Text enhancing images are used extensively as well to enhance the meanings of specific language in the text. Images nine through thirteen all appear on two pages where facts are given about Québec. The rich meanings are created through the visual dimension that each one adds to the textual presentation of facts, and the factual information adds meaning that is not apparent in the visual alone. The overall effect of the positioning of the text and visuals is a textured collection of various modes of meanings about Québec. Its coherence, created by the cohesion of image and text, is very rare across all the textbooks. A second pocket of coherence includes images 20 through 25, which picture aspects of the texts and activities within the theme of memories. The central text is 'The Hockey Sweater' narrative. Images support and add vivid visuals to enhance students' perception of the main ideas. One image does not enhance the texts specifically, but rather helps to build the theme of memories. Image 25 showing a store front in Montréal with signs in French is in the section of the book with a lot of Québec content which is developed through the theme of memory, including 'The Hockey Sweater' text, which is narrated as a text that the author remembers as an event from childhood. The image with its caption 'La boutique Marché de souvenirs à Montréal' indicates a souvenir store. 'Souvenir' means memory.

Four of the images are used to provide a general orientation. Three are the maps that appear at the beginning of the text. There are three of them, but in terms of the multimodal analysis of meaning, they all perform the same meaning making function, which is to orient readers to the geographical locations that are included in various parts throughout the textbook. All of the images in *Paroles* have an identifiable purpose in multimodal meaning making, and therefore, none was judged as requiring meaning construction based on a single image.

Table 4.7 Descriptions of images, their captions, and their connections with the text and activities in *Paroles* (Magnan, Berg, Martin-Berg, & Ozzello, 2007)

Image description	Caption	Connection with text and activities
1. Map of the world showing where French is the official language (inside cover)	Le Monde	General orienting: The map contains geographical names that appear in texts and images later in the chapter.
2. Map of the North America showing where French is the official language (inside cover)	L'Amérique du Nord	General orienting: The map contains geographical names that appear in texts and images later in the chapter.
3. A decorative cylinder with posters attached on a city walkway (p. 2)	Canada	General orienting: The image from Canada accompanies images from other parts of the world to create a visual introduction to the chapter.
4. Four business cards from places in Québec (p. 13)	None	**Task essential:** Students are asked to try to figure out the meaning of the text on the business cards.
5. A business card from Trois-Rivières in Québec (p. 40)	None	**Task essential:** It is among the business cards that students are asked to try to interpret.
6. A drawing of a red and white Canadian flag (p. 42)	None	**Task essential:** It is one of the seven flags used in an activity asking students to ask a question about nationality. The correct response is 'ce sont des Canadiens. Ils habitent à Québec.'

(*continued*)

Table 4.7 (continued)

Image description	Caption	Connection with text and activities
7. Gabrielle Roy, a francophone Canadian author (p. 193)	Gabrielle Roy	**Task enhancing:** The provides an image of the subject of the text.
8. A street protest (p. 306)	Manifestion au Québec contre les OGM	**Task essential:** The images is used as the basis for discussion.
9. Le Château-Frontenac (p. 396)	Le Château-Frontenac	**Text enhancing:** Provides a view of Québec to accompany a page with facts about Québec, including that Le Château-Frontenac is in the capitol, Québec.
10. La Place Jacques Cartier à Montréal (p. 396)	La Place Jacques Cartier à Montréal	**Text enhancing:** Provides a view of Québec to accompany a page with facts about Québec, including that Montréal is a principal city.
11. Landscape (p. 396)	Le Québec: pays riche en ressources naturelles	**Text enhancing:** Provides a view of Québec to accompany a page with facts about Québec.
12. Québec license plate (p. 397)	None	**Text enhancing:** Provides an image containing the Motto for Québec, which is also given in the list of facts about Québec.
13. Building with fresque painted on the side in downtown Québec (p. 397)	La fresque des Québéois	**Text enhancing:** Shows the building containing the fresque whose contents are used for a matching exercise on the following page. The fresque is described in the text adjacent.
14. Drawing of Louis Jolliet (p. 398)	None	**Task essential:** Used in a matching exercise
15. Drawing of Felix Leclerc (p. 398)	None	**Task essential:** Used in a matching exercise
16. Drawing of Gabrielle Roy (p. 398)	None	**Task essential:** Used in a matching exercise

(continued)

Table 4.7 (continued)

Image description	Caption	Connection with text and activities
17. Drawing of Thaïs Lacoste-Frémont (p. 398)	None	**Task essential:** Used in a matching exercise
18. Drawing of Alphonse Desjardins (p. 398)	None	**Task essential:** Used in a matching exercise
19. Drawing of Jacques Cartier (p. 398)	None	**Task essential:** Used in a matching exercise
20. Drawing of children getting dressed to play hockey (Illustration from *The Hockey Sweater*) (p. 406)	Tirée du livre Le chandail de hockey (c) 1984, Sheldon Cohen: illustration publiée aux Livres Toundra	**Text enhancing:** Full page images forecast a reading from and information about the text, *The Hockey Sweater*.
21. A woman as a teacher in a park instructing young people seated on an outdoor deck (p. 409)	Institutrice au Québec	**Text enhancing:** Used to illustrate the topic of the activities (responding to question about being young) for students in the adjacent text
22. The *Je me souviens* motto spelled out in plants (p. 410)	Le devise du Québec en fleurs devant le Manège militaire à Québec	**Text enhancing:** Accompanies a dialogue about memories of school using the expression *Je me souviens*
23. People on ice skates outside on an ice rink within a city (p. 414)	Québec	**Text enhancing:** One of four pictures used for an activity asking student to describe one of the pictures as the location where they spent their vacation.
24. Hockey player and hero in Québec, Maurice Richard, with a trophy honoring his achievements (p. 419)	Maurice Richard avec le trophée nommé en son honneur	**Text enhancing:** The culture note that accompanies *The Hockey Sweater* story and activities, which are about Maurice Richard

(continued)

Table 4.7 (continued)

Image description	Caption	Connection with text and activities
25. A store front in Montréal showing signs in French (p. 437)	La boutique 'Marché de souvenirs' à Montréal	Theme building about memories
26. Sign on the street in Montreal reminding people to recycle cans (p. 442)	Panneau d'affichage à Montréal	**Text enhancing:** Accompanies activities asking students to respond to questions on the topic of pollution
27. Exhaust from factories over the city at dusk or dawn (p. 443)	Usines au Québec	**Text enhancing:** Accompanies activities asking students to respond to questions on the topic of pollution
28. A traditional stone house with a red roof in the snow and by the water (p. 552)	Une maison au Québec	General orienting: Used on a full page of three images of homes in different francophone countries to start the unit on *Qualité de vie*

6.4   Summary: Images in Multimodal Meaning Making

In the three texts described in this section, multiple contributions of images were apparent to the process of meaning making. Within each of the three texts, a variety of uses of the images was evident, but a shift in the uses of images for more precisely orchestrated multimodal meaning was seen in the progression of textbooks across the three decades. The terms I used to classify the degree of multimodal meaning making helped to show the shift toward selection of images most supportive of specific elements of texts as well as images that play an important role in the learning tasks. The numbers of images across the three texts were not the same, as shown in Table 4.8, but the shift from no task essential meaning in the 1970s case to eleven in the 2000s is probably significant. It probably reflects an increase in the specificity of interests on the part of the textbook producers in addition to expanded capacity for gathering the specified images.

Table 4.8 Number of images categorized by degree of text essentiality in the three case study textbooks

	Textbook cases		
	Parole et Pensée (1970s)	*Son et Sense* (1980s)	*Paroles* (2000s)
Independent	0	2	0
Generally orienting	0	3	4
General theme building	8	10	1
Text enhancing	7	5	12
Task essential	0	1	11
Total images	15	20	28

To explain the variation in the multimodal meaning potential of the textbook images, I used Kress and van Leuveen's (2006) idea of interest on the part of the producer. A variation in the specificity of the meanings to be constructed and the cohesion to be achieved with other elements on the page(s) indicates a variation in specificity of interests, as illustrated in Fig. 4.10. In selecting images, textbook producers have interests that vary from the general to more specific, and the level of specificity of their interest affects the precision with which the criterial aspect of the chosen image is determined. As the interest is more specific, the criterial aspect can be defined more precisely, and the chosen image can be most closely coupled with that text and activities.

Some of the selection of images appears to have been driven by a general interest in placing images that express something about Canada in the textbook. In these cases the criterial aspects of the images are as general as something about Canada or Québec. Examples of these appear in *Son et sense* with the images of the birthday party and the children in a tent in a store. A general interest may motivate images with iconic value (or stereotypes) that are expected to be immediately recognizable by readers. In some of the textbooks, for example, hockey players are used to denote Canada. Since there is no specific coupling of image with text, and no specific meaning to be conveyed, the image itself has to convey a message recognizable without any multimodal support. Even if a caption is used, such images simply evoke ideas that must be already known rather than teaching something new. When selection of images is driven

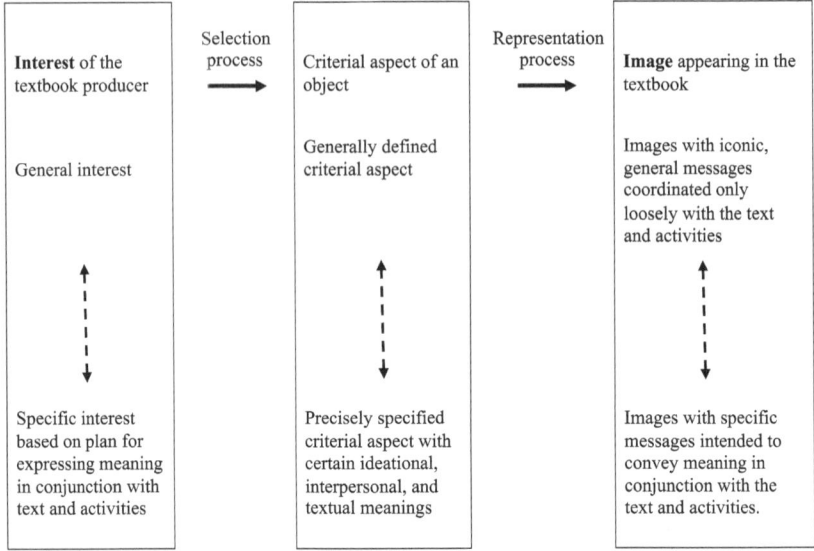

Fig. 4.10 Theoretical conception of the meaning making process resulting in textbook images

by a more specific interest in using the image in conjunction with text and activities to engage students in multimodal learning, their criterial aspects are more precisely defined. The ideational meanings conveyed by the participants (e.g., the horse), processes (e.g., drinking water), and circumstances (e.g., at the fountain with the carriage driver in the background) need to be specified.

7   Conclusion

The analysis of images presented in this chapter describes the visual presentation of Canada and Québec as it has emerged over an important fifty-year period. It added a detailed look at the content of images that had been shown to increase over this period, with a notable jump in numbers in the most recent decade studied. In addition to the increase in percentages of images of Québec and Canada over this period, this chapter showed an increase in the variety of images as well with, for example the types of Canadian and Québecois characters presented (identity) and the level and variety of activities people engaged in (activity). In the three case studies, the multimodality of the meaning creation increased in the most recent case. In *Paroles* (Magnan, Berg, Martin-Berg, & Ozzello, 2007) from the 2000s subsample, the images of Canada and Québec cohered with the texts and activities that the students were asked to do in a way that would help the students to gain a richer understanding of the text and language of the activities.

Although these general trends were apparent throughout the entire sample of texts, an important finding is that there is a great deal of variation with respect to the amount of coverage of Canadian and Québec content. The variation can be explained by elaborating on Kress and van Leuveen's (2006) concept of interest with the idea that interests can be general (interest in a picture of Canada) or more specific (interest in a picture of Maurice Richard winning a literary award); where the textbook producer's interests seem to be more specific, the nature of the content varies considerably. In other words, where the images are intended for use in multimodal learning, what is to be learned about Canada and Québec varies considerably. Because of the variability in the sample of textbooks, the large number of books in the sample is an essential feature of this study. Any individual observation needs to be interpreted in terms of how prevalent it is relative to other textbooks of the time period as well as to other textbooks across time. In particular, the variability in the decade subsamples precluded selection of a typical case from each decade, and instead motivated my selection of cases that provided the most examples in each of the three decades.

These findings were possible because of my use of the social-semiotic theoretical conception of how to read images developed by Kress and van Leuveen (2006). The framework is a general one, pointing to types of meanings that can be made in images, and therefore it can be used for other foreign language textbook analysis. The analysis revealed some political meanings that are pertinent to Québec's cultural narrative. In the following chapter, I pick up that thread of the analysis to look more closely at how politics has been constructed through both text and image in the textbooks across all five decades.

References

Bennett, D., Bennett, J., Joiner, E., & Shinall, S. (1984). *Horizons—nouvelle langue, nouvelle culture*. New York: Holt, Rinehart and Winston.

Bragger, J. D., & Rice, D. B. (1988). *Allons-y! le français par étapes* (2nd ed.). Boston: Heinle & Heinle.

Byrnes, H., Maxim, H. H., & Norris, J. M. (2010). Realizing advanced foreign language writing: Development in collegiate education: Curricular design, pedagogy, assessment. *The Modern Language Journal, 94*(Supplement), 1–122.

Butturff, D. L., & Coffman, M. E. (1976). *French: Language and life styles*. New York: McGraw-Hill.

Clarke, K. M., & Holt Editorial Staff. (1974). *À la française*. New York: Holt, Rinehart and Winston.

Comeau, R. F., & Lamoureux, N. J. (1982). *Échanges: Première année de français*. New York: Holt, Rinehart and Winston.

Fouletier -Smith, N., & Le Zotte P. (2000). *Le parallèles: communication et culture*. Upper Saddle River, NJ: Prentice Hall.

Hagiwara, M. P., & De Rocher, F. (1985). *Thème et variations: An introduction to French language and culture* (3rd ed.). New York: Wiley.

Heilenman, K. L., Kaplan, I., & Tournier, C. (1989). *Voilà*. New York: Harper & Row.

Jarvis, G. A., Bonin, T. M., Corbin, D. E., & Birckbichle, D. W. (1980). *Connaître et se connaître: A basic reader for communication* (2nd ed.). New York: Holt, Rinehart, and Winston.

Kress, G. (2010). *Multimodality: A social semiotic approach to contemporary communication*. London: Routledge.

Kress, G. R., & Van Leeuwen, T. (2006). *Reading images: The grammar of visual design*. London: Routledge.

Lafayette, R. (1988). Integrating the teaching of culture into the foreign language classroom. In A. J. Singerman (Ed.), *Toward a new integration of language and culture* (pp. 47–62). Middlebury, VT: NCTFL.

Lenard, Y. (1977). *Parole et pensée: Introduction au français d'aujourd'hui*. New York: Harper and Row.

Magnan, S. S., Berg, W. J., Martin-Berg, L., & Ozzello, Y. (2007). *Paroles* (3rd ed.). Hoboken, NJ: Wiley Custom Services.

Mondelli, R. J., François, P., & Terry, R. M. (1984). *Accent: Conversational French one*. Boston: Heinle & Heinle.

Muyskens, J. A., Omaggio, A. C., Chalmers, C., Imbarton, C., & Almeras, P. (1982). *Rendez-Vous: An invitation to French*. New York: Random House.

Mitschke, C., Tano, C., & Thiers-Thiam, V. (2007). *Espaces: Rendez-vous avec le monde Francophone*. Boston: Vista Higher Learning.

Oates, M., & Oukada, L. (2006). *Entre amis* (5th ed.). Boston: Houghton Mifflin.

Ollivier, J., Morran, M., & Howard, C. M. (1983). *Appel: Initiation au Français*. New York: Harcourt Brace Jovanovich.

Pimsleur, P. (1970). *C'est la vie*. New York: Harcourt, Brace and Jovanovich.

Risager, K. (1991). Cultural references in European textbooks: An evaluation of recent trends. In D. Buttjes & M. Byram (Eds.), *Mediating languages and cultures: Towards an intercultural theory of foreign language education* (pp. 181–227). Clevedon, UK: Multilingual Matters.

Siskin, H. J., Williams-Gascon, A., & Field, T. T. (2007). *Débuts: An introduction to French*. Boston: McGraw-Hill.

Terrell, T., Rogers, M. B., Kerr, B. J., & Spielmann, G. (2005). *Deux mondes* (5th ed.). Boston: McGraw-Hill.

Thompson, C. P., & Phillips, E. M. (2004). *Mais oui!* (3rd ed.). Boston: Houghton Mifflin.

Valdman, A., Barnett, M. A., Holekamp, E., Laronde, M., Magnan, S. S., & Pons, C. (1986). *En Route: introduction au français et au monde francophone*. New York: Macmillan.

Valdman, A., MacMillin, G., Lavergne, M., & Gahaka, E. (1984). *Son et sens* (3rd ed.). Glenview, IL: Scott Foresman.

Valdman, A., & Pons, C. (1997). *Chez nous: branché sur le monde francophone*. Upper Saddle River, NJ: Prentice Hall.

Weninger, C., & Kiss, T. (2013). Culture in English as a foreign language (EFL) textbooks: A semiotic approach. *TESOL Quarterly, 47*(4), 694–716.

Wodak, R., & Meyer, M. (Eds.). (2009). *Methods for critical discourse analysis*. Thousand Oaks, CA: Sage.

5

A Closer Look at Language Politics

This chapter continues the qualitative analysis with a focus on the content of the political messages in Québec's cultural narrative conveyed through text and image in the textbooks across the five decades. Following from the observation that teaching about French language in Québec provides a natural opportunity to teach about language politics and ideology, I look at how these topics have actually been covered in the textbooks. Cultural narrative is the collective story of a people that expresses their past experience in a way that shapes their current understandings of local and global events. The cultural narrative that I outlined for Québec in Chap. 2 showed the centrality of language politics to the experience and everyday reality of the people of Québec and their identity. The sketch of the cultural narrative revealed 400 years of events creating a supermarket of topics that authors could choose from as they select content, texts, themes, and ideas for presentation in their textbooks. The analysis in this chapter is carried out in two stages. First, the image analysis examines images with political content. On the basis of the image analysis and consideration of the political content of the texts, I selected one textbook from each decade to serve as a case study of political content in each decade subsample. Having provided a discussion of politics in

© The Editor(s) (if applicable) and The Author(s) 2016
C.A. Chapelle, *Teaching Culture in Introductory Foreign Language Textbooks*, DOI 10.1057/978-1-137-49599-0_5

the cultural narrative and Québec's language politics in Chaps. 1 and 2, respectively, I focus on methods and results to reveal (1) how images were used to convey political messages and (2) how text and image were used within individual textbooks to express political meanings of Québec's cultural narrative.

1   Images with Political Messages

Images reflecting politics and history require a measure of interpretation to select. I approached the search open to any type of messages that I thought could invoke in viewers the thought of politics or history of Canada and Québec. The images I selected were of six types. First, I included as political any appearance of a Canadian or Québec flag. In Québec politics the blue and white flag with the fleur de lys is an iconic symbol of Québec identity, whereas the red and white Canadian flag symbolizes Canadian unity and Canada. Flags are the most frequent category of political and historical images, perhaps because of their strong iconic value and the flexibility of locations in which they can appear. Flags are a prototypical symbol of a nation, a people, and their ideologies.

Second, images containing the motto of Québec, 'Je me souviens' is another iconic Québec image that symbolizes Québec identity and a connection with the historical French heritage. 'Je me souviens' meaning 'I remember' is interpreted as meaning I remember our heritage as *Canadiens*, whose solidarity over time has maintained our language and heritage. The third type is the collection of images of political figures in Québec and Canada. This includes political leaders and cultural icons who are depicted in the text as playing a political role in contemporary events.

Whereas the first three types of images are specific people and objects, the fourth type of images includes the group demonstrations or protests that appear in some of the textbooks. The fifth type also captures a variety of different images consisting of political and historical places, events, and activities.

Finally, I counted maps as containing a political message about where French is spoken, which Gray (2013) argues is a political statement, and Québec's cultural narrative would attest to as well. Maps of Canada and

Québec appearing in the foreign language textbooks can be used to express political and historical meaning. In addition to expressing the facts about how bodies of land, countries, and language boundaries are placed, maps can be presented with a level of objectivity that comes in part from the top-down angle used to present the way the world is divided up. Maps can be more or less objective, depending on how official-looking the rendering of the geographical regions is. Maps can depict a less objective attitude when the geography is presented at an angle, cartoon-like lines and colors are used, or other types of images are added such as products, weather symbols, or any text or graphics that would add a signal of subjective interpretation to the basic depiction of the geography.

1.1   The 1960s and 1970s

The only Canadian image in any of the 1960s textbooks is a map of North America showing the French possessions in the middle of the sixteenth century (Fig. 5.1). By today's standards, the map would have too much of a hand-drawn quality to be considered highly objective, but a direct top-down view is presented and the facts are clearly represented: The French possessions through Canada and the USA were enormous. The caption under the images states in words what the visual presentation says. In this only image of Canada and Québec, neither Canada nor Québec is designated. North America appears as one undifferentiated space marked only with the shaded area denoting the French possessions. All but one of the other textbooks in the 1960s contain maps, but none of them include Canada.

In the 1960s, no Canadian flags appear in any of the textbooks in the sample, but in the 1970s, Canadian flags appeared in four of the textbooks. In three of the images the Canadian flag with its red maple leaf is the only or most prominent participant in the image—in two cases, the flag is the whole image. In the third, the Canadian flag appears over a marching band of people dressed in red uniforms, which highlight the red in the flag. The fourth image in the 1970s depicts the Canadian flag at a border crossing between Québec and Vermont. The Canadian flag is waving only slightly and is therefore difficult to see. It is on a pole on the Québec side of the border. There is another flag, but it is not waving at all and therefore it is impossible to detect what flag it is, but the most likely inference is that it would be a US flag. Overall, then, the 1970s display the political national symbol, but the nation is Canada, and the symbol is the maple leaf.

In the 1970s the other political and historical images are the national motto, 'Je me souviens,' which appears on a coat of arms in one image and in the garden in front of the parliament building in the other. The parliament building itself is another image that symbolizes the history and politics of Québec. The two images appear in the one book of the 1970s with a large majority of the images, *Parole et pensees*. They sit side by side on a single page, with the coat of arms picture tilted to one side like a photograph tossed onto the table. The 'Je me souviens' on the coat of arms is small but the cohesion between it and the 'Je me souviens' in the garden in front of the Parliament emphasizes that this is the primary message to be seen in the two images.

In the 1970s, maps including Canada and Québec as areas where French is spoken appear in only two of the eleven textbooks, in a small map section inside the back cover of the textbooks. The two maps where Canada appears are actually world maps where French-speaking territory (including Québec, but not Canada) is colored in a contrasting color. Like in the 1960s, most of the textbooks in the 1970s subsample (all except two) contain maps, but Canada is not on them.

1.2   The 1980s

In the 1980s, flags are notably infrequent as symbols of Canada and Québec in images. Of the fifty-four images that appear in the texts in the 1980s, only two contained flags. In *Son et sens*, the book with the greatest number of Canadian images, the Québec flag, blue with the fleur de lys, appeared along with the red Canadian maple leaf flag over a ski hill with two skiers. The flags are in the background, but they are large and salient waving outstretched against the blue sky, on two separate poles, but with the red Canadian one above the blue Québec fleur de lys. The only other instance of flags in the 1980s is the same picture of the US-Canadian border that was in the 1976 edition of *Practical Conversational French* with the Canadian flag hanging limp at this official government check point.

The 'Je me souviens,' symbol appears four times across two textbooks in the 1980s. *Connaître et se connaître* displays three images containing the motto. One is a line drawing of Québec's coat of arms which includes 'Je me souviens' sketched visibly on the ribbon at the bottom (p. 171). The second two instances of 'Je me souviens' appear at the bottom of Québec license plates. The same license plate is pictured in images on two pages of the book, once on p. 175 next to a picture captioned 'Une rue à Québec.' A second textbook, *French for Communication*, also displays the 'Je me souviens' motto on a license plate (p. 205).

Other images with political and historical messages include important political and historical figures. The most explicitly political message across all of the textbooks is the page in *Horizons* (p. 345) containing the two separate pictures—an attention grabbing one with the big Canadian flag held by celebrating people and a second smaller one shows sad faces on people holding signs, depicting the outcome of the 1980 referendum vote.

Rendez-vous shows the political figure of René Lévesque facing a large group of reporters (p. 447). A key figure in modern cultural narrative, René Lévesque was the leader of the Parti Québécois who led Québec to the 1980 referendum vote. A second image in *Rendez-vous* pictures the former French president, Charles de Gaulle, standing on a balcony in Montreal, where he uttered the famous 'Vive le Québec libre' (p. 453) This is an important historical cultural event. A third image in *Rendez-vous* is a reproduction of a piece of artwork called 'Coureurs des bois au Canada' (p. 444). It shows the early French explorers in the North America living out in the woods with animals. The coureurs des bois played a key role in the foundation of Québec because of the way they integrated with the native people and learned to live in the challenging climate, affording them a central role in Québec's cultural narrative. *Accent* pictures the face of Gilles Vigneault in a close up (Fig. 4.3) showing him singing with his gaze set in a dream-like position, perhaps contemplating the liberation of Québec (p. 304). In *Conaitre et se connaitre* a cartoon drawing shows the three trips of Jacques Cartier as he discovered Canada and made his way each time a bit farther into the continent while encountering the native people (p. 142). Two pages later, a drawing shows Jacques Cartier in greater detail (p. 144). *Theme et variations* shows the famous historic Place Royale where the first French settlers built a settlement in Québec

(p. 209). All of these specific people and places figure into the political cultural narrative of Québec.

In the 1980s, maps of Québec appear in a variety of forms and for varying uses, but overall there is a dramatic increase in their number, with twelve of the twenty-three books containing at least one map of Canada and Québec. In *Accent* (p. 88), a neat hand-drawn map of streets in one area of Québec is presented. The site of the hotel Château Frontenac is shown with a little drawing of the hotel and its name printed. The site of a restaurant is also indicated, along with a few other landmarks. The map is to be used by students in an activity describing how to walk from the hotel to the restaurant. The top-down view of the city is authoritative, but the selection of what to include on the hand-drawn map adds subjectivity to the rendering. It is unlikely that a student using this map in class would consider it as depicting an objective presentation of the downtown area of Québec.

A second map of Québec appears in *Accent* (p. 433). This one shows the outline of the province of Québec as a contrast between the white Québec and the dark gray surrounding territories, which are named also in dark lettering so that the lettering does not stand out visually. What does stand out distinctly is the topological detail in Québec, where the lakes and rivers appear as dark gray spots of varying shapes, and dark veins, respectively, through the white Québec. Dark, thin, relatively smooth lines denote the main highways, and lighter weight lines with regular crosses are marked as the railroad lines. The airports are marked with triangles, and the ports are marked with diamonds. Many cities are named on the map. It is a serious map that offers considerable information to viewers in an objective fashion.

A less objective map of Québec appears as the backdrop to two whimsical photos, one of a clown in the carnival and a second of Le Bonhomme waving to a crowd in *Son et sens*. The map has Québec fully outlined and in light blue to distinguish it from the surrounding unnamed areas (Ontario, the Northeastern USA, and the Eastern provinces). Québec is named 'la province de Québec' and several cities in the south of the province are named on the map. The pale blues of Québec and the bodies of water with the white territory outside of Québec create a pale background that lessens the objectivity conveyed by what can be objective-appearing material. *Son et Sens* also contains a map of the world on the inside cover, with France and its departments shaded in orange and francophone countries or regions marked in green. Canada is colored as a whole in green. These examples show the variety of the types and styles and functions of maps of Québec and Canada that make their appearance in the textbooks for the first time in the 1980s.

1.3   The 1990s

In the 1990s, again two images contain flags. One is a street scene with several flags including a Canadian one and a Québec one. The second is an image of a cartoon figure holding a flag with a red maple leaf intending to symbolize that she is Canadian. The other political and historical image in the 1990s is a single image of Brian Mulroney, with the caption 'Brian Mulroney, Premier minister au Canada.'

In the 1990s, maps start to take on their modern role as objective presentations depicting where French is spoken in the world. Four of the five texts that have images of Canada and Québec also contain at least one map. Overall, six of the nine texts in the 1990s subsample have maps of Canada and Québec. In *Chez nous*, authoritative maps that look as if they could have come from textbooks in geography or history appear on the inside front and back covers. The inside front cover has a map of the world with Québec highlighted in lavender to indicate that French is an official and/or material language and the rest of Canada in green, to indicate that French is an official and administrative language. The map states in objective-looking terms the political statement of Québec's distinctness. The inside back cover contains two frames, one with a map of Canada showing the names of the Canadian provinces and the other with a map of Québec. A map on p. 15 of *Chez nous* shows the world with French-speaking regions highlighted in orange to contrast with the dull purple of the rest of the countries. On p. 143 of *Chez nous*, a map of Québec appears as a pale blue watermark behind a text printed in black about the education system in Québec. On p. 157, a weather map complete with rain clouds shows the region of Québec by the St. Lawrence River and including New England in the USA.

Entre amis contains two maps showing Québec as a French-speaking region. One on the inside back cover shows the western hemisphere with North America and South America. The territories where French is the maternal language, including Québec, is colored in pink. The regions where French is marked as having a significant presence includes Louisiana, the northern states of New England, but not the rest of Canada. A second map on p. 142 shows Québec as the object of interest, with the surrounding provinces in Canada each named and in a lighter color, and the northern part of the USA shown in a different color with the states not marked individually.

Rapports displays a map of the world on the front inside cover entitled 'Le Monde Francophone' with the area colored in pink and numbered. The numbers refer to a key, where the specific regions are named. The colored area includes the eastern part of Canada and the key for that section defines it in French as Canada (New Brunswick, Nova Scotia, Québec, Newfoundland). Regions of the USA are also colored in pink and the key names the region as The United States (Louisiana, New England). Again, this map does not include the rest of Canada in 'Le monde francophone.'

Voilà includes three maps, one of which shows all of Canada with Québec colored in pink to indicate the focal region. The key identifies the region as a 'Francophone province.' A second map in *Voila* shows 'Regions francophones du monde.' This like those in *Entre Amis* and *Rapports* shows Québec and the Eastern Provinces shaded as indicating they are francophone regions, as are New England and Louisiana in the USA, but the rest of Canada is not shown as Francophone. A third map in *Voilà* shows a map of New England east of New York with Canada marked above and Québec City. The caption reads, in French, French is spoken in New England. The map has clearly arrived in the 1990s as a means of expressing a range of meanings.

1.4   The 2000s

In the 2000s subsample, the number of images conveying political and historical meanings was substantially greater. There was a total of seventeen images in nine of the eleven textbooks in the sample showing

Canadian or Québec flags. Six of these images show the Québec flag pictured without the Canadian flag, eight show the Canadian flag pictured without the Québec flag, and in three pictures the Canadian and Québec flags appear together. In the 2000s, the Canadian maple leaf flag images remain in the majority as symbols of Canada in the textbooks, but by the 2000s, the Québec flags had clearly gained a position that they had not held in these textbooks in the previous decades, appearing frequently as well. In three of the images showing Québec flags, the image has clearly been selected to depict a political message about the ongoing battle to preserve the language and heritage. The one in *Entre amis* (p. 84) accompanies a short text written in English that presents a brief cultural narrative beginning with the founding of Canada through the continued aim of ensuring the maintenance of Québec society and French in North America. The ones in *Horizons* (p. 132) and *Espaces* (p. 427) show Québec flags as instruments in demonstrations, one of which includes a uniformed police officer in the foreground, who looks off to the side while the flag-waving crowd persists. Aside from these three images in three books, the Canadian and Québec flags are presented as if they are neutral symbols of a place where French is spoken.

The other political and historical images in the 2000s include two pictures of protests without flags. One is a line drawing in *Deux mondes*, p. 428, with four cartoon figures, three of whom hold a sign intended to indicate a group that risks loss of identity due to its minority position. The signs say 'Basque,' 'Québec,' and 'Breton.' No flags are used as props for this protest. A second protest appears in *Paroles*. This one is not about language, independence, or even Québec. The crowd is protesting genetically modified organisms (GMOs). The protest, according to the caption, took place in Québec. Some of the signs are in French.

In the 2000s, several of the textbooks contain historical figures from Québec's cultural narrative. *Horizons* places a painting of Jacques Cartier, the French explorer who discovered Canada, above the image of the Québec protesters on a page. The brief text in French on the page ties together the founding of Canada with the continuing battle to maintain the French language despite the domination by the English. Jacques Cartier is also pictured in *Deux mondes* and in *Paroles*; Jacques Cartier is one of six historic figures appearing in an image in *Paroles*. *Vis-à-vis* contains an image of Samuel de Champlain, founder of Québec. Despite the relatively rich collection of images presented in the 2000s, the important political figures are notably absent.

Paroles contains an image of the 'La fresque des Québécois,' which covers the side of a large building in Québec (p. 397). The text indicates that the fresque contains significant historical characters, six of whom are pictured in six separate rectangles, and lettered A through F, to be used as a matching game. The six images are of Jacques Cartier, the founder of Québec for the French in 1534; Felix Leclerc, an important Québec singer; Alphonse Desjardins, founder of the first bank in Québec; Thaïs Lacoste-Frémont, a women's rights activist; Louis Jolliet, discoverer of the Mississippi river for France; and Gabrielle Roy, an important franco-phone writer in Canada.

A final historical image that appears in *Horizons* is a painting 'The meeting place' showing a port city from 1866 (p. 102). Three images across two textbooks contain the historical reference, the national motto, 'Je me souviens.' Like in the previous two decades, the motto is displayed on Québec's license plates in two of the images and outlined by plants in the garden by the Québec Parliament building in the third. All of the textbooks in the 2000s subsample have maps that show Canada and Québec and include at least Québec in the French-speaking world.

1.5   Summary of Images with Political Cultural Narrative

This analysis provides a chronological look at the way that the political messages in images have developed over the five decades included in the sample. When flags first appear in the 1970s, they are all red and white maple leaves, suggesting that Québec is not portrayed as having a politi-cal identity as a flag-bearing nation. Québec's blue fleur de lys appears in one of the twenty-three textbooks in the 1980s alongside the maple leaf flag of Canada. In the 1990s, flags appear in two of the books, and one of these contains the blue fleur de lys in addition to the maple leaf and flags from several other countries.

The presence of maps develops in sophistication throughout the five decades. In the sample of 1960s textbooks, the one single image depicting Canada is a map of the French colonies in North America. Other political symbols and people are rare in the 1970s and begin to appear in the 1980s, most notably in the image of René Lévesque that appears in one textbook. In the 1990s, political images are very rare, but then they increase in the 2000s. The appearance of maps of Canada and Québec shows a similar trajectory, beginning with a single North American map in the 1960s that shows France's North America of the 1600s. Canada appears in only two maps in the 1970s sample, with Québec marked as a French-speaking territory. Maps with Canada and Québec appeared in about half of the 1980s subsample and in two-thirds of the 1990s subsample. In the 2000s, maps of Canada and Québec appear in all of the textbooks in the subsample.

The ideational analysis of these images reveals the political and historical messages that the images may convey to the viewer. In doing so, they may contribute to the education in politics and history that some educators have hoped would permeate foreign language education. This analysis of the visual presentation of Québec's language politics complements the analysis of the textual representation of Québec's cultural narrative in Chap. 3. It also adds to the image analysis of Chap. 4 with a focus on a particular interest and how it has been instantiated in actual textbooks. What remains to be shown is the way that the text and images combine to create political meanings in a single book.

2 Politics in Text and Image: Case Studies

The methodology used for the analysis is a qualitative case study, which presents the opportunity to examine how the coherence of Québec's cultural narrative is built throughout a textbook from each of the decades included in the study. Identifying the relevant textbooks for the case study required a review of the textbooks in the sample. Because of the centrality of politics and its somewhat amorphous nature, I had not attempted to code the texts as 'political' but rather had codes that were useful in looking for texts containing aspects of the cultural narrative. As I described in Chap. 3, I reviewed all of the textual content that had been tagged with any of the labels for the content pertaining to Québec's internal linguistic and cultural evolution (e.g., Canadian history, Quiet Revolution, bilingualism). Any of the texts that contained politically related content were selected to form the initial pool of potential candidates for the case studies. The numbers and percentages of textbooks with such political content in each of the five groups and the totals are displayed in Table 5.1.

The amount of political content is shown to grow over the five decades, but the qualitative analysis is needed to look at the nature of that growth. To choose the cases for analysis for this study, I reexamined the content of the textbooks containing political content in each decade to identify the one with the most substantial treatment of Québec's cultural narrative (e.g., four in the 1960s, three in the 1970s). The results should therefore be interpreted as showing the maximum treatment of Québec's cultural narrative in beginning-level French textbooks in the USA for each decade. They do not show the typical treatment of the topic in textbooks. Description of the 'typical' in subsamples with such great variation is not plausible because there is no typical. Moreover, examination of the maximum presentation offers more insight into the possibilities for presentation of cultural narrative, provided it is interpreted in view of the quantitative summary showing the place of each case in the overall subsample.

Table 5.1 Number and percentages of textbooks containing political content

Decade	Number of books in decade subsamples	Number (%) of books *with* political content	Number (%) of books *without* political content
1960s	11	4 (36 %)	7 (64 %)
1970s	11	3 (27 %)	8 (73 %)
1980s	23	12 (52 %)	11 (48 %)
1990s	9	5 (56 %)	4 (44 %)
2000s	11	11 (100 %)	0 (0 %)
Sample total	65	35 (54 %)	30 (46 %)

2.1   The 1960s Case: *Beginning French: A Cultural Approach*

Textbook producers in the 1960s had over 300 years of Québec history that they could have selected from to introduce students to Québec's language politics, as outlined in Chap. 2. However, at that time, the study of Modern European languages including French was focused exclusively on Europe, and therefore whatever was going on in other parts of the French-speaking world was unlikely to capture the attention of textbook producers. In four of the textbooks in the 1960s subsample, however, some aspects of Québec's cultural narrative were revealed.

The textbook containing the map is the one that was selected for the case study, *Beginning French: A Cultural Approach* (Hendrix, & Meiden, 1961). Québec is mentioned in a historical narrative of France's ventures beyond its borders for colonization and exploration. In a 642-word essay, France and the French are clearly the main topic. Canada and Québec are presented as France's discovery. Some of the pre-1960s events are included in a text titled 'Les Français en Amérique' as are some of the general statements about language and society. 'Les Français créèrent une civilisation et une culture toutes différentes de celles des autres nations d'Europe. D'autre part, bien que la France ait perdu presque toutes ses possessions dans le nouveau monde, elle y a laissé des traces caractéristiques de son influence' (p. 342).

France and French people are the agents who do things to the new world:

- la France envoyât des explorateurs au Canada. (p. 342)
- en 1534, Jacques Cartier fut chargé par le roi François Ier de chercher … au nord du continent américain un passage vers les Indes. Il traversa l'Atlantique et découvrit le Saint-Laurent. Au cours d'un second voyage. (p. 342)
- il remonta ce fleuve et prit possession au nom du roi de la « Nouvelle France ». (p. 342)

- En 1608 Champlain fonda la ville de Québec. Des missionnaires français atteignirent la région des Grands Lacs. (p. 342)
- Plus que les Anglais, les Français explorèrent les plaines inconnues de l'intérieur du vaste continent. Au milieu du dix-septième siècle la France possédait une grande partie du Canada et tout le centre des États-Unis, connu sous le nom de Louisiane. Après une série de guerres malheureuses, il fallut que la France livrât le Canada à l'Angleterre en 1763. (p. 342)

Unique to this particular case in the 1960s is the shift to Canada and Québec as the main topic in the final 113-word paragraph, which includes some general statements that reflect aspects of cultural narrative including the distinction of French Canadians:

> Au Canada toute la province de Québec parle français. Montréal est la deuxième ville du monde au point de vue de la langue française. Mais la prononciation du canadien-français est différente du français de Paris, et le vocabulaire du canadien-français a subi l'influence de la langue anglaise. Les Canadiens français se distinguent nettement des autres Canadiens. Ils conservent leurs vieilles traditions. Dans les villes de la province de Québec on trouve partout l'influence de l'architecture française. Aucune ville d'Amérique n'est plus pittoresque que la ville de Québec; aucune ville n'a gardé autant de traces de la colonisation française en Amérique. Tout le pays a un aspect bien particulier qui rappelle la France elle-même. (p. 344)

This text is also unique in its presentation of an image containing Canada. This image of France's holdings in America presents a piece of the Québec narrative, as shown in Fig. 5.1.

Overall, however, in this time period there was little if any space in the texts for Canadian and Québec culture in a French language curriculum that was all about French in France. *Beginning French: A Cultural Approach* was the only textbook in the 1960s subsample that contained any such information.

Au milieu du dix-septième siècle, la France possédait une grande partie du Canada et tout le centre des États-Unis

Fig. 5.1 Drawing of a map showing the French possessions in North America in the early 1600s (Hendrix & Meiden, 1961, p. 343)

2.2   The 1970s Case: *French: Language and Life Styles*

In the 1970s, textbook producers had just begun to look beyond Europe for cultural content for their textbooks and Québec's Quiet Revolution with its continuing repercussions might have provided rich material for textbooks in the USA. A cultural revolution encompassing all facets of social life could have provided consciousness raising materials for students while teaching them about Québec's cultural narrative. In the 1970s subsample of textbooks, however, pieces of Québec's narrative appear in only three of the eleven textbooks.

The cultural narrative is supported by images in one of the textbooks, *French: Language and Life Styles* (Buttruff & Coffman, 1976), making it the best selection for the 1970s case. *French: Language and Life Styles* is an extreme outlier in the 1970s subsample because it contains a text of 797 words followed by questions that offers an analysis of Québec in Canada. It begins with the touristic opening that was and still is familiar in beginning-level textbooks:

> Le Québec, la « Belle Province » avec ses lacs, ses rivières, ses montagnes, ses forêts, ses villes et ses plaines inhabitées. Il vaut la peine de connaître ce pays de l'Amérique du Nord dont 33 pour cent de la population est francophone. (p. 184)

The touristic turns toward the academic with a shift to an analysis of the French Canadian:

> Le contraste entre le vieux et le nouveau rend difficile à définir le caractère du Canadien français. Entre la France et l'Amérique, le Québec connaît une vie originale. Tous les Québécois en sont conscients. Tous sont attachés à leurs traditions culturelles, à leur manière de vivre. L'originalité du Canadien français résulte du fait qu'il tente d'assimiler deux cultures et deux civilisations, et deux langues. (p. 184)

The introduction of tension in the analysis marks the author's shift into the relatively recent events of the Canadian bilingualism policy and Québec's own official French policy. In the course of the essay, the author touches upon a number of the recent events such as the Quiet Revolution, the idea of national independence, the need to make French the official language of Québec, movements toward international engagement, and establishment of educational and cultural exchanges with France. Two images, one shown in Fig. 5.2, accompany the text without necessarily supporting any of the textual presentation of language politics.

2.3   The 1980s Case: *Rendez-vous: An Invitation to French*

By the 1980s, language politics had been strongly established in Québec's cultural narrative. The establishment of the charter of the French Language in 1977 and its predecessors as well as the activities of the Parti Québécois would have provided provocative cultural content for textbooks. For the first time, a sizable number (about half) of the textbooks in the subsample included some information about Québec's cultural narrative. The one with the strongest presentation selected for the case study was *Rendez-vous: An Invitation to French* (Muyskens, Omaggio, Chalmers, Imbarton, & Almeras, 1982).

The first presentation of Québec's cultural narrative appears in a grammar exercise on the past subjunctive. The opening line of the dialogue includes the subordinator 'avant que' which takes the past subjunctive of the verb in the subordinate clause in this case: 'Corinne: Parfois, j'envie les aventures des coureurs des bois français avant que l'Amérique du Nord n'ait été entièrement explorée' (p. 443). This presentation is accompanied by a drawing showing 'coureurs des bois au Canada' (p. 444), as seen in Fig. 5.3. The drawing shows the early French explorers in the North America living out in the woods with animals. The coureurs des bois played a key role

Des jeunes gens sur la rue Sainte-Anne à Québec   *Arthur Sirdofsky from EPA*

Fig. 5.2 Young people pictured on Sainte Anne Street in Québec (Butturff & Coffman, 1976, p. 183)

in the foundation of Québec because of the way they integrated with the native people and learned to live in the challenging climate.

The next section of the text is titled 'Alternatives to the Subjunctive,' and its content is the following dialogue:

Gilles: Nous Québécois, nous sommes fiers, mais il est bon de se rappeler que nous avons de bonnes raisons de l'être.

Marianne: Tu veux dire que vous avez toujours dû vivre entourés d'Anglais mais que vous avez pu garder votre langue intacte.

Gilles: Nous avons gardé intactes notre langue, notre culture et notre identité collective. J'espère que nous saurons regagner la force politique que nous méritons. (p. 447)

The dialogue appears alongside an image of René Lévesque, and the caption reads 'René Lévesque, chef du Parti Québécois' (p. 447). René Lévesque was the leader of the Parti Québécois that led Québec to the

Coureurs des bois
au Canada

Fig. 5.3 An image showing the early French settlers who worked closely with the native people, 'coureurs des bois au Canada' (Muyskens, Omaggio, Chalmers, Imberton, & Alméras, 1982, p. 444)

first sovereignty referendum vote, earning him a starring role in Québec's cultural narrative (Fig. 5.4).

Two pages later, Québec content is used in another grammatical exercise. Students are to change the grammatical structure of the following statements:

> 1. Il est important que nous soyons fiers d'être canadiens-français. 2. Il est essentiel que nous continuions à parler français. 3. Il est nécessaire que nous maintenions nos traditions. 4. Il est essentiel que nous protégions *(protect)* notre identité. 5. Il est important que nous restions unilingues. 6. Il est nécessaire que nous ayons des échanges avec la France. (p. 449)

René Lévesque, chef du
Parti Québecois

Fig. 5.4 An image showing René Lévesque (Muyskens et al., 1982, p. 447)

After students have encountered Québec in these grammar illustrations and exercises, they are provided with *Commentaire culturel* (p. 452–453) in English that begins with an introduction to the French heritage in the USA and Canada focusing on the recognition of French place names such as Baton Rouge and Detroit. It continues with a historical overview of the French presence in the USA for one paragraph (200 words) and then goes on to a second paragraph about Canada (247 words). A lot of cultural narrative is packed into those 247 words including the separatist movement of the 1960s, the visit of Charles de Gaulle, the growth of the

Charles de Gaulle en 1967:
«Vive le Québec libre!»

Fig. 5.5 An image showing Charles de Gaulle (Muyskens et al., 1982, p. 453)

Parti Québécois, as well as the establishment of the office of the French language and then French as the official language in 1974. It ends with an interesting statement: 'Nonetheless, separatist feelings remain strong in Québec, even in spite of the defeat in 1979 of a bill in the Canadian Parliament that sought to make Québec a separate entity (p. 453). The paragraph about Canada is positioned next to the image of Charles de Gaulle, shown in Fig. 5.5.

2.4   The 1990s Case: *Rapports: Language, Culture, Communication*

In the 1980s, the first sovereignty referendum had found a place in Québec's cultural narrative, which had developed a clear story line. Five of the nine textbooks in the 1990s subsample revealed some of the aspects of Québec's language politics. The textbook selected for the case study, *Rapports: Language, Culture, Communication* (Walz & Piriou, 1990), contains some of the most detailed information of any of the textbooks.

The introduction to Québec's cultural narrative appears on pp. 126–128, where readers are introduced to Québec in the context of la francophonie. The pre-reading text in English introduces Jacques Cartier as a player in the spread of French language. The political nature of Québec's French is forecast: 'Despite political turmoil, French remains the official language in the province of Québec' (p. 126). The text in French juxtaposes the fact that French is the official language of Québec with the fact that the rest of Canada is officially bilingual and that even the national anthem is in both French and English. The second mention appears in a cultural note in English stating, 'We generally associate one or two languages with any given country: English with the United States, English and French with Canada, and French with France.' (p. 387)

On pp. 417–419 in *Rapports: Language, Culture, Communication*, readers are presented with more information relevant to Québec's cultural narrative. The text titled, *Le français aux Etats-Unis*, begins in English with the point that French is not really a foreign language in the USA because of the significant number of Americans of French origin. It then corrects the lineage by explaining that most French heritage in the USA is the result of immigration from Québec. This information provides background for students to embark on the text in French, which describes multiple waves of immigration from Québec. Another short text about poet Léo-Albert Lévesque uses English to describe his work and then implies that he is an example of the people of Québec who are 'proud of their origins, their language, and their customs' (p. 423). It explains that Québécois feel an attachment to the land and that this is therefore often the subject of their work. The image shown in Fig. 5.6 is used to support this idea.

Mon pays

Fig. 5.6 An image illustrating the attachment to the land of Québécois(e) artists (Walz & Piriou, 1990, p. 421)

The heart of the political story is presented in an 1100-word text and activities on pp. 439–443 entitled 'Le débat linguistique au Québec.' The pre-reading for the French text is provided in English. It introduces some of the most poignant pieces of Québec's cultural narrative including Pierre Vallières book, *Nègres blancs d'Amérique*, Charles de Gaulle's 'Vive le Québec libre' speech, the Parti Québécois, the idea of separation from the confederation, and the negative vote on 'independence' in 1980 (p. 440). The French text is cited as adapted from a lecture by Paul-André Comeau for a group of American French teachers. It provides an engaging account of the dynamic forces at play in contemporary language politics, including the role of immigrants and their attraction to English, the key mandates of the Charte de la langue française, and the controversy it prompted including the 1988 Canadian supreme court finding that the French sign law was unconstitutional. It ends with an authentic note of uncertainty: Québec francophones feel threatened, the government is taking measures to offer advantages for families who have a third child, and even the francophone immigrants prefer to use English. It concludes, 'Si rien ne se passe, on peut se demander s'il y aura encore des francophones au Québec en l'an 2060' (p. 443).

Québec, Montréal, même pays

A Québec, cité-refuge des valeurs
francophones, et surtout à Montréal,
on est en « presque Amérique ».
Mais tout est dans ce « presque ».

Fig. 5.7   Image showing newspaper headlines (Walz & Piriou, 1990, p. 422)

Rapports: Language, Culture, Communication contains Québec-related images, but the only two that support the cultural narrative are the linguistic map on the inside cover showing Québec among the pink areas indicating the French-speaking world and a text simulating a newspaper headline about a story of Québec's distinctness (Fig. 5.7).

2.5   The 2000s Case: *Mais Oui!*

By the 2000s, Québec's narrative had developed an intriguingly equivocal plot with both successes and failures. The commitment for the support of French was stronger than ever, efforts to raise the status of Québec French to make it the workplace norm had essentially succeeded, and Québec's global presence had expanded. However, the second sovereignty referendum had failed, this time by an extremely narrow margin. The Parti Québécois had lost power, and 'la question nationale' continued to place uncertainty about the future at center stage for many. In short, textbook producers had a wealth of modern history to select from to introduce students to Québec's language politics. All eleven textbooks of the 2000s subsample present some aspects of Québec's cultural narrative. Although the amount and types of treatment these topics receive varies across the books, this was the subsample from which one case was most difficult to select because treatment of the issues is qualitatively rather than quantitatively different across the cases. The textbook selected for the case study was *Mais oui!* (Thompson & Phillips, 2004) because its presentation seemed to be among the most substantial and creative of those in the subsample.

Québec's narrative is developed gradually throughout the *Mais oui!* text through a variety of strategies including various forms of historical narrative, some in English and some in French, presenting historical facts and interpretation, introducing the fictional character, Isabelle, from Québec, who provides insight into being Québécoise today, an extensive presentation and analysis of *The Hockey Sweater* text by Roch Carrier, and a few images.

Readers' first encounter with Québec's narrative is in English in a short text entitled 'L'identité québécois' (p. 36). This text provides history in a nutshell to get to the point: what it means to be Québécois(e) today:

> Settled by French explorers in 1534, the eastern part of Canada was known as la Nouvelle-France for over two centuries before Great Britain took it over in 1763. Les Canadiens francais, however, held firmly to their language and traditions, forming the province of Québec, the only French-speaking province in English-speaking Canada. Linguistic and cultural tensions between Anglophones and Francophones are still very much an issue, as many of the 7 million Québécois still talk of independence. What is a Québécois(e)? Here are a couple of answers from some Québécois. 'Surrounded by English speakers, a Québécois defies cultural assimilation through personal inner strength–strong emotions, a strong will to preserve one's heritage, and a good sense of humor!' (I.L., Student). 'The Québécois can never rest on their laurels, for the survival of their culture is never assured. This pressure brings on a sense of insecurity at times but most often an abundance of energy and creativity' (H.D.F., university professor). (Thompson & Phillips, 2004, p. 36)

This text ends with a question for readers, also in English, which asks them to imagine what they would do if their town were culturally and linguistically isolated.

Readers meet Isabelle a few pages later, when she appears as one of the respondents to a question about the main characteristics of identity for someone from her culture. Her response is clear and precise relative to the others, who refer to gender, family, education, and religion. For Isabelle, 'Le fait que je suis québécoise joue un grand rôle dans l'image que j'ai de moi-même car je me considère premièrement québécoise et ensuite canadienne … C'est plus le fait que je suis une femme *québécoise* qui m'influence.' (p. 47)

The next point where Québec's narrative is mentioned is on p. 354, where the expression 'Je me souviens' is introduced:

> La présence du passé se manifeste certainement dans la devise officielle du Québec, «Je me souviens». De quoi les Québécois se souviennent-ils? De leurs origines françaises, d'un pays qui de 1535 à 1763 s'appelait la

Nouvelle-France, de la domination anglaise (1763–1867), puis de la création de la Fédération du Canada permettant aux «Canadiens français» une certaine autonomie. Depuis 1974, la seule langue officielle du Québec est le français, mais les tensions linguistiques et culturelles entre les francophones et les anglophones continuent. Comment la devise «Je me souviens» peut-elle aider les Québécois à préparer leur avenir? (Thompson & Phillips, 2004, p. 354)

This introduction is accompanied by an image of a license plate (p. 354), as shown in Fig. 5.8.

Fig. 5.8   Image of license plate (Thompson & Phillips, 2004, p. 354)

Isabelle: Depuis que je suis toute petite ma mère nous amenait[6] au marché chaque semaine pour faire les courses. Elle cultivait aussi un grand jardin, donc nous mangions souvent des aliments frais. À cause de cela j'ai développé un goût pour les aliments frais. Aussi lorsque nous allions chez mes grands-parents, la première chose qu'ils nous offraient c'était de la nourriture. Il me semble que tout ce que nous faisions c'était de manger en discutant. Pour eux, le fait de nous donner de la nourriture c'était leur manière de nous donner de l'amour. Aujourd'hui je me surprends[7] à faire la même chose. Si je veux montrer mon amour pour quelqu'un, je lui offre de la nourriture. Aussi, parce qu'au Québec il y a tellement de lois qui protègent[8] la langue française, pour moi aujourd'hui c'est très important de conserver ma langue.

Fig. 5.9   Image of Québécoise character, Isabelle (Thompson & Phillips, 2004, p. 370)

On p. 370, Isabelle returns as a respondent this time to a question about a past event that continues to influence her thoughts and actions today. She responds with an example about her family, but concludes with 'Aussi, parce qu'au Québec il y a tellement de lois qui protègent la langue francaise, pour moi aujourd'hui c'est très important de conserver ma langue' (p. 370). Each time Isabelle appears in the text, readers see her image next to her words (Fig. 5.9).

The previous bits of information might serve as a preface providing background for what is the main event for Québec in this textbook. The textbook producers have authored a 2250-word episode in which Roch Carrier is introduced as an artist within the political context of the 1970s and sufficient excerpts from his classic story, *Une abomina-*

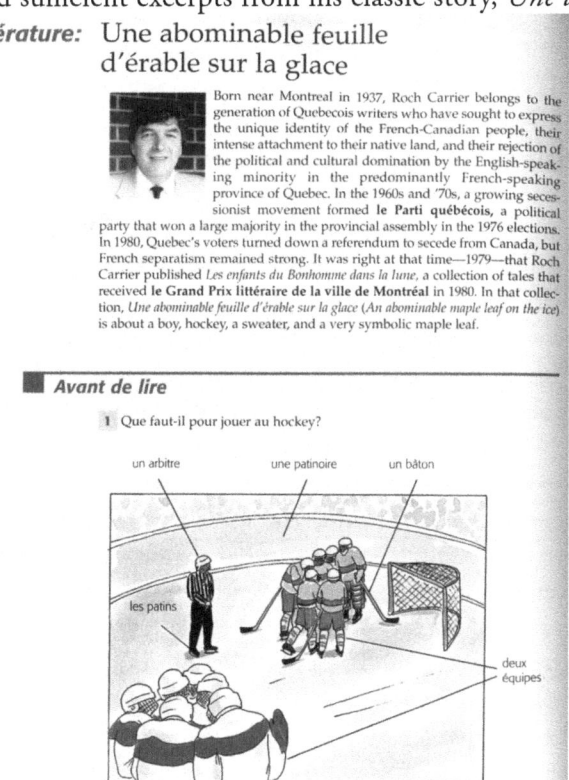

Littérature: Une abominable feuille d'érable sur la glace

Born near Montreal in 1937, Roch Carrier belongs to the generation of Quebecois writers who have sought to express the unique identity of the French-Canadian people, their intense attachment to their native land, and their rejection of the political and cultural domination by the English-speaking minority in the predominantly French-speaking province of Quebec. In the 1960s and '70s, a growing secessionist movement formed **le Parti québécois**, a political party that won a large majority in the provincial assembly in the 1976 elections. In 1980, Quebec's voters turned down a referendum to secede from Canada, but French separatism remained strong. It was right at that time—1979—that Roch Carrier published *Les enfants du Bonhomme dans la lune*, a collection of tales that received **le Grand Prix littéraire de la ville de Montréal** in 1980. In that collection, *Une abominable feuille d'érable sur la glace (An abominable maple leaf on the ice)* is about a boy, hockey, a sweater, and a very symbolic maple leaf.

Avant de lire

1 Que faut-il pour jouer au hockey?

un arbitre   une patinoire   un bâton

les patins

deux équipes

Fig. 5.10   Image of Roch Carrier and hockey artifacts (Thompson & Phillips, 2004, p. 400)

ble feuille d'érable sur la glace [*An abominable maple leaf on the ice*] (also known as *The Hockey Sweater*). This segment also contains extensive post-reading exercises for comprehension, discussion, and extension. This section starts out in English, and then shifts to French for the pre-reading questions, the story, and some of the post-reading questions. The introduction to Roch Carrier includes his photo, and the pre-reading exercise uses images to introduce the hockey terms that are used in the story, as shown in Fig. 5.10.

2.6   Summary

The case study analysis shows how the political aspects of Québec's cultural narrative are developed in a textbook from each of the decades. It revealed some important changes such as the shift from the single France-centered historical narrative to a more recent development of the cultural narrative through a mix of texts, languages, and modalities in the textbooks from the 2000s. Table 5.2 attempts a summary showing an evolution of topics that are included in each of the cases selected for their maximum treatment of politics in each decade subsample. It is difficult to discern a clear pattern of selections made by authors, but I would note a few interesting findings from the overall picture. First, there is only one theme that is present in all of the cases, and it is the general statement about the French and Francophone presence in Québec and Montreal, whose degree of political statement could be questioned. Even beyond the 1960s case, only one common theme appears across the other four decades, which is the pride and memory of French Canadians (symbolized by 'Je me souviens'). The other details of the historical political people, events, and ideas appear sporadically even in the textbooks with the maximum political treatment.

The second observation I would make about the case studies focuses on the case from the 2000s, which has a multiphase introduction to Canada and Québec, but which seems to miss some of the core elements of the political story. It contains the historical signposts of dates prior to the Quiet Revolution, but omits the more cultural history of the coureurs des

Table 5.2 Themes from Québec's cultural narrative that appear in the French textbook from each of the five decade samples

Cultural narrative themes for Québec	Decade subsample source for textbook				
	1960	1970	1980	1990	2000
Chronological list					
Founding of Canada (1534) or Québec (1608) by the French	x		x	x	x
1535–1763 Nouvelle France					x
First exposure of native people to French (1632)	x				
Coureurs des bois français			x		
Plus amis des Indiens que les Anglais	x				
Treaty of Paris and royal proclamation (1763)	x		x	x	x
1763–1867 domination anglaise					x
Federation (1867) gives some autonomy to French Canadians					x
Quiet Revolution		x			
International engagement		x			
Exchanges with France		x	x		
1961 Office de la langue française			x		
Charles de Gaulle's visit to Montréal in 1967, 'Vivre le Québec libre'			x	x	
1974 Loi sur la langue officielle (loi 22)			x		x
Parti Québécois and the rise of nationalism			x	x	x
René Levesque				x	
1977 Charte de la langue française (loi 101)				x	
Roch Carrier's *Une abominable feuille d'erable sur la glace*					x
1980 Referendum				x	x
1990 La langue, au cœur de la politique québécoise de l'immigration				x	
1995 Referendum					
General statements about language and society					
The French and Francophone presence in Québec and Montreal	x	x	x	x	x
Pride and memory of French Canadians (symbolized by 'Je me souviens')		x	x	x	x
Attachment to the land				x	x
Distinctness of French Canadians	x	x	x		x

(continued)

Table 5.2 (continued)

Cultural narrative themes for Québec	Decade subsample source for textbook				
	1960	1970	1980	1990	2000
Language-related tensions and negative aspects of the situation			x	x	x
Differences in Canadian French	x		x		
Bilingualism in Canada		x	x	x	

bois and the integration of the French explorers with the native people to create a Canadien identity that was distinct from European French people. It is also missing the Quiet Revolution and the internal Québec politics that unfolded during that era, except for the 1974 Official languages act and founding of the Parti Québécois. It does not mention immigration as an issue for the French language in Québec of the 1990s and beyond, nor does it mention the 1995 referendum, even though it did mention the 1980 referendum. The 1995 referendum is at least as interesting as the 1980 referendum because it represents the tenacity of the sovereignty movement, it failed by only a fraction of a percent, and it represented a recent important political event at the time that *Mais oui!* was published. It would be worth looking more carefully at the other texts in the 2000s to assess the variation in the political content covered within this subsample.

The examples provided in these case studies provide a glimpse at the type of presentation that is likely to be at the heart of any real changes in foreign language textbook production. Information about Québec's cultural narrative can be conveyed through a number of different pedagogical text types including the encyclopedic description of places and events, the academic analysis, the voice of characters in a dialogue or excerpts from interviews, as well as the student's own words that have been prompted by questions or topics for discussion. All of these devices are used in the examples, with a notable shift in sophistication in the example from the 2000s over those in the previous decades. These text types are needed to make content accessible to beginning-level students, and therefore any fruitful integration of Canadian Studies and the teaching of French will need to engage with the issues of not only what should be taught to build a beginning-level of cultural knowledge for students but also the text types and images required to do it.

3 Conclusion

The results of the political content analysis demonstrate increasing interest in Canadian Studies on the part of producers of French language textbooks. The proportion of textbooks with cultural narrative content in the 1960s and 1970s was around one-third. This proportion jumps to approximately half in the 1980s and 1990s, and then to the entire sample in the 2000s. The political images reveal some aspects of political recognition of Québec as a nation, with the addition of the Québec flag next to the Canadian flag in the 1980s and to a single Québec flag in some images by the 2000s. The maps of Canada and Québec in the textbooks are also revealing. Moreover, the results show changes in the way Québec's language politics has been presented, with shifts from a single historical narrative (with France as the main topic) in the 1960s to a variety of text types including literary text, the voice of a person from Québec, and opportunities for students' discussion in the 2000s. The analysis also reveals remaining challenges for fruitful integration of Canadian Studies into beginning-level French language learning materials.

Despite the apparent increase in cultural narrative over the five decades, the amount of space given to Canadian and Québec content in first-year French textbooks is an issue that deserves continued attention in the field. Relative to the past, Canadian content is abundant in current textbooks, and in some cases, important cultural stories are conveyed and cultural artifacts are presented thoughtfully. Another picture would emerge, however, if we were to look at the amount of Canadian and Québec content in the textbooks relative to all content in the textbook. For example, in the case from the 2000s subsample, *Mais oui!,* the presentation of Roch Carrier's *Une abominable feuille d'érable sur la glace* continues for six pages. Other Québec political content may add an additional page for a total of seven pages conveying Québec's cultural narrative in a book that is 496 pages long.

Moreover, the Canadian and Québec content throughout all of the textbooks analyzed tends to be brief and general. It is not evident that textbooks contain sufficient detail to help students interpret and engage with contemporary life in Québec. Perhaps most critical is the near absence of the people responsible for building Québec's cultural narrative. Many of the textbooks contain the name of Jacques Cartier, but René Lévesque is named in only three of the sixty-five textbooks that I examined across the five decades. Two of those instances were in the subsample of twenty-three textbooks in the 1980s, and one was in the 1990s textbook chosen for the case study. The former was an unusual textbook in its inclusion of more political detail than the others, and it even contained a picture of René Lévesque. He is not mentioned in any of the textbooks in the 2000s subsample. Only slightly more prevalent is the introduction of the Parti Québécois by name in eight of the sixty-five textbooks (three in the 1980s, two in the 1990s, and three in the 2000s). The Parti Québécois continues to be relevant in Québec, and in fact held power again from 2012 to 2014. It is difficult to imagine that students would be prepared to attempt to interpret contemporary life in Québec without knowing who René Lévesque is and what the Parti Québécois is about. Moreover, a trend toward downplaying language politics is evident throughout the textbooks of the 2000s.

References

Gray, J. (Ed.) (2013). *Critical perspectives on language teaching materials*. New York: Palgrave Macmillan.

Butturff, D. L., & Coffman, M. E. (1976). *French: Language and life styles*. New York: McGraw-Hill.

Hendrix, W. S., & Meiden, W. (1961). *Beginning French: A cultural approach*. Boston: Houghton Mifflin.

Muyskens, J. A., Omaggio, A. C., Chalmers, C., Imbarton, C., & Almeras, P. (1982). *Rendez-vous: An invitation to French*. New York: Random House.

Thompson, C. P., & Phillips, E. M. (2004). *Mais, Oui! (3rd edition)*. Boston: Houghton Mifflin.

Walz, J., & Piriou, J.-P. (1990). *Rapports: Language, culture, communication* (2nd ed.). Lexington, MA: D.C. Heath.

6

Strengthening Cultural Content in First-Year Textbooks

In Chap. 1, I claimed that analysis of beginning-level foreign language textbooks from the perspective of cultural narrative could help teachers and materials developers to select and develop materials for students at the beginning level. Through the following chapters, I elaborated on this claim by demonstrating what is entailed in such a textbook analysis. Chap. 2 demonstrated the background that would have to be established to begin to undertake such a textbook analysis. It included both the building of a version of the cultural narrative through historical and cultural research and the construction of a relevant sample of textbooks to analyze. Chap. 3 illustrated how the language of cultural narrative in textbooks can be analyzed in a way that allows teachers and materials developers to select, create, and critically analyze the appropriateness of the materials for beginning-level learners. Chap. 4 showed how the same theoretical perspective can be used to examine the meanings contributed by images in the textbooks. Chap. 5 took a closer look at the presentation of political aspects of cultural narrative as it has been presented through multiple fragments about Canada and Québec within a textbook. In Chap. 6, what remains is to interpret the findings from this research for improving the teaching of cultural narrative in foreign language classes in

© The Editor(s) (if applicable) and The Author(s) 2016   **213**
C.A. Chapelle, *Teaching Culture in Introductory Foreign Language Textbooks*, DOI 10.1057/978-1-137-49599-0_6

the USA. Prompted by this study, I also present a challenge to the field of foreign language teaching and assert the role of textbook analysis in meeting the challenge.

1   Implications for Teaching

Systematic textbook analysis should uncover a wealth of detailed findings at the macrolevel revealing what is included and what is omitted from textbooks as well as at the microlevel showing the language in particular genres and visual aspects of certain images. Accordingly, results should be useful as guidance for materials developers and teachers who want to include cultural content in beginning-level materials. I therefore begin with a summary of the main findings of the study and make suggestions for teachers and materials developers in French that are based directly on the findings. I then extend beyond French to make suggestions for the field of foreign language teaching more broadly and present a theory of foreign language materials development that includes the role of knowledge of culture on the part of developers.

1.1   Findings: Québec's Cultural Narrative in Textbooks

My research investigating Québec's cultural narrative in beginning-level textbooks revealed six findings that may be particularly useful for future materials development about Québec for French language learners. In this section, I elaborate on the potential implications of the findings, and I provide suggestions for materials developers particular to French language teaching.

1.1.1   Increases in Canadian and Québec Content

The amount of Canadian and Québec content in beginning-level French textbooks has definitively increased over the fifty-year period included in this study. Increases in Canadian and Québec results are evident in Chap. 2, where the amounts of textual and visual content were reported. Those results indicate two important increases in the amount of content, one in the 1980s and the other in the 2000s. Increases in Canadian and Québec content are evident in every metric used in this study including the counts of various types of content (Chap. 2), cultural narrative content (Chap. 3), images (Chap. 4), and political content (Chap. 5). Despite this trend in the average counts for each decade subsample, variation also appeared in every decade subsample. Textbook authors varied considerably in the amount and nature of the Canadian and Québec content they chose to include, with some textbook producers opting to leave Canada out. The exclusion of Canada was apparently no longer an option in the 2000s, when all textbooks were found to have some Canadian or Quebec content.

This clear trend of increase suggests that materials developers wishing to represent Canada and Québec in teaching materials can feel confident that they are working within the overall trend in the field. Canadian and Québec content in French textbooks is not a radical idea. It should therefore not be an insurmountable project to continue the trend to increase representation of Canada and Québec. This study did not set out to compare the cultural representation of various places in la francophonie, but in the case study for the 2000s case in Chap. 5, I noted that what seemed to be an extensive cultural presentation of Québec content was actually about 6 pages of the 496-page textbook. In the current environment, where the goal is to increase the relevance of French language study for all students, it seems that more attention to the local North American context would be warranted. This is a project that would benefit from a better conceptualization of what the important content consists of and how it can best be included to meet the goals of culture teaching at the beginning level.

1.1.2   Cultural Narrative at the Beginning Level

Aspects of Québec's cultural narrative appeared in thirty-five of the sixty-five textbooks studied, representing 54 % of the entire sample (Chap. 3).

Therefore, examples showing cultural narrative exist that materials developers can consult if they want to teach Québec's cultural narrative including its political dimensions in beginning-level foreign language courses. These examples are important in view of the fact that the beginning level has remained on the periphery of professional discussion of culture teaching in foreign languages. The MLA report explicitly calls for a revision of foreign language curricula to better incorporate the beginning-level courses. However, the discussion of culture teaching in the MLA report, like that in the ACTFL *Standards*, is pitched at the intermediate and advanced levels. The assumption in the professional literature appears to be that it is really not possible to communicate significant and interesting aspects of culture to students until they have studied the language for a year, at least. This assumption is not useful for textbook producers creating materials for the beginning level, and in view of the fact that textbook producers attempt to provide cultural content, it is probably not accurate. Some authors have attempted to incorporate aspects of cultural narrative into their textbooks, providing a starting point for authors wishing to explore the inclusion of cultural narrative at the beginning level.

I showed in Chap. 3 how the examples in previous textbooks can be usefully examined from the perspective of the genres that have been chosen to convey aspects of cultural narrative. The two most frequent genres conveying aspects of cultural narrative were the historical narrative and the casual conversation. The textbooks provided a number of examples of each of these, and the texts illustrate aspects of French language that couple with these genres. The genres are not deterministically linked to Québec's cultural narrative, but instead various aspects of the cultural narrative appear well suited to particular genre patterns. Such an analysis should prove useful for text analysis during materials development. Moreover, this perspective connects with the extensive work on curriculum materials accomplished by Byrnes, Maxim, and Norris (2010), who also provided concrete suggestions about the accessibility of various genre patterns.

This theorized concept of text seems essential as materials developers address the more complex demands of multimodal materials development that they meet today. Even in the 2000s subsample, the examples showed multiple genres and images were curated to develop a coherent presentation. In such mixes, the authors attempt to communicate with beginning learners in part by providing a stage-setting introduction to the topic (often in English) and sufficient background for the genres presented in French to make sense. The examples in textbooks going back to the 1970s present concrete examples that should provide food for thought to anyone who assumes that culture teaching necessarily begins after the beginning level.

1.1.3   Limitations in Past Work

Despite the presence of materials intended to convey Québec's cultural narrative in some of the textbooks, important limitations were identified as well in Chaps. 3, 4, and 5. The detail provided about the content, texts, and images in these chapters suggested many areas for improvement that could better convey cultural narrative to students at the beginning level. First, the genre analysis revealed that the autobiographies and biographies that should be best for beginning learners had been underused in the textbooks. Instead, the more complex historical narratives were used. A review of the cultural narrative could help materials developers to identify potential characters, such as René Lévesque and Pierre Trudeau, for use in constructing biographies. Pierre Trudeau's son, Justin, became Prime Minister of Canada in November of 2015, when the Liberal party regained power returning the topic of his legendary father to the public's attention. The analyses of historical narratives in Chap. 3 showed the potential to develop beginning materials that are good examples of a particular genre, in a way that uses the language to transparently reflect the genre. The analysis in Chap. 3 also provided a starting point for constructing dialogue. The analysis showed the need to make clear who the speakers are because who people are determines what they can contribute to the conversation. There is a need for more québécois voices expressing their sentiments and understanding of events from the perspective of cultural narrative. For example, how does the election of Justin Trudeau invoke memories of the past for a Québécois(e)? How do aspects of the cultural narrative affect the conversation that a Québécois(e) has with an American? How should it affect what an American asks about in a conversation? The textbooks tend to contain dialogues between people of unknown origins or with people from France, but the more important insights might be gained through dialogue among Québécois(e), between Québécois(e) and Canadians, or between Québécois(e) and Americans.

The image analysis suggested room for improvement in the integration of the images into the language learning activities of textbooks. Moreover, it showed that the images often seemed to be chosen based on a general interest of the textbook producer rather than a specific interest that is tied to the text and the activities. If the images are to play a role in language learning, they should be selected in view of their specific connection to the text. Images are more likely to be able to provide scaffolding for students' comprehension if the text refers to specific people, places, and events that have meaning for the cultural narrative. For example, the student protests of 2012 in Québec involved particular student leaders and politicians that appeared in the news every day in particular places. A fictional autobiography of a student involved in the protest (or one who chose not to get involved) could refer to these people and places, making the selection of images based on a specific interest. Such images would be more likely to scaffold understanding and memory than would general images of places in Québec.

The selection of political content was shown to be somewhat haphazard and lacking in the detail needed for students to understand current events. Even textbooks that present a historical account of language politics do so in an impersonal way with the groups, institutions laws, and events as the subjects of sentences. This 73-word excerpt, from a 558-word text in *Entre amis*, provides an example of the impersonal treatment of the work of the Parti Québécois:

> Entre 1974 et 1985, *le parti québécois* est le parti majoritaire au Parlement québécois. En 1977, *la Loi 101* fait du français la seule langue officielle au Québec. Si une entreprise a plus de cinquante employés, *il* faut utiliser le français pour toute correspondance commerciale. *Les écoles* vont être presque toutes francophones. Même les *enseignes des magasins* doivent être en français. En 1980, par contre, *les Québécois* rejettent l'indépendance dans un référendum provincial.

[Between 1974 and 1985, the *Parti Québécois* is the majority party in the Quebec Parliament. In 1977, *Bill 101* makes French the only official language in Quebec. If a company has more than fifty employees, *it* is necessary to use French for all commercial correspondence. *The schools* will be almost all francophone. Even *the signs in stores* must be in French. In 1980, in contrast, the *Québécois* reject independence in a provincial referendum.] (Oates, Oukada, & Altman, 1991, pp. 144–145. my emphasis)

This kind of person-less presentation of events is typical of the textbooks, but does not reflect the more engaging cultural and political historical accounts that one reads in works of history and Canadian Studies. The latter would include René Lévesque as the leader of the Parti Québécois, who was morally defeated by the outcome of the 1980 referendum. Including people in the cultural narrative at the beginning level would also create a syntactically more transparent text, a potential for students to remember key figures, and a specific interest for the textbook producer to select relevant images. The critique of existing materials provides a basis for developing stronger materials for teaching Québec's cultural narrative, but as a starting point, it was critical to examine the actual cultural narrative of Quebec outlined in Chap. 2.

1.1.4 Contributions from Canadian Studies and Québec Studies

Among the most serious limitations in the textbooks investigated was the need for a more coherent and deliberate presentation of Québec's cultural narrative. In Chap. 2, I outlined briefly some of the intricate twists and turns in the cultural narrative to provide a basis for examining textbook content. Canadian Studies and Québec Studies provide a strong basis for outlining a cultural narrative for Québec. High-quality scholarly work exists to let materials developers gain an understanding of Québec's cultural narrative and to provide sufficient detail for materials development. Materials developers need to consult the resources produced by scholars of Canadian Studies and Québec Studies to develop an understanding of Québec's cultural narrative.

Canadian Studies and Québec Studies are international areas of scholarship that create knowledge about Canada and Québec, respectively. Each encompasses cross-disciplinary perspectives that welcome discovery and analysis on topics of culture-specific facets of history, politics, and society, as well as the humanities and arts. Canadian Studies and Québec Studies are each the subjects for international organizations as well as American organizations, which host conferences and sponsor academic journals. A look at the scholarship produced by researchers in Canadian Studies and Québec Studies reveals a range of interesting topics with useful detail and valuable perspectives for foreign language materials developers. A good point of entry for the study of Canada is an edited volume, *Canadian Studies in the New Millennium,* Second Edition (Kasoff & James, 2013). This volume provides an introductory overview that allows readers to learn enough to be able to go deeper. For example, the chapter on Québec begins by clarifying for an American audience the use of the term 'nation' to refer to Québec. Because it is written for an American audience by scholars of Canadian Studies who have taught Canadian Studies in the USA, it anticipates the points of confusion by recognizing points of difference across the two countries.

For Québec Studies, an excellent introduction titled *Québec Questions* was compiled by Gervais, Kirkey, and Rudy (2011), and another one titled *Le Québec à l'aube du nouveau millénaire* was edited by Weidmann-Koop (2008), the latter in French. Both of these volumes contain more than one chapter on language politics. Like Kasoff and James' (2013) volume that introduces Americans to multiple aspects of Canada that typically need to be explained to Americans, *Québec Questions* is also appropriately pitched to an American audience. There are five chapters on language in Québec, which include the topics of sociolinguistics, politics, planning and policy, philosophical reflections on politics, and the role of popular music in Québec's linguistic journey. The topic of identity is covered in six chapters. Among the five chapters in a section on Québec's international relations, one addresses the relationship between Québec and the USA: 'The Ottawa-Québec-Washington Dance: The political presence of Québec in the United States.' In the chapter, political scientist Balthazar reveals what the USA's position has been toward the question of Québec independence since Jimmy Carter stated it in 1977 in response to the formation of the Parti Québécois.

These books introducing Canadian Studies and Québec Studies provide a wealth of orienting information and detail about the nations as multifaceted cultural entities that are distinct from the USA in many important respects. One such difference is the treatment of language policy as something to be legislated by the state. The cultural significance of language policy in Canada and Québec converges with its educational significance for students studying French in the USA to suggest this as an area of critical importance to elaborate in beginning-level French textbooks.

1.1.5   Guidance from Social-Semiotic Theory

Area studies alone do not provide a sufficient basis for developing, revising, or analyzing language learning materials for beginning-level learners. The point of foreign language teaching is centrally about language, and therefore it is the language used to express ideas about cultural narrative that has to be part of the analysis. In this textbook analysis, I analyzed both the cultural content and the language that was used to express the cultural content. Content and language are inherently connected, so it is not necessary to link language and content. Instead, what is needed is a means of analyzing the language in a way that takes into account the content that the language expresses, as I did in Chap. 3. By building on the work of Byrnes et al. (2010), I was able to benefit from their insights about the analysis of materials in addition to their conceptualization of the way that language level can be linked to text accessibility. I extended the analysis of meaning making to include the nonlinguistic representation of Canada and Québec in the textbooks as well in Chaps. 4 and 5.

My research demonstrated how these analytic tools can be used for textbook analysis, but textbook analysis is necessarily limited to how others have chosen to represent Canada and Québec. Such analytic tools can also be used to create materials based on rationales for the meanings that should be conveyed and the language and images that should be selected to do so. With a reconceptualized set of goals for beginning French learning, teachers and materials developers should be able to use the categories of meanings, genres, and language from social-semiotics to design beginning-level French materials that introduce students to the relevant cultural and linguistic materials through selection of appropriate genres. Byrnes et al. (2010) suggested particular genres that would be ideally suited to beginning-level learners. Their analysis of genre included useful specification of levels of linguistic accessibility. With respect to the language, this entailed the degree of congruence between language and meaning.

The genre that Byrnes et al. (2010) identify as the most accessible for learners is autobiographical and biographical historical narrative. Recent scholarship in Québec Studies uses materials from primary sources to produce interesting biographical and autobiographical narrative particularly of immigrants from Québec. For example, there was a panel on Franco-Americans at the 2014 meeting of the American Council for Québec Studies. Researchers described results from their interviews and oral history projects conducted with decedents of immigrants from Québec. Such studies convey history and cultural narrative at the personal level of letters written by Franco-American clergy (Richard, 2014), women removed from the poverty of rural French Québec (Blood & Duclos-Orsello, 2014), historically grounded stories of language shift (Stelling, 2014), and stories of life as Francophones in the USA (Bernard, 2014). The same social-semiotic analysis that is critical of existing materials can help to suggest alternatives.

1.1.6   Reconceptualizing Politics in French Textbooks

Findings from my research indicated that the political aspects of Québec's cultural narrative were only minimally included in the textbooks. This finding is most evident in Chap. 5, where I looked at the political messages in both image and text in the textbooks, as well as taking a closer look at five textbooks. Québec's cultural narrative is principally a political one, but the apolitical approach of typical foreign language textbooks results in a haphazard presentation of the political story. As a result, students are provided with little if any prompting to develop interest in the political aspects of language acquisition and use. Moreover, they are not provided with a basis for making sense of current events in Canada and Québec.

New approaches should be developed for conceptualizing how political aspects of cultural narrative can be included in beginning-level textbooks. The monologic presentation of cultural information such as one finds in reference materials lacks both the language and a sense of currency regarding the relevance of the cultural topics. For example, some of the textbooks mention the separatist movement in Québec, but they do not give an idea of where the movement stands now or how its results play out today. For example, does anyone *talk* about Québec independence today? Dialogues showing the day-to-day discursive construction of cultural topics are needed if students are to build a foundation they can use for learning through conversation. More generally, political genres need to be selected, revised, and created to provide students with the genres of language use that will teach them how to use the language to make sense of the culture. Students need to learn the interpersonal language of dialogues in addition to the knowledge that is typically presented in monologic text.

1.1.7 Summary

The six findings with their implications and recommendations are summarized in Table 6.1. This discussion of implications is necessarily specific to teaching French in the USA even if some of the ideas may be useful for French teaching in other locations. The cultural narratives and students' needs are specific to particular places, and progress in the teaching of culture requires careful examination of specific cultural materials. The overall approach of my analysis, however, has implications for teaching of foreign language more broadly.

Table 6.1 Summary of research findings, implications, and recommendations for beginning-level French textbooks

Finding	Implication	Recommendation for beginning-level French textbook producers
The amount of Canadian and Québec content in beginning-level French textbooks has definitively increased (Chap. 2).	Material developers wishing to represent Canada and Québec in teaching materials can feel confident that they are working within the overall trend in the field.	Continue the trend to increase representation of Canada and Québec by strengthening the presentation of Québec's cultural narrative.
Aspects of Québec's cultural narrative appeared in some of the 65 textbooks studied (Chap. 3).	Materials developers can consult examples showing cultural narrative including its political dimensions in beginning-level foreign language courses.	Use examples from previous years to see how cultural narrative can be included in the beginning level.
Some important limitations were identified in the presentation of Québec's cultural narrative in text, image, and their coherence (Chaps. 3 and 4).	Improvements are needed in the presentation of Québec's cultural narrative, including selection of genres well suited for presentation of both content and language and selection of images in fragments.	Critique existing materials and develop stronger materials for teaching Québec's cultural narrative based on revised objectives for students' culture learning.
Canadian Studies and Québec Studies provide a strong basis for outlining a cultural narrative (Chap. 2).	High-quality scholarly work exists to let materials developers gain an understanding of Québec's cultural narrative and to provide sufficient detail for materials development.	Consult resources produced by scholars of Canadian Studies and Québec Studies to develop an understanding of Québec's cultural narrative to use in materials development.
Social-semiotic perspectives on the analysis of text and image provided a means for examining text and image (Chaps. 3 and 4).	Analytic tools can be used to create materials based on rationales for the meaning that should be conveyed and the language and images that should be selected to do so.	Use the categories of meanings, genres, and language from social-semiotics to design beginning-level French textbooks.

(continued)

Finding	Implication	Recommendation for beginning-level French textbook producers
The inclusion of political aspects of cultural narrative is minimal (Chap. 5).	Students are provided with little if any prompting to develop interest in the political aspects of language acquisition and use.	New approaches should be developed for conceptualizing how political aspects of cultural narrative can be included in beginning-level textbooks.

1.2 Suggestions for Teaching Cultural Narrative

The suggestions for improving the content of French language textbooks are based on the motivation to improve the content of the beginning-level course to interest students in the places and people whose language they are studying and to prepare them to learn more through conversation and future study. To meet those objectives I have outlined some suggestions that arose from my textbook analysis.

1.2.1 Cultural Narrative

Materials developers should investigate the cultural narratives that are relevant to the people whose language they are teaching. The content of cultural narrative is packaged with the language used to express meanings about the cultural narrative. The starting point for materials development, therefore, needs to be discovery of the cultural narrative of the people who speak the language. This process of discovery necessarily begins by identifying the cultures relevant to the language and the learners—a difficult issue in view of the many cultural narratives in which some languages play a role. It is an issue that needs to be tackled, however, if materials are going to go beyond the superficial fragments of culture that have typically been found in textbooks. Teaching cultural narrative requires making a commitment to learn and teach particular cultural narratives because language is packaged with particular meanings. In my study, I did not make the commitment, but instead analyzed the existing materials. However, if I were creating new materials for students in the USA, I would include Québec's cultural narrative, in view of the geographical location and interconnections between Québec, Canada and the USA.

Discovery of cultural narratives can be undertaken by seeking resources produced in area studies. Like Canadian Studies and Québec Studies, other areas of the world have scholars devoting their attention to understanding their history, politics, society and people relevant to the world languages taught at universities. It is plausible for foreign language materials developers to become educated about the important cultural narratives that are critical to the people who speak the languages they teach. In particular, foreign language courses should highlight the strand of political narrative that pertains to language policy.

Recent work in applied linguistics has explored the connections between language policy studies and language acquisition with, for example, a symposium called 'Bridging Language Acquisition and Language Policy' held in June of 2015 at Lund University in Sweden. The symposium was convened to create a dialogue about a territory of shared relevance to both areas of applied linguistics. The organizers had their sights set on improving education and political action with respect to language education, but equally pertinent is the need for language teachers and materials developers to learn about language policy in their particular languages of expertise.

Language policy studies are important for improving how cultural narrative is introduced in foreign language textbooks. All languages play a critical role in someone's cultural narrative. It is probably connected to the evolution of a national identity. It may have been used as an instrument of power and coercion, and it is probably the result of a standardization process that was instrumental in nation-building. Languages play roles in interesting and important political stories that students can learn from while they are studying foreign languages.

1.2.2   The Role of Existing Textbooks

Materials developers can look to existing textbooks from the past to see how important cultural messages have been conveyed by other authors.

In my study of French textbooks, existing examples were useful in demonstrating how textbook genres and images communicate important meanings about cultural narrative. The analyses shown in Chaps. 3, 4, and 5 illustrate how existing textbook materials can be analyzed by authors to understand their semiotic and linguistic contribution to the textbook and to students' potential learning. For example, in Chap. 3, the historical narratives from the textbooks provide concrete examples of the language used to express a variety of different types of historical texts. The casual conversations illustrated how participants can use aspects of the cultural narrative in their talk. Eggins and Slades' (1997) analysis of casual conversation as a means for socially constructing reality suggests that such conversation is the ideal site for expressing meanings about the cultural narrative. Accordingly, the examples showed that the participants in the casual conversations affect the social reality that can be constructed by making it possible to express some aspects of the cultural narrative. In particular, important messages about the connection between French, identity, and pride were discursively constructed when one of the characters was Québécois(e). The examples of both historical narrative and casual conversations showed that materials including aspects of cultural narrative can be developed around topics of tourism. In particular, the dialogue that develops between a character who is showing the city of Québec mixes the pragmatic goals of the tour guide with casual conversation that prompts social construction of important moments in Québec's history.

In this dialogue *in Horizons* (Bennett, Bennett, Joiner, & Shinall, 1984, pp. 362–365), a man and woman from Paris are visiting Québec with a Québécoise host, Pierrette. Together they tour the city and their host points out some of the geography that is connected to Québec's cultural narrative.

Promenade dans Québec
    Nos deux Parisiens et leur hôtesse québécoise sont maintenant sur la Terrasse Dufferin, qui domine le Saint-Laurent de 300 mètres devant le superbe hôtel Château Frontenac. [Our two Parisiens and their Québecoise guide are now on the Terrasse Dufferin, which overlooks the Saint Laurence River 300 meters in front of the wonderful hotel Château Frontenac.]

Marie: Quel panorama! Quelle hauteur! C'est vraiment impressionnant!

Pierrette: Je savais que tu aimerais la vue d'ici, Marie, et que tous les deux, vous vous intéresseriez à l'histoire de cet endroit. En effet, nous amis sont entourés de témoignages° du passé du vieux Québec. C'est ici qu'en 1608 Samuel de Champlain a fondé la ville de Québec qui devait plus tard devenir la capitale de la province.

Marie: Passe-moi tes jumelles, s'il te plait, Pierrette. Jean a laissé les nôtres à Paris. (Elle regarde.)

Pierrette: L'ile que tu vois en face, c'est Lévis. C'est là que les Anglais ont campé pendant trois mois avant de prendre la ville de Québec en 1759. Les Américains auraient, eux aussi, aimé prendre la ville de Québec! Ils ont essayé en 1775, mais sans succès. (Bennett et al., 1984, pp. 362–365)

1.2.3   Extending Beyond Existing Textbooks

Past materials provide a useful starting point for developers wanting to create new opportunities for learning from foreign language materials. But if future materials developers are to extend and expand beyond existing practices in culture teaching at the beginning level, they will need to take a broader view that includes a curriculum with more relevant goals for foreign language learning at this level. In Chap. 1, I presented an argument for improving culture teaching that is relatively uncontroversial in the profession, at least among foreign language teachers in the USA. The profession has regularly sought ways to reconceptualize and improve culture teaching. More recently, the need to include the beginning-level courses in the reconceptualization has been recognized. Such a motivation might best be guided by taking into account that (1) the majority of students in beginning-level foreign language classes are not majors, (2) a primary goal of the language class is to interest the students in the specific cultural issues of the speakers of the language, and (3) the first year should prepare students for communication with speakers of the language and with interlocutors from a variety of different cultures.

The fact that the majority of students in beginning-level foreign language classes are not majors means that for well over half of the students in beginning foreign language classes, their exploration of foreign language study is likely to consist of only the first-year language course. The profession has plenty of experience with these students, who get through the beginning course(s), decide that foreign language is too difficult for them, and then recall their unsuccessful experience in trying to learn a language with dissatisfaction for the rest of their lives. These are the people who, later in life as parents and university administrators, decide where funding cuts should be made when there is insufficient time and money to teach everything. In other words, the first-year language courses have played an enormous public relations role for the profession over the past decades. They leave lasting impressions on the many Americans who took them while they were a requirement. These are the people who today do not vote to continue to require them.

In view of the critical public relations role played by beginning-level foreign language courses, I would argue that a primary goal should be to interest the students in the people and places of the speakers of the language. Materials about people and places can be found in resources from area studies. In a language class, students should learn something about language policy as it pertains to the language that they are studying. Language policy as it intersects with other historical and cultural issues is an appropriate domain for language classes, and it is also a topic of human interest that may create positive memories of a language class and useful knowledge that will enhance students' international knowledge. Students' interests are varied, but so are the facets of current culture that students might be guided to discover in the cultures that they are studying. Teachers can learn more about all facets of culture—from sports and cooking to history and international relations—through the scholarship in area studies.

The first year needs to prepare students to communicate with speakers of the language and with interlocutors from a variety of different cultures. This preparation does not consist of solely linguistic preparation, and in fact few first-year students are going to use their language knowledge to communicate with international interlocutors. Our students communicate with their interlocutors in English. I would argue that the fact that students typically do not learn enough language in one year to carry on a conversation in the language should not relieve their foreign language teachers of the responsibility for preparing them for communication. The type of monolingual conversation that foreign language classes seem to be exclusively interested in does not reflect the type of co-constructed, multilingual dialogue that learners actually engage in when they have the opportunity to use their language. Rather than the exclusively monolingual dialogue in textbooks, students need to see how they might actually engage in conversation through the use of English and the foreign language. Rather than an apolitical presentation of language and culture that appears in most textbooks, students need to be introduced to topics that would provide them with a basis for communicating and learning more about the speakers of the language. The research on study abroad that finds students are treated as children or pets because of their lack of knowledge and language provides a compelling image of a situation that should be improved upon.

1.2.4 Area Studies

Every language that is taught in university courses is connected to someone's area studies, and therefore foreign language materials developers should be able to find scholarship about cultural narratives. Area studies in different parts of the world undoubtedly offer different types of resources and opportunities, but based on my experience working in Canadian Studies and Québec Studies, I can offer two observations. First, research in area studies yields resources that are both interesting and relevant as potential topics, genres, language, and images for students of foreign languages. Unlike the superficial, disconnected content that students are accustomed to in first-year textbooks, area studies can help to target interesting and important cultural materials. In order to select good content for language materials the developer needs to understand the big story of culture and select detail that helps to convey the story to the students. Scholarship encompasses historical, political, and cultural facets of an area. It inevitably connects with the USA in some way that the student studying in the USA should know about. It touches on language and the connection between language and nationalism in some way even if the linguistic aspects of the story are not well developed.

Second, the nascent scholarship on language within area studies represents an opportunity for applied linguists in foreign languages to contribute to the scholarship on the role of language in developing the national cultural narrative. Research in applied linguistics provides some examples of the study of language in societies in the areas of language policy, which includes historical studies of language management, but this is an area of applied linguistics that would also benefit from the knowledgeable scholarship of applied linguists across the various languages of the world. A second opportunity for applied linguistics scholarship within area studies is the type of textbook analysis that investigates teaching culture in language classes. In Québec Studies the current scholarship on French is heavily literature-focused because of the absence of applied linguists in this arena, but because of the inherent cross-disciplinary nature of area studies, applied linguists have been welcomed. Canadian Studies has a strong strand of teaching Canada scholarship where my work on teaching Canada in French language classes has been welcomed for many years. I am certain that the applied linguistics niche in area studies for other parts of the world can be discovered by applied linguists interested in pursuing this path.

1.2.5 Social-Semiotic Analysis

In my experience, the foreign language professionals who actually create language learning materials are typically not very familiar with social-semiotic theory because their education has typically focused on different aspects of language, linguistics, and language education. What is needed then for materials development is a concrete way into an analysis of prospective materials that will provide a social-semiotic lens for materials developers wishing to strengthen the basis for their selection and creation of texts and images. The frameworks for analysis of language learning materials that I outlined in Chaps. 3 and 4 may provide a useable introduction to help these materials developers take advantage of the analytic tools developed within a social-semiotic perspective to meaning and to help them access the more extensive work of Byrnes, et al. (2010) and Kress and van Leuveen (2006).

A social-semiotic perspective on language learning materials is impor-tant because it requires the materials development process to begin with decisions about what meanings the author is trying to create in the mate-rials, which in turn requires motivated decisions about the meanings that the student needs to be able to create. The process of analyzing students' needs is of course fundamental to materials development in language teaching, but needs analysis alone does not include an analytic perspec-tive on meaning making in language and image that can be used to make sense of the analysis of students' needs in sufficient detail to create materials. Needs analysis can be undertaken through research methods examining students' future language needs from their perspective, from teachers' opinions, and from discourse analysis of language users in the field, for example. Such research needs to be coupled with an analytic perspective that affords the materials developer a way of describing the relevant aspects of meaning. From the perspective developed by Byrnes et al. (2010), the analytic categories of meaning theorized in systemic functional linguistics serve well because they prompt the analysis of multiple dimensions of meanings, particularly focused on the ideational (who the participants are and what the text is about), the interpersonal (the relationships and attitudes depicted through the language), and the textual (the role of the language and particular wordings chosen). They draw upon a rich tradition of analysis that elaborates on how these types of meanings are constructed in texts through the use of genres, and the genres in turn are made up of particular linguistic features. The contribu-tion of social-semiotic analysis with refined goals for the first-year course would provide a much needed advance in the materials creation process.

1.2.6   The Role of Politics

Materials developers working in all foreign languages need to conceptual-ize the role of politics even beyond language policy in the cultural content of their teaching. The role of politics should be articulated in a way that allows students to appreciate the political dimensions of language in the cultural narratives and that gives them a foundation for understanding current events. Students have access to news and other information about politics on the Internet without even going on study abroad. Politics in all democracies is continuously newsworthy and therefore students have access to political aspects of culture, but they need to be taught enough about how the politics work in a particular country to be able to watch and learn from the news. Some of the textbooks in my study contained an introduction to the political aspects of Québec's cultural narrative, but even in the books with the most extensive political coverage, students were not introduced to the main players and political parties that form the basis for news today in Québec.

Comprehension of the day-to-day coverage of the news requires some basic knowledge about the artists, the issues, and the political players in the news. Most textbooks produce a new edition every five to seven years, making it a challenge to introduce up to the minute coverage of who's who. However, the Internet does provide such coverage for teachers and students who know how to find and interpret the relevant current information from Québec. If textbook authors carefully choose their historical and political cultural content, they can provide the foundation required for teachers and learners to find and interpret current events. For example, political actors can be interpreted in view of the ideology and history of the political party they represent. Research is needed to identify the topics that will help students to comprehend the everyday cultural and linguistic input that they can access on the Internet or on a study abroad program. With respect to the language of the news, recent work in applied linguistics offering methods targeting news discourse may be useful for better understanding the semiotic resources that students should ideally learn to navigate (Bednarek, & Caple, 2012).

1.3   Theorizing Materials Development as Meaning Making

The recommendations for materials development offered in this chapter need to be placed into a broader conceptualization of meaning making. Kress and van Leeveun's (2006) theoretical conception of how the design of images is composed by an artist, photographer, or curator provides a useful starting point for doing so. As summarized in Chap. 4, Kress and van Leeveun's social-semiotic theory of images posits that the creator of the image begins with an interest, which prompts the choice of a criterial aspect of an object, which in turn materializes into a specific image in the textbook. In Chap. 4, it was evident that some of the criterial aspects of objects were more precisely specified by interest than others. The level of specificity of the image affects its utility in supporting the language of the textbook. I therefore attempted an explanation of image specificity by the specificity of the interest of the textbook producer. However, specificity of interest is prompted by motivation.

The recommendations for materials developers in this section target the motivation for the interest of the developer. They suggest that the materials developer study about cultural narrative, learn from existing textbooks, and analyze the texts and images intended to convey aspects of cultural narrative. All of this is intended to stimulate some specific interests that can in turn specify criterial aspects of objects and texts so that appropriate selections and creations can end up in the textbooks. Figure 6.1 illustrates this idea that includes motiva-

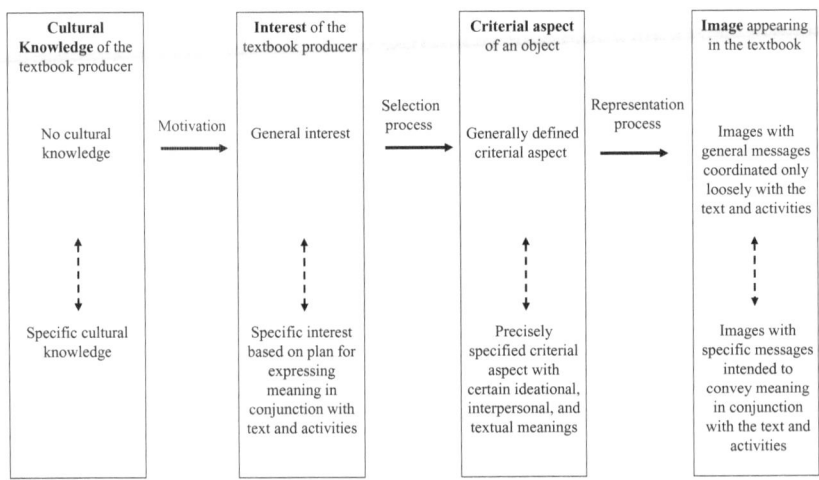

Fig. 6.1 Revised theoretical conception of the cultural meaning making process resulting in textbook images

tion with a theory of materials development from a social-semiotic perspective.

This theoretical conception of materials development as meaning making places the cultural knowledge of the textbook producer at the genesis of the process. This starting point encompasses a number of people and processes, but together they marshal their collective knowledge to articulate their interest in a text or image (or both) about Canada or Québec. Placing this collective knowledge at the start of the process highlights the challenge for the profession.

2   The Challenge

The theoretical model of materials development presents a challenge for the profession because it suggests that creating good materials for communicating cultural narrative requires that developers have knowledge of cultural narrative. This requirement is not insurmountable, but it will require a significant change in the status quo, that is, foreign language teachers who become materials developers do not know anything about politics and have no interest in it. Moreover, many foreign language teachers have not studied applied linguistics in a way that would teach them about language policy, social-semiotic analysis, or language acquisition. Nevertheless, without a change in the level of knowledge and interest in the cultural, historical, and political aspects of language, foreign language seems likely to continue to be seen as irrelevant by the large majority of Americans.

This is a concern that has been raised repeatedly over the past thirty years as the institutional support has eroded away from foreign languages in higher education. Diminishing institutional support is the result of decisions made by faculty and administrators who themselves have undoubtedly sat in foreign language classrooms as college students. Based on their experience in higher education and then in the world, other areas of study are more important than foreign language study. Even people who are deeply interested in history and cultural studies do not see their interests in connection with foreign language. I had the opportunity to meet some of these people while attending a 'French' cultural event in Michigan in the summer of 2015.

I met a number of American history enthusiasts who had not studied French at the university level. These Americans are deeply interested in cultural history, and particularly the history of the French presence in America. I found them at Fort Michilimackinac at the northern point of the lower peninsula of Michigan on French history and culture day during the 300-year anniversary of the construction of the fort. Today's fort is a replica of the one built by the French fur traders in the 1600s. It now serves as a state park for visiting tourists who come to learn about the past in this location. Its history is connected with the beginning of the Québec story that I outlined in Chap. 2 because it is one of the many forts that was built as an outpost for the *coureurs des bois* as they explored the Great Lakes area. On August 8, 2015, I visited because the theme was advertised as 'Bienvenue à Michilimackinac: French History and Culture.' The publicity on the web page for the park announced the theme as follows:

> French soldiers and traders were the European first residents of Michilimackinac, and French culture still remains important in the Straits of Mackinac area. Reenactors from Fort Des Chartres, Illinois will join the interpretative staff to present the historic foods, fashions, songs, dances, and crafts of Michilimackinac's thriving French community. (Michilimackinac 300, 2015)

The Americans working there on French history and culture day, who had never appeared in any university French classes, were working as interpreters and reenactors of the historical events that took place during the construction of Fort Michilimackinac by the French fur traders until the time that the British took over in 1760. I chose to visit that day to see the fort, while looking at how the planners of the exhibit had chosen to present to the public aspects of French language as it was significant for the history at that site. My tangible findings consisted of a map of the French settlement in Michigan showing geographical locations originally named by the French. The map contained a sampling of familiar (Detroit and Sault Ste. Marie) and less familiar (Au Gres and Seul Choix) place names in Michigan, including some with the French as annotations such as Whitefish Point (Pointe au Poisson Blanc). Another display 'Becoming Canadian' expressed the ways that the French settlers at Michilimackinac adapted to the environment. It presented the key points as 'families,' 'food,' and 'clothing.' There was nothing about language. Overall, the designers of the exhibit had planned the event without including the way the fur traders communicated with the native people or with each other.

I sought more information by talking to some of the many historical interpreters and reenactors about language. I met *coureurs de bois* just outside the fort. These French Canadian enthusiasts had come from Kansas to play the role of the *voyageurs* on this special weekend at Fort Michilimackinac. They were set up with tee-pees and dressed the part. I asked, 'Who are you?' The response was, 'We are voyageurs,' so I said, 'Oh, *vous parlez français, n'est pas?*'

The content of the response did not surprise me, but the degree of the categorical denial did: 'Ah no—no French. No one speaks French any-more.' He went on to say, 'We speak a little of the lingua franca of trade that all of the voyageurs used in working with all of the native people.' And then he demonstrated that with a three-turn conversation. 'I used to know more than that, but if you don't use it...'

'Yes,' I agreed, and I dropped the topic of French to let him tell me what the voyageurs did. He knew a lot about the voyageurs, where and how they traveled, what they wore, what they ate, and what they did for fun. He was able to talk about the fur trading business in that era, and seemingly every-thing that it meant to be a voyageur—everything except French language.

As I walked, I met two local voyageurs from Michigan. I started the same way. 'Oh, *voyageurs, donc, vous parlez français.*' One voyageur responded, 'No, but I know some words that voyageurs used.' And he stated a list of about eight or nine words about boats and water. I asked him how he had learned those words. He responded, 'We learn those when we learn about voyageurs, plus I took French for two years in high school. That's how I know how to pronounce the words. But I can't speak French.' This is a familiar line in a conversation that I have with many people: I studied French, but I cannot speak it at all. Some people have studied it in high school and cannot speak it. Some people have studied it in college for any number of years, but cannot speak it. I continued.

I entered a house where the women dressed in French attire were cooking, and there was a Metis man who was fully in costume, and playing the part with great animation. '*Bonjour,*' he greeted me when I entered. 'Ah, Bonjour,' I responded, '*On parle français ici! J'ai cherché par toute ici pour quelqu'un qui parle français, et je n'ai pas encore trouvé personne.*' Stunned, he watched me while signaling with his hand over his head. I stopped. 'No French?' I said.

'No,' he said. 'Are you from France? or Canada?'

'No,' I replied, 'I'm from Michigan.'

'Michigan?' he said. 'But your French.... I was afraid that you only spoke French.' I assured him that it was possible for someone from Michigan to speak French, but the idea seemed incredible to him. He was another of the voyageurs who had traveled across states to come to this event, where he played the role of a voyageur without speaking any more than a word of French. Moreover, I got the clear message that the idea that an American could speak French was something that he had not encountered in his many travels.

I went to a house where two women were dressed in French-style clothing. I started talking to them, and then slipped in a question about French, this time in English. 'So, does anyone speak French at the exhibit?' They both insisted that neither of them spoke French. 'I speak a little Spanish,' one told me. She went on to say, 'One of the people who works at the fort speaks a little French, but she is not here today.' I was the only one to see the irony in the fact that the only person who spoke French was not working on the French culture day at the Fort. It was French culture day, but language was absolutely irrelevant.

No one working at Fort Michilimackinac, the French Canadian fort, on French culture day saw French language as having anything to do with the exciting and interesting historical time period and events that they were depicting. The people whose vocation or avocation is retelling the story of the French Canadian explorers in America had never taken a university French class. The one person working at the park who knew a little French was not working that particular day because French language was apparently irrelevant. How did the irrelevance of French language become unanimous among all of these enthusiasts of the French exploration of North America?

One interpretation of this story is that it simply provides support for a pessimistic statement about the hopelessness of monolingual Americans. Such statements are a standard line to language teachers and applied linguists. But there is another possible interpretation. An alternative interpretation affords our profession with the agency, insight, and responsibility to change the role of foreign language study to make it relevant. Taking this challenge will require connecting the first-year course, where four out of five students study all of the French they will ever take, with something of interest to them. Students studying in the first-year course typically learn that foreign language is difficult and that they are not good at it. They do not learn that is it is connected to any of their interests.

French makes a particularly poignant example because of its past strong presence in the northern USA, which diminished to being, at best, a relic of the past, or at worst completely irrelevant, as it was on French culture day at the fort. But every language in the university catalogue has a social, political, and cultural narrative that in some way connects with the USA. Intersections include stories of immigrants welcomed to the USA, as well as less desirable but equally educational stories of poverty, discrimination, internment, and military force. The challenge for the profession is to reinvent the beginning-level language course in a way that makes it so relevant and interesting to students that it sparks their interest in language.

3   Implications for Textbook Analysis

Every textbook in the most recent decade in the study claimed to teach culture of the francophone world. Indeed, every textbook contained at least something about Québec's cultural narrative. However, a closer look at exactly what was taught in textbooks revealed that still in the 2000s the cultural narrative was sporadic. Looking at any one of the textbooks next to the coherent cultural narrative as sketched in Chap. 2 revealed what Singerman (1996) so aptly described as fragments. The images of Canada and Québec were used in many cases it seemed just to include an image of Canada to accompany a text that made reference to Canada. Missing from some images was a particular criterial aspect of an object or person that worked with the text to help convey a specific message. Moreover, with respect to politics, the textbooks provide little if any basis for allowing students to understand current events, talk to Canadians and Québecois about their culture, and become engaged in the interesting story of Québec's national cultural narrative. It is only through a careful analysis of these textbooks that I was able to identify some concrete limitations that future textbook producers might seek to address. Moreover, I was able to apply a social-semiotic perspective to analysis that can inform deliberations about textbook content in the future. My textbook analysis yielded these useful perspectives because it attempted to meet the goals for textbook analysis that I identified in the first chapter: (1) cultural and historical grounding, (2) theoretical and practical relevance, and (3) methodological credibility.

3.1   Cultural and Historical Grounding

My research demonstrated the necessary interdisciplinarity of textbook analysis, which is one of the assumptions underlying textbook analysis that was identified by Gray (2013). In addition to the research methodology from social science and semiotic analysis from linguistics, the research relied on knowledge from Canadian Studies and Québec Studies. Area studies are themselves interdisciplinary fields of inquiry, each relying on knowledge from a range of disciplines including history and political science. In Chap. 2, I sketched Québec's cultural narrative as it has been written and taught in Québec for many years. By drawing upon resources from Canadian and Québec Studies, I was led to the government of Québec document as well as relevant history and political texts to make sense of the government's story and modify it to bring it more in line with the scholarly work. I used Québec's cultural narrative as the basis to examine the content in the textbooks, and in doing so I took an important step in textbook analysis: I started by identifying the cultural content of interest. This allowed me to set aside the many texts in the textbooks that mentioned Canada and Québec without touching on cultural narrative, and left some of the examples worth examining in more detail. This narrative necessarily touched on political aspects of cultural narrative and therefore provided a good basis for identifying the relevant political aspects of the cultural narrative as well, which was done in Chap. 5.

By beginning with area studies rather than solely the research in applied linguistics, my study also raised an important issue about analysis of the cultural dimensions of foreign language textbooks: foreign language textbooks in the USA (and perhaps globally) are different from their English as an international language counterparts. Weninger and Kiss (2015), based on their review of textbook analyses investigating English as an international language, concluded that English cannot be conceptualized as connected with any particular culture(s) and instead, they argued, that culture needs to be reconceptualized to take into account the transnational character of language use and language ownership. They cite the postmodern critique emanating from the research investigating EFL and ESL textbooks that problematizes the practice of analyzing the representation of national cultures in textbooks, as I have done. This practice

> presumes a somewhat static notion of culture in two different senses. On the one hand, culture is often taken to mean national culture or thought of in terms of mutually exclusive binaries such as Asian-Western, foreign-nonforeign, downplaying the existence of hybrid, subcultural, or global cultural representations.... On the other hand, it is assumed that the analyst's interpretation will match that of the readers of the textbook—students and teachers—or the intention of the author (Weninger & Kiss, p. 700)

This idea may appear to connect with the conception of transnational cultural competence that Risager (2007) defined. Both want to recognize cultural issues beyond any one culture.

However, the idea of cultural competence as transnational, or national cultures as unworthy of analysis, seems at odds with the MLA report's position that cultural narrative should be considered as an organizing framework for the development of curriculum. By examining an actual cultural narrative, my research demonstrated that the connection between French and Québec's cultural narrative was absolutely critical both for gaining an understanding of Québec and for providing important content in a beginning-level textbook. French language use in Canada can be presented without explicit reference to the cultural narrative by introducing, for example, vocabulary contrasting with that of France and ecological education programs in Canada. They can describe bureaucratic language laws that appear to discriminate against English speakers. Canadian and Québec characters can be presented in transnational conversations and places playing roles that could as well be filled by any other transnational person who works on solving mysteries, engages in tourism, and sits in cafés talking about who speaks what language. There are plenty of examples of these transnational texts in the textbooks I analyzed. But they are not particularly interesting. More seriously, they present French as neutral and homeless with the same functional uses as English or any other language. French is anything but neutral and homeless in Québec. It would be inaccurate to treat it as neutral in textbooks.

Québec's cultural narrative holds the potential to serve as the basis for content. Moreover, I would argue that a transnational cultural competence as described by Risager (2007) requires that language learners understand the significance of language in a world where people do associate languages with nations. 'Transnational' appears to signify to Risager that language users know how languages are connected to nations and states. She argues that if learners are to use language to act as independent agents, they need to have an understanding of the political and ideological meanings of nation, state, and identity, in a world where these are regularly connected to language. This sense of transnational cultural competence elevates the value of the insights that American students might gain from learning about the meaning of French in Québec's cultural narrative. It also underscores the difference between analysis of textbooks of English as an international language and those of foreign languages.

3.2   Theoretical and Practical Relevance

My research intended to provide results that would be useful to textbook producers who are attempting to improve beginning-level foreign language textbooks by better creating cultural content. At the same time, it is intended to contribute toward moving forward the profession's understanding of a range of issues pertaining to cultural content in beginning-level textbooks. To make clear the implications for practice, I restated the findings and elaborated on their implications first for developing French language learning materials (Sect. 1.1) and then for foreign language learning materials in general (Sect. 1.2).

One of the most important contributions that I hope to have made is in the connection between professional knowledge and commercial interests in textbook production. Theoretical discussion of culture in the profession exists in a parallel universe with the everyday work of producing foreign language textbooks. Theoretical papers in applied linguistics offer rich insights into the meaning of culture and its importance for language learners. Research on learners attempting to engage in cross-cultural situations provides plenty of examples of issues, which in turn, can be theorized. In the meantime, textbook producers work diligently to produce high-quality materials tailored to the needs of the market. It is a worthy goal to bring these two worlds closer together.

3.3   Methodological Credibility

Gray (2013) argued that there is a need for more textbook analysis. My research was prompted in part by this assumption, which also suggested to me the need to contribute to inspiring others to conduct textbook analysis. The key to inspiring future research is to start with an approach that will be theoretically and practically relevant to the field of applied linguistics and textbook producers, respectively. The other key ingredient is to construct a study in a manner that is methodologically credible. In order for my study to serve as input to others' methodologically, I have explicitly discussed the rationales for methodological choices throughout the study.

In the first chapter, I laid out the problem in the field that helped me to formulate the study. I described my interest and background in studying French, studying in Québec, teaching in Québec, developing language learning materials, and conducting research. All of these factors converged to develop the goal of the study. The overarching methodological approach was justified in terms of the need for both quantitative and qualitative methods and the existence of a credible mixed-methods tradition of research methodology that would give me a way to articulate a rationale and explain my approach.

The quantitative thinking behind the definition of the population and sample was explained in Chap. 2. The population was identified systematically because I wanted the results to be interpretable to a known population of textbooks. In order to interpret the results, I wanted to measure how adequately the sample represented the population. This is particularly important because the content I was investigating was very rare in the textbooks, and therefore results would be subject to a great deal of influence from unrepresentative textbooks if the sample were very small. Having obtained 50 % of the population for my sample, I can be relatively confident about the stability of the overall results. I was also concerned about the stability of the results for each of the five decade subsamples. Because of the uneven availability of textbooks across the decades, the level of confidence in results varies, with the 1990s being the least trustworthy sample (with 33 %), whereas the other subsamples were all adequate for representing their respective subpopulations.

Because analysis of cultural representation in textbooks is centrally about meaning, a qualitative approach is needed to first identify relevant meanings for further analysis and then to examine the meanings through the use of a relevant theoretical framework. Combining the quantitatively oriented sampling of textbooks with the need for qualitative analysis is a challenge which must be met with analytic frameworks. In Chaps. 3 and 4, I introduced the way that the social-semiotic theoretical perspective would be operationalized in my qualitative analysis of text and image, respectively. I did not invent new theories and frameworks for analysis, but instead drew from the complexities of social-semiotic theory as they have been operationalized by Byrnes et al. (2010) and by Kress and van Leuveun (2006), respectively. As a result, I was able to analyze a relatively large number of texts and images across sixty-five textbooks, illustrate how these frameworks can be operationalized in textbook analysis, and direct other materials developers and analysts to the large store of concepts and methods of analysis that can be applied to other textbook analysis problems.

The categories in the analytic frameworks provided guidance on how to analyze the text and images, but it was the historical research that was needed to identify what to analyze. The knowledge gained from my study of Canadian and Québec Studies was foundational in identifying the Canadian and Québec content, sorting out the content containing cultural narrative, and interpreting the political aspects of the narrative. Chap. 5 draws extensively on the cultural narrative, using it to build a content framework for recognizing what aspects of politics the textbooks contain, what they mean, and what is missing.

Finally, the diachronic analysis of Canadian and Québec content in the textbooks adds an essential perspective for seeing a trajectory of interest in Québec overall, in addition to identifying specific content-related trends that are important to consider for the future. The most important finding was that the small amount of cultural content in the textbooks in the 2000s actually reflects a definitive increase in representation of Canada and Québec relative to previous decades. This provides a very different picture of textbook producers' interest in inclusion of Canada and Québec from what one sees with a look at the 2000s alone. In view of the need for perspective on these little researched issues, a chronological perspective is very useful.

4   Conclusion

Only time will tell what the payoff will be from my attempt to create convergence between theory and research in applied linguistics with practice in foreign language textbook production. However, the time has never been better for taking a look back on how materials have incorporated the cultural narrative and particularly its political dimensions into materials. Teachers and materials developers recognize that their students are ready for more engaging content, as foreign languages are increasingly dropped as requirements from academic programs. The profession continues to discuss changes in foreign language curricula. The theoretical and analytical tools exist for examining prospective new materials, and a new generation of applied linguists is being educated to question existing practices and conduct mixed-methods research. I hope that my contribution will help to bring these strands of activity together in a productive synergy that will include textbook producers in the process of reshaping the representation of cultural narrative in beginning-level textbooks. It seems unlikely that beginning-level textbooks can change dramatically without a clear understanding of the current practices within the profession and what kind of change is desired. Textbook analysis should be central to this process.

References

Bednarek, M., & Caple, H. (2012). *News discourse* (Vol. 46). London/New York: Continuum.

Bennett, D., Bennett, J., Joiner, E., & Shinall, S. (1984). *Horizons—nouvelle langue, nouvelle culture*. New York: Holt, Rinehart and Winston.

Bernard, I. (2014, October 16). *Bates street and beyond*. Paper at ACQS 19th biennial conference, SUNY Plattsburg.

Blood, E. A., & Duclos-Orsello, E. A. (2014, October 16). *Language and identity in Salem's Franco-American community*. Paper at ACQS 19th biennial conference, SUNY Plattsburgh.

Byrnes, H., Maxim, H. H., & Norris, J. M. (2010). Realizing advanced foreign language writing: Development in collegiate education: Curricular design, pedagogy, assessment. *The Modern Language Journal, 94*(1), Special Issue.

Eggins, S., & Slade, D. (1997). *Analyzing casual conversation*. London: Equinox.

Gervais, S., Rudy, J., & Kirkey, C. J. (Eds.). (2011). *Quebec questions: Quebec studies for the twenty-first century*. Don Mills, ON: Oxford University Press.

Gray, J. (Ed.) (2013). *Critical perspectives on language teaching materials*. New York: Palgrave Macmillan.

Kasoff, M. J., & James, P. (Eds.) (2013). *Canadian studies in the new millennium*. Toronto, ON: University of Toronto Press.

Kress, G. R., & Van Leeuwen, T. (2006). *Reading images: The grammar of visual design*. London: Routledge.

Lenard, Y. (1977). *Parole et pensée: Introduction au français d'aujourd'hui*. New York: Harper and Row.

Michilimackinac 300. (2015). *Mackinac: State, Historic, Parks*. Retrieved from http://www.mackinacparks.com/michilimackinac-300/.

Oates, M. D., Oukada, L., & Altman, R. (1991). *Entre Amis: An interactive approach to first-year French*. Boston: Houghton Mifflin.

Richard, M. (2014, October 16). "Sunk into poverty and despair: Franco-American clergy letters to FDR during the Great Depression." Paper at ACQS 19th biennial conference, SUNY Plattsburgh.

Risager, K. (2007). *Language and culture pedagogy: From a national to a transnational paradigm*. Clevedon: Multilingual Matters.

Singerman, A. J. (Ed.) (1996). *Acquiring cross-cultural competence: Four stages for students of French*. Lincolnwood, IL: National Textbook Company.

Stelling, L. E. (2014, October 16). "Perspectives on language shift in two Franco-American centers." Paper at ACQS 19th biennial conference, SUNY Plattsburgh.

Weidmann-Koop, M. C. (Ed.). (2008). *Le Québec à l'aube du nouveau millénaire: entre tradition et modernité*. Québec, QC: Presses de l'Université Laval.

Weninger, C., & Kiss, T. (2015). Analyzing culture in foreign/second language textbooks. In X. Curdt-Christiansen, & C. Weninger, (Eds.) *Language, ideology and education: The politics of textbooks in language education* (pp. 50–66). London: Routledge.

Appendix: English Translations for French Texts

Text 2.1

Vacation plans

...

– If possible, I would want to go to America. It would be wonderful to spend a few days in Canada, to stay in Quebec, to travel to the United States, to stay in New York for eight days, and to see California. (Hendrix & Meiden, 1961, p. 205)

Text 2.2

Sportspeople

Michel and Danielle are French tourists in Canada. They are attending, along with thousands of other spectators, an ice hockey game. Danielle is not saying anything while everyone is shouting. She is sitting while everyone is standing. She looks bored while everyone seems to be enthusiastically enjoying themselves.

Danielle:	But what is going on? Why are all these people screaming like that? They have a toothache?
Michael:	What are you talking about?
Danielle:	Why do they shout so loud?
Michael:	Because the Quebec team just scored a goal! I beg you, make an effort to understand. Do not be discouraged so easily!

© The Editor(s) (if applicable) and The Author(s) 2016
C.A. Chapelle, *Teaching Culture in Introductory Foreign Language Textbooks*, DOI 10.1057/978-1-137-49599-0

Danielle promises to try. She watches carefully the movements of the players, but they are propelling the puck so skillfully that it is hard to follow. After a few minutes, she has really had enough.

Danielle: Why do they rush like crazy behind this little thing? They are afraid of losing it?

Michael: Look, be nice! If you do not like this, do not make the others sick of it!

Danielle: Good! I'm going. I'm going for a drive. I'll meet you after the game. Hand me the keys, please.

Michel: Well, here they are. Do not lose them for me, whatever you do!

Danielle: Don't worry … I'm not completely crazy. (Clarke & Holt Editorial Staff, 1974, pp. 306–307)

Text 2.3

Letter to a Québécoise

My dear Louise,

A big Merry Christmas! I envy you in your Québécoise house out in the country. It should be white everywhere! But, frankly, after a youth of shoveling snow to no end, I'm not complaining. Here, I exchanged my shovel for an umbrella!

What's happening with you these days? Do you cross-country ski often? Did you make your cipâtes and pies? I imagine you spending a quiet Sunday listening to your Vigneault and wondering if your Bizou will leave Monday morning. Let me know what's going on with you!

Here, things are not bad. I especially want to tell you about the presentation I made to students in French class last week: "What is French Canada?" Well, I tried to make them understand (in 45 minutes!) the difference between a Franco-Ontarian like me, and a Quebecer like you. It was not easy, I swear. For them, French Canada is completely uniform. Anyway, how can they speak of a culture exclusively "Canadian"—French or English—when you are flooded by US media from morning to night? I gave them the main ideas, anyway. In addition, finally, I read them Tremblay. They understood very little but, while laughing, they quickly found out that joual is not at all the language of Racine, no more than "cockney" is the language of Shakespeare.

Apart from this episode, there is not much worth telling. The end of the semester approaches, and I am preparing for exams. Write me as soon as possible!

Until then!

Michel

(Bragger & Rice, 1988, pp. 442–443)

Text 2.4

Montreal

The city of Montreal is the center of the *francophonie* in North America; two-thirds (2/3) of the population speak French as their mother tongue. Montreal, home to 20% of the population of Quebec, is situated on an island. This is the second largest city in Canada after Toronto. And this is the second largest French-speaking city in the world after Paris.

Each year many tourists visit Montreal, a city both modern and historical. In the center of the city, Old Montreal is a tribute to the past. Its churches, old houses, and restaurants attract many visitors. But Montreal is also a very modern city. Under the skyscrapers of downtown is a whole underground city of restaurants, shops, cinemas, cafes, and even a subway!

For you to respond

1. What is the largest French speaking city in the world? And the second?
2. Is there a subway in your city?
3. Imagine why there is an "underground city" in Montreal. Are there shops and underground restaurants in your city? (Oates, Oukada, & Altman, 1991, pp. 142–147)

Text 2.5

Gabrielle Roy was born in 1909. She was educated in Manitoba, and she became a teacher. Then in 1937, she left for Europe, and she began writing in France. Then she returned to Canada and in 1945, she published her first novel. In 1950, she returned to Europe and continued to write novels. Gabrielle Roy died in Quebec City in 1983. She had a rather discrete life. She is a very great novelist. (Magnan, Berg, Martin-Berg, & Ozzello, 2007, p. 193)

Text 3.3

It was during the sixties that French Canadians began to question the Anglophone dominance and their isolation from the rest of Canada. Thus, the French in Canada first became French Canadians and then *Québécois*. "Vive le Québec libre" became the rallying cry of Quebecers and "I remember" their official motto. A song by Gilles Vigneault, "Gens du pays," became the national anthem of Quebec.

But how are they different from other Quebecers and Canadians? Why do some *Québécois* ask for their independence? First, because their traditions, lifestyle, and value system come from their French heritage, but they live in a country of Anglophone domination. Also, *Québécois* are traditionally Catholics in a generally Protestant country. Economically, Quebecers feel at a disadvantage, too. Historically, most companies have been controlled by English speakers who favor people who speak English.

It may be in the linguistic domain that the *Québécois* feel most isolated. As Pierre Trudeau, former Prime Minister said, "The Québécois want to be at home everywhere in Canada, and only a bilingual Canada will allow them to feel comfortable from Vancouver to St. John." (Jarvis, Bonin, Corbin, & Birckbichler, 1980, p. 175)

Text 3.4
Welcome to La Belle Province

Bill: Do you think you're a little French?
The driver: Do you think you're a little English? No, of course not. We're totally *Québécois*, and you are completely American! But we do not forget our origins. (Lenard, 1977, pp. 269–275)

Text 3.5
The School in the Great North
Francine, a *Québécoise*, teaches in one of these schools. She recalls her impressions.

"**We** arrived on 10 September. The next day, the first permanent snow was falling. **We** thought we would start teaching right away. That was a mistake: everything is slow out there. First, **we** <u>settled</u> into our house. Then **we** met the principal and the parents' committee." (Jarvis et al., 1980, pp. 210–211)

Text 3.6

The French in America

You already know that we speak French in Canada, especially in Québec. When did the French arrive in North America? The history of French Canada goes far back in the sixteenth century. Between 1534 and 1541, **Jacques Cartier** made three long trips to Canada. During his second trip, **he** *discovered* the St. Lawrence. **He** *planted* a large cross on a hill and named the hill Mont Réal. **Another explorer**, Samuel de Champlain, explored the Gulf of Mexico, New England, and then the East of Canada. **He** established the French colonies in Acadia—now the Canadian Maritime provinces of Nova Scotia and New Brunswick—and he founded **Quebec** City in 1608. Quebec subsequently became the capital of New France, a vast French territory in North America.

The seventeenth century was the most active period of exploration in America.

Exploration continued in the following century. (Hagiwara & De Rocher, 1985, p. 208)

Text 3.7

The history of Quebec: Discovery and colonization

It is in 1535 that **the French explorer Jacques Cartier** discovers the St. Lawrence River and the land surrounding it. **Cartier** takes possession of the new land in the name of the King of France. In 1608, **Samuel de Champlain** builds a house on a rock which forms a natural fortress near the St. Lawrence. It is the first French community in North America, and **Champlain** is the founder of New France. This first city is called Québec.

As a result of the Seven Years War in Europe, **the British** wage war against the French in Canada. In 1759, **the English army** is finally victorious on the Plains of Abraham in Québec City. **Montreal** also **falls** several weeks later. In 1763, **France** signs the Treaty of Paris and hands over to England its colonies located east of the Mississippi. In addition, **the English** force many of the French who live in Quebec and Acadia (now, New Brunswick) to leave Canada. **Many of these Francophones** settle in Louisiana, another French colony. It is the descendants of these Acadians then we now call "Cajuns." (Oates, Oukada, & Altman, 1991, pp. 144–145)

Text 3.8

The situation in 1971

In 1971, **many Quebecois** speak French and English. But **bilingualism** leads to assimilation, and **almost all francophone communities in western Canada and New England** gradually became Anglophone.

English was the language of business and industry in Quebec. The **Anglophones** were often in charge of businesses. The **immigrants** preferred to send their children to English schools. In 1971, **79 % of children of immigrants** were in an English school. Since the conquest, **French Canadian** had been adopting many English words. In English-speaking regions, there was little respect for the North American French. In Toronto, in Vancouver, even in the English schools in Quebec, what is generally taught is the French of Paris.

1977: The Charter of the French language

The **"Charter of the French language"** was a unique act of cultural policy in the world. **Its goal** was to give the French language the leading role in Québec society and to allow French to survive in North America. (Siskin, Williams-Gascon, & Field, 2007, pp. 457–459)

Text 3.9

Quebec

Around 1960, **French-speaking Quebecois** experienced what they call "the Quiet Revolution." This is a great economic development accompanied by social and profound political changes. **The Catholic Church,** which dominated Quebec life for centuries, now plays a less important role. **The Quebec government** established a system of very ambitious social measures. **It** began the nationalization of some sectors, such as energy and health care. **The government** also tried to encourage the development and dissemination of Québec culture through literature, theater, and song. Finally, it gave great importance to the French language by making laws to insert French into the economic life—banks, offices, factories. (Valdman, Barnett, Holekamp, Laronde, Magnan, & Pons, 1986, p. 540)

Text 3.10

...

Melissa:	Apart from France, I know one, it's Quebec.
Ken:	Yes. Who has not heard of Jacques Cartier! (Ollivier, Morran, & Howard, 1983, 371–373)

Text 3.11

French adventurers in the New World

Corinne: Sometimes I would like to have the kind of adventures that the French trappers had before North America had been fully explored.

Jacques: Imagine! There was not a single European in the St. Lawrence before Cartier led his men.

Corinne: You know, although New Amsterdam had had a Dutch settlement from 1626, it's a Frenchman, Peter Minuit, who was the first governor and who bought Manhattan from the Indians.

Jacques: I admire even more the explorer Toussaint Charbonneau, who guided Lewis and Clark up until they arrived at the Pacific! (Muyskens, Omaggio, Chalmers, Imbarton, & Almeras, 1982, p. 443)

Text 3.12

- Our visit to Canada, George, piqued my curiosity. Do you know the time period of the French presence in America?
- I have a small book on the subject just at hand, Good. I quote: "The French presence in North America has been seen since 1534, the year when Jacques Cartier discovered the Gaspé Peninsula, which was made part of the current province of Quebec."
- Were there also French colonies in America outside of Canada?
- Yes, well. I will continue: "From 1699 to 1803, Louisiana was a French territory. But Napoleon sold the territory to the United States, who would buy it for about twenty-seven million dollars."
- Twenty- seven million! But that's not much for such a territory!
- Indeed, well. Napoleon was a great general but a horrible businessman! (Comeau & Lamoureux, 1982, p. 447)

Text 3.13

Separatism in Canada

Gilles: We Quebecois, we are proud, but it is good to remember that we have good reason to be.

Marianne: You mean you've always had to live surrounded by English but you have been able to keep your language intact.

Gilles: We kept intact our language, our culture and our collective identity. I hope we will regain the political strength we deserve. (Muyskens, Omaggio, Chalmers, Imbarton, & Almeras, 1982, p. 447)

Text 3.14

In the land of Descartes

...

Ms. Morin:	That's right. Human reason, intellect, art ... But soon a Disneyland near Paris, a pyramid in the heart of the Louvre and mahgrébisation of our major cities, you can't know what to think any more!
Jessica (*Francoise*):	In your home, between English Canada and the United States, you must be familiar with the same crisis.
Françoise:	Yes, but for us, it strengthens us in our culture.

...

(Pucciani & Hamel, 1983, p. 637)

Text 3.15

Peter:	Yes, but <u>you</u> know, today in Europe, in all professions the practice of foreign languages is very useful and sometimes even indispensable. You're lucky to live in a bilingual country.
Françoise:	You know, in Canada its only us French-Canadians who are really bilingual.
Pierre:	What language do you use at the university?
Françoise:	Me, I go to the University of Montreal, which is a francophone university. I have friends who go to McGill, which is an English language university.
Pierre:	I have heard talk about *joual*. What is it exactly?
Françoise:	This is the French that many people speak, especially in the Montreal area. It comes from the local pronunciation for "horse."
Peter:	And you speak this variety of French?
Françoise:	With my friends, of course. But at home, since Mom is French and Dad lived a long time in France, we speak the French of France. Mom was born in the south, and as she has a little southern accent, we tease her about it every time she complains about how people in Montreal speak. (Valdman, 1975, pp. 547–548)

Text 3.16

Montréal Reportage:

Live in French

Speaking French in a French atmosphere, but in the Americas, is that possible? Of course!

There is a Francophone territory close to you. It is the province of Quebec in Canada. In this region, French is the official language of government, labor, trade and communications.

How many members are in this community? Six million people. Very active and passionate Francophiles, they want to protect their French cultural heritage.

American student, Deborah, studies French at the University of Montreal to become a teacher. Every day she reads "Le journal de Montreal" or " La press." On television, she looks for French programs broadcast by the Réseau de l'Information (RDI).

She likes to walk in the quiet streets of the old town. "I feel like I'm in Europe," she said. We understand why: Montreal was founded by the French in 1642. Its origins are evident in its architecture, in the names of streets in the Old Port. But above all, in Montreal, we attach paramount importance to the beauty of the environment and quality of life. Just like in Paris, Rome or Madrid. (Amon, Muyskens, & Omaggio Hadley, 2004, p. 103)

Index

© The Editor(s) (if applicable) and The Author(s) 2016

C.A. Chapelle, *Teaching Culture in Introductory Foreign Language Textbooks*, DOI 10.1057/978-1-137-49599-0